Word of Mouth

Word of Mouth

SIMON ELMES & MICHAEL ROSEN

With illustrations by Rowan Barnes-Murphy

OXFORD
UNIVERSITY PRESS

OXFORD
UNIVERSITY PRESS

Great Clarendon Street, Oxford OX2 6DP

Oxford University Press is a department of the University of Oxford.
It furthers the University's objective of excellence in research, scholarship,
and education by publishing worldwide in

Oxford New York

Auckland Bangkok Buenos Aires Cape Town Chennai
Dar es Salaam Delhi Hong Kong Istanbul Karachi Kolkata
Kuala Lumpur Madrid Melbourne Mexico City Mumbai Nairobi
São Paulo Shanghai Singapore Taipei Tokyo Toronto

Oxford is a registered trade mark of Oxford University Press
in the UK and in certain other countries

Published in the United States
by Oxford University Press Inc., New York
By arrangement with the BBC

© Simon Elmes and Michael Rosen 2002
© Programme material BBC 2002

The BBC logo is a trade mark of the British Broadcasting
Corporation and is used under licence
BBC logo © BBC 1996

The moral rights of the author have been asserted

Database right Oxford University Press (maker)

First published 2002

All rights reserved. No part of this publication may be reproduced,
stored in a retrieval system, or transmitted, in any form or by any means,
without the prior permission in writing of Oxford University Press,
or as expressly permitted by law, or under terms agreed with the appropriate
reprographics rights organization. Enquiries concerning reproduction
outside the scope of the above should be sent to the Rights Department,
Oxford University Press, at the address above

You must not circulate this book in any other binding or cover
and you must impose this same condition on any acquirer

British Library Cataloguing in Publication Data

Data available

Library of Congress Cataloging in Publication Data

Data available

ISBN 0-19-866263-7

10 9 8 7 6 5 4 3 2 1

Typeset in Poppl-Pontifex
by George Hammond Design
Printed in Great Britain by T. J. International Ltd,
Padstow, Cornwall

Contents

Preface   ix

CHAPTER 1: OFFICIAL CURRENCY   1

    Spun Gold   3
    Moolah Makes the World Go Round   10
    Dear Sir, I Wish to Complain . . .   15
    Cut and Thrust   22
    Lies, All Lies   29

CHAPTER 2: PERSUASION   39

    The N-Word   41
    Heart to Heart   43
    From Soap to Serum   46
    Cover Story   56
    Working It Out   64

CHAPTER 3: HOMEWORK   67

    Toujours la Politesse   69
    Of Mogs and Dogs   74
    Icky Bitty Babytalk   80
    Never Say *Die*?   87

CHAPTER 4: MINDING YOUR SPEAK   93

   Nicely Spoken   95
   To Er ... Er is Human   99
   Rude!   104
   Crack the Whip and Put Your Foot Down   112
   All-Purpose Filler   118
   Kersplatt!   125

CHAPTER 5: MUSCULAR LANGUAGE   133

   Football United   135
   Surfin' NSW   139
   A Little Birdie Told Us   144
   Paying Court   149

CHAPTER 6: WORDING YOUR EATS   153

   Words of Mouth   155
   Organic Panic   160
   Summer Sizzle   164
   Cakes and Ale   167
   The Naming of Tarts   171

CHAPTER 7: BETWEEN OURSELVES   177

   Ssshh! Don't Let On   179
   Puts Words on Your Chest   182
   Jazzin' it Up   187
   The Ire of the Beholder   190
   How Nice to Vada Your Eek   195

CHAPTER 8: THE NAME GAME 205

Naming Names 207
Coffee-Breaking the Mould 210
True Brit 212
How to Name a Plane 221
Appeal of Bells 227

CHAPTER 9: COUNTRY NATTERS 235

Writes of Spring 237
A Rose by Any Other Name 239
Woodcraft Folk 245
Flights of Fancy 248
Under the Weather 253
Fall Tales 258

CHAPTER 10: THE WORD HAS LANDED 263

Seated One Day at the Mouse-Mat 265
In-Flight Entertainment 271
Indeed to Goodness, Look You 275
Whizz-Words of Oz 282

Word of Mouth transmission dates 289
Acknowledgements 290
Index 291

Preface

Travel challenges our capacity to survive boredom. On a flight across the Atlantic in 1990 I heard Mike & the Mechanics sing a moderately hard number whose refrain ended, 'If you believe in the word of mouth'. To beat off the inflight tedium, I began to play with the idea, 'Word. Of. Mouth.' From this uncoiled the ordinary idea that just as all brain action is expressed chemically, all speech is a function of human music. Or, to be specific, vocal sound.

Next thought: 'sound'—can I turn this into anything? I recollected that as a child I felt comforted by certain words because of the 'lumps' they made in my mouth. I remembered 'portmanteau', and 'the Caucasus mountains', and 'lobby' and 'perseverance'.

Thus the genesis of the ten-year-old BBC Radio Four programme, *Word of Mouth*: no medium suits language and mouth-lumps better than radio, in which I had been working for, by then, 25 years. Now the question arose—'Can I sell this programme idea?' I had recently sued the BBC for theft of copyright and even though the case never hit the news I reckoned on small likelihood of success with new proposals.

Wrong: the Radio Four Controller (such interesting titles BBC executives have) was Michael Green and my agent and I went to see him on, by coincidence, my birthday. The propitiousness came through—he bought the series in an instant and Simon Elmes, with whom I had first worked in 1979 and who was the only producer I ever considered for the idea, was put on board.

PREFACE

We recorded a pilot at, among other places, Wimbledon where we talked to Max Robertson. He was reputed to broadcast every point played in tennis and our pilot programme's theme enquired as to the speed of delivery at which language loses meaning.

Those are the historical facts. I presented the programme for three years until a serious illness took me for a time out of everything. Now *Word of Mouth* sails on and I love that it does.

History, though, offers only facts. Successful broadcasting, like managing your money, is also a matter of emotion. *Word of Mouth* interested me as much as anything I had done at that point because it aired something long configured in me—an English-language awareness so exuberant that I had often been in danger of sacrificing content to form. Perhaps I had never—have never—grown out of that joy children take in bending language to all sorts of shapes. As a reporter I had long delighted in watching politicians use evasive language (they were amateurs in those innocent days!). Also, I was lucky enough to span the eras of Johnny Mercer and Cole Porter and Noel Coward and the Beatles and Bob Dylan, so I had a storehouse full of clever, appealing lyrics. Therefore and thereby, my motivation in drafting the programme idea that became *Word of Mouth* was, quite simply, the lovely and almost unbearable excitement that comes of investigating English.

Begin with the 'lumps'. We all have favourite words. Usually—or typically—they may be euphemisms for swear-words. *Jeepers* needs no translation, nor does (a Dublin expression) *James's Street*; the full expletive runs, *James's Street, Christchurch and the Coombe*—three well-known working-class districts serving their time as stand-ins for the name of the Holy Family of Nazareth. And that's another thing; the necessary constrictions of religion have made English so vivid—how else might *damn*, also a thrilling 'lump' in a child's mouth, have become such an expletive?

Move this idea on and add something even more fascinating: here's the thought process. Ballads and folksongs, primary native music, depend on 'lumps' and riffs of 'lumps'; *Are you going to Scarborough Fair?/Parsley, sage, rosemary and thyme.* Now add some formal intent, via poetry—in other words, bridge the gap between the natural rhythm of the ballad and the erudition of the poet. In this matter the gatekeeper, for my money, is Kipling; *What is a woman if you forsake her,/And the hearth and the home-acre,/To go with the old grey Widow-maker.*

So, is it the case that we have within us a mysterious natural rhythm—as though something in the brain keeps pace with the beat of the heart? Or some other unknown but vital cadence? I think something of that order must reside somewhere in the psyche. How else can we explain the way in which certain phrases, spoken melodies, continue to haunt us—in the same way as snatches of music? *They told me, Heraclitus, they told me you were dead,/They brought me bitter news to hear and bitter tears to shed./I wept as I remembered how often you and I/Had tired the sun with talking and sent him down the sky.*

By now the trove was wide open—making radio programmes about language promised Ali Baba levels of excitement. Once, in a German museum, a curator invited me to plunge my hand into a huge funerary cauldron, which had been filled with mead in the summer of 552 BC. At the bottom lay several inches of tender sediment. When I trickled this powder through my fingers I caught the whiff of the flowers from which the ancient honey had originally been made. The experience served as a metaphor for what I hoped *Word of Mouth* might also become—a trawl through language's antiquity, routes to roots through usage and definition.

Such fun! Early in the series we launched into false etymologies. Sadly, we found that *kangaroo* is not an aborigine word for *I beg your pardon?*, as one myth had it (an officer of Captain Cook's was alleged to have asked what the bounding animal was, but the native Australian to whom he addressed the question didn't hear fully). And no, perhaps even more sadly, *sincere* did not come from the goldsmiths of Tuscany stuffing their air-bubbled statues with gold-powdered wax, therefore to be *without wax*, i.e., *sine cere*, was a good thing. But who cares what's true and false? The hunting of the etymology provided the fun. (Thought association—did Lewis Carroll truly coin *chortle*? He did.) On and on we went, looking here, there, and everywhere; we were like lottery winners in a flea market, picking up everything and anything and bringing it all home just for the sake of it.

Accordingly, a major problem soon surfaced. The field proved almost destructively rich. In any one week up to a hundred ideas might appear as Stick-It notes on Simon Elmes's wall. Everywhere we turned, everything we heard, gave us a new treasure. A trade union worker called a boss, *a very silly man*. Ping!—short piece on the origin of *silly*; it once meant *holy* or *saintly*, not at all what was intended by its utterer on this occasion. *Sleaze* was all the rage then; from Silesia long ago came a cloth of open weave, worn by the impoverished: the implication was that it was of low caste and you could see through it. Our greatest task became one of selection. I likened it to looking up a definition in the twenty-volume *Oxford Dictionary*; you find your word, you trace it—and then, alongside it, you find something even more interesting and this diverts you from your chosen path. We soon knew we had a programme that could have been broadcast several days a week—and an audience to match it.

PREFACE

Word of Mouth's adventures in the word trade have been merrily detailed in this book by Simon Elmes and the current presenter, Michael Rosen. I should imagine they have had the same difficulty of selection—but at least this gives, as it gave me, the benefit of range. In these pages you will find—I pluck at random—words that come from golf and words that come from falconry. How can such a programme subject be anything less than exhilarating? Yet, from the beginning, a wonderfully serious point lay beneath the great enjoyability. We moan—we all do—about the dogs towards which civilization has long been going. Artists and politicians, debutantes and clergy seem hell-bent downwards from the standards we all hold dear. So we say, so we chant ritually. The English language, though, keeps the watch, watches the keep. Sturdy listeners told us time and again that they hold their language dear, that it is their bastion, their touchstone, their mascot, their pride. When I seemed to pander elsewhere, to fall for some new and exotic usage, shoals of letters washed to my feet, typically beginning, 'Dear Mr Delaney—oh dear, Mr Delaney'. Thus was that week's blonde held to be peroxide.

I found this hugely comforting—because, truth telling, when it comes to accurate usage I acknowledge myself conservative to the point of being reactionary. I'll even confess to pangs of regret that Dr Johnson—or someone else—didn't succeed in creating a confinement of usage that we might have called, 'ideal English'. Yes, the punchy shorthand of new terminology can be exciting and tempting. Yes, the fresh colloquialism invigorates—and this book is filled with such enjoyable specimens. But, for me, nothing compares finally with the beauty of an elegant sentence, spoken clearly, all meaning made plain, with, if possible, form harmonized to content. In other words—and I use the phrase in every sense—I like my 'lumps' to have lovelier shapes now, especially as we get more surrounded every day by the galloping unlovely.

Frank Delaney
August 2002

Chapter 1
Official Currency

SOMEONE ONCE DESCRIBED *Word of Mouth* as a 'keyhole' programme. What they meant was that via the relatively restricted aperture of language, the listener was offered an opportunity to eavesdrop on whole roomfuls of ideas, issues, and angles on the contemporary condition. Leaf through this book and you will catch a flavour of that very diversity which has been the programme's trademark. And amongst more timeless notions, *Word of Mouth* has offered, from its very first editions, a fascinated commentary on the heavy-duty aspects of public life—politics, business and all that *Today* programme stuff— though always with a wry smile, naturally.

So, political observers are still dissecting the intricacies of political waffle and deconstructing the ways of Westminster's spin machine. Likewise, Chancellors come and go, yet the manipulation of our money never changes. So money, moolah, dibs, dosh, and spondulicks prove a rich trove for linguistic analysis.

And once you've spent the dosh, if you don't get the performance/return/lifespan/satisfaction/pleasure/efficiency (delete where applicable) what better to do than complain? But how do you negotiate the dragons of the Customer Complaints Department?

Now, no one is for a moment suggesting that you are trying to get your money back because you are (a) greedy or (b) dishonest, but *Word of Mouth*'s expert says that we progress every day through a veritable jungle of half-truths, untruths, and downright lies. Just part of the currency of daily life, I guess, and not just for politicians. Ah well.

Spun Gold

Pity the poor foreign student of English. Sitting on his or her bus in the morning, laden with tomes full of practice dialogues about life in Britain today—'On the Train', 'At the Bank'—you know the sort of thing. Opposite, a studious fellow traveller (no, not in *that* sense) has his face buried deep in the newspaper. The headlines on front and back pages are presented to view. The Page One lead screams *TOO MUCH SPIN, SAY TORIES*. Dead opposite, the sports headline reads *ENGLAND ATTACK LACKS SPIN*. Ah, the eccentricities of the English language! What a joy to behold for us who know. What puzzling ambiguities for the non-Brit who doesn't.

Before one even makes a start on untangling the different meanings of *spin* in those headlines, English presents the unwitting student with so many semantic elephant traps. All those phrasal verbs for a start. (Have *you* ever thought of the differences between *stand up* and *stand down*, between *stand out* and *stand in*, between *stand off* and *stand on*? It must be a complete horror even to begin to make sense of it all.)

Now, Americans confronting the phrasal verb nightmare at least have a good idea how to handle it. But I suggest that even they, when confronted with those strange *spinning* headlines and unacquainted with the ins and outs of cricket, would be mystified. (And as for those for whom English is still a learning experience, well, my sympathies!)

But if cricketing spin is likely to flummox them, it is not entirely inconceivable that a transatlantic reader might still today be puzzled by political spin. Because *spin* in this sense is a very recent phenomenon. On the other hand, as the term is originally American—from the game of baseball—they are clearly more likely to have come across it. (A *spin doctor* or particularly clever pitcher will apply special spin to the ball. Others have attributed the word to the game of pool, with similar meaning.)

I confess that the first time I encountered the term it was, I subsequently discovered, already well established in the political lexicon. I can remember feeling a particular sense of 'lostness' when a columnist in my newspaper, whom I admired and read regularly, suddenly dropped the term *spin-doctor* into his copy, without the merest gloss, explanation or 'so-called'—simply no qualification whatsoever. For him, it was clearly an established term, yet one which did not make any sense to me at all. I could like it or lump it. Sure, I could understand roughly from the context that it referred in some way to the enhancement of the interpretation of political events, but why *spin* exactly and who were these *doctors*? Couldn't get it at all. I do sympathize with those foreign students.

According to the reference books, *spin* in the sense of 'a bias or slant on information, intended to create a favourable impression when it is presented to the public' dates from at least as long ago as 1978 and probably quite a bit earlier, while *spin doctor* is first recorded in print six years later. This particular little confection is doubly mystifying to the initiated as it blends narrow specialized meanings of *both* its components.

On *Word of Mouth*, lexicographer Betty Kirkpatrick told the history of how *spin* originated with an Old English term, *spinnan*, which had no flavour of the sort of rotary motion with which it subsequently became synonymous. It was merely the drawing out and braiding together of threads to form a yarn. *Spinning a yarn* in the figurative sense of 'telling a story', Betty explained, originated, it is thought, with sailors who, while braiding their ropes, would tell tales to while away the time. *Spinning* in the sense of rotational motion originates in the mid-seventeenth century, and that confusing-to-foreigners cricketing association (just what picture is conjured up to the uninitiated by the phrase *left-arm spin* is wondrous to imagine!) does not appear until Victorian times.

Doctor in the famously puzzling expression is being used, not Hippocratic-oath fashion meaning to practise the medical arts, but as in 'to alter or disguise the appearance, flavour, or character of, falsify, tamper with, adulterate or "cook"', a sense which dates from the late eighteenth century.

But if *doctoring* in this sense is 200 or so years old, politics itself has been a black art since governance began, and the idea that political deeds or facts are open to different interpretations is almost as primordial. It was, though, the fact that the Labour administration from 1997 onwards, which started in a blaze of favourable headlines and optimism, soon became deeply bogged down in the mire of spin and accusations of spin that caught the political analyst's eye for a contemporary phenomenon. In fact *New Labour spin* became such a useful piece of ammunition to the Opposition that it itself became one of those other political weapons, the *sound-bite* and the *slogan* (and then became itself a piece of weaponry in the spin war).

Andrew Rawnsley, as chief political commentator for the *Observer* newspaper, has been watching the rise and rise of spin and the spinners since the term was minted: 'What the spin doctorate would say in their defence is that any event is open to interpretation. So, "We as the government—and we as spinning on behalf of the government—have every right to put the best gloss we can on a particular event or a particular policy announcement."'

And, turning to the lessons of history, we discover that this particular political black art has been around even since before Niccolò dei Machiavelli (1469–1527) gave his name to what subsequent generations might call *spinning*. Thomas Langley was, argues historian Ian Sharman (who has written a study of him entitled *The First Spin-Doctor*), one of the earliest political fact manipulators in British history. 'Langley was the son of a peasant farmer who rose to become, in turn, Keeper of the King's Signet, Privy Seal, Bishop of Durham, Chancellor to two English kings, a billionaire (he made £10.5 billion a year in today's money) and, above all, was the first spin-doctor,' says Sharman. 'In order to seize power in the first place and then maintain it, one has to always be one step ahead and manipulate in advance, which is what was the genius of Langley as a spin doctor—to manipulate the events in advance.'

It was during the reign of the young King Henry V that Langley operated, and Sharman tells the story of how he manipulated the facts of a visit to the French court in order, in the long run, to gear the public up to the notion of a war with France.

> 'Langley came back to England and he was questioned by Parliament. They asked him in particular what was the demeanour of the French—how did they view our king? Langley said: "they found our king to be indolent; they thought he was young inexperienced and juvenile." Of course, the Commons erupted because of the insult, and the subsidies were voted through the next day. War ensued, and from that we got Agincourt.'

But if the notion of putting a positive gloss on neutral or even on negative facts is not new—and we are all too aware of what happens to facts at times of war, for example—the way that spin doctoring in a more ritualized sense has developed on the British political scene is a product very much of the modern communications environment. With the ever-gathering pace of social life, televisual zapping, snack-food 'grazing' and the development of that late twentieth-century cliché the *sound-bite culture* (the word *sound-bite* is recorded from 1980 onwards), the need to make an impact with policy and be seen to be doing something has become imperative.

We want action now! Do something! Make it happen! The cry is all about us, and the impatience that we frequently display across almost all sectors of life at the start of the third millennium (road rage, air rage, surf rage, and the rest) means that the pressure to 'do something' in politics—and, above all, to be *seen* to be doing something—is at the top of the agenda. Not surprising therefore that the name of Alistair Campbell has become, during the Labour administrations that have straddled the millennium, a significant part of the New Labour project. Andrew Rawnsley comments:

> I think what's happened now is that *spin* has got associated with all sorts of other things which come quite close to lying. It's a word we don't often use in politics (you're even banned from using it in the House of Commons by the Speaker), but people feel spin's almost got to the point of lying. Certainly a deliberate attempt to deceive. That spinning is in some way not simply putting your best gloss on a fact, but actually in fact *creating* the truth.

The problem too is that the more the western world has become plugged in, connected, cabled, and internetted, the more we know what can be done to facts. Just as image manipulation, computer enhancement of photographs, the 'morphing' of faces on video and on TV, *Walking with Dinosaurs* and the special effects wizardry of Industrial Light and Magic, *Buzz Lightyear*, *Monsters Inc*, and the rest in the film industry, so facts are manipulable too. And we know it. We've been shown how they do the SFX magic on screen and we are rightly suspicious that our politicians are up to it right, left, and centre. It is an aspect of contemporary political process that has been effectively exploited by the Conservative Party to attack the powerful government of Tony Blair. 'I think that part of their problem is that the modern audience—which is the voters in our period—are now far too literate about the techniques, agrees Andrew Rawnsley. 'I mean they have seen Bill Clinton looking the people in the eye, pointing his finger, oozing sincerity and saying, "I didn't have sexual relations with that woman, Miss Lewinsky."'

Not so, in the really quite recent past. All those so-called 'fireside chats' that our political masters used to indulge in on both sides of the Atlantic. Cosy and intimate, Harold Wilson puffing on his pipe and relaxing into an armchair, full of comfortable northern vowels and homespun wisdom. 'For a while it worked, this idea that politicians, particularly the leader, whether it was Tony Blair or Bill Clinton—whoever it was—would directly communicate to the people through a set event like the "fireside chat". It was a technique pioneered in America by Franklin Roosevelt, and in the radio addresses of Stanley Baldwin in Britain in the 1930s. They would be able to communicate directly with the public—unmediated by all those reptiles in broadcasting or the newspapers: this direct connection.'

Now, of course, that doesn't work. The surprise that John Major sprang on the public in the 1992 election when he mounted his soapbox and harangued the crowd through a loudhailer was exactly the right sort of 'anti-spin' that was cleverly calculated to counterbalance the highly stage-managed spectaculars mounted by Neil Kinnock's Labour Party. But it was a trick that Major could not pull off twice: the highly efficient spin machine of the New Labour team saw off the tactic in 1997. But spin is dangerous stuff, and the lesson of John Major's modest proposals delivered by apparently the most modest of means in the general election campaign of 1992, has not always been remembered. The current disenchantment with politics that is much spoken of and worried over has been ascribed in some quarters to 'nobody being able to believe anything any more', as a result of over-spinning.

'Modern politicians now are desperately searching for ways of proving their authenticity,' says Andrew Rawnsley. And perhaps John Major's anti-spin soapbox was one of the first manifestations of the true postmodern form of the art.

> Now of course, sometimes appearing *un*spun can be the most clever spin of all. I think Ken Livingstone is the classic example. One of the reasons Ken Livingstone won the contest for mayor of London was because he marketed himself as an 'anti'-politician. He kept saying again and again to us, 'You know, I'm just poor old Ken against the great New Labour machine with all its spin doctors...' I don't know a politician who's cleverer at manipulating the media or deploying some of its darker arts than Ken. He was the fantastic example of somebody who marketed himself as 'unspun'. Which, in itself, was brilliant spin.

Moolah Makes the World Go Round

As we know, money makes the world go round but doesn't grow on trees. It's the root of all evil but can't buy love. Time is money, though a fool and his money are soon parted. Money talks, but that's the way money goes, pop goes the weasel.

Technically speaking, money is a general and agreed measure of value so that we can exchange it for goods and services. However, it doesn't disappear after the exchange, which means we can store it, lend it, or sell it. It makes it seem very real. Yet, in a way money's a fiction, says Kevin Jackson, editor of *The Oxford Book of Money*. Like fiction, it works by us all collaborating in the business of believing in it. Believing in money makes it possible to render all things, places, processes, skills, attributes, even people themselves, equivalent. Money can make a quantity of bread equal an area of land equal a period of time of a person's work equal a footballer's leg equal a beautiful beach equal a gemstone equal a divorcee's contribution to a family equal a slave equal a pile of another country's currency. In short, money is magic, though Francis Bacon (the sixteenth-century essayist) said that money was 'like muck'. This wasn't a disparaging comment: he was trying to make the egalitarian suggestion that money was mostly not a good thing, apart from when 'it be spread'.

Money has to be recorded. In the past this has involved such things as cowrie shells, pelts, pieces of paper and, more recently, sequences of ones and zeros in the memories of electronic machines. The British Museum has one of the world's finest collections of the metal system of accounting that we call coins. It's where the *Word of Mouth* team met the curator of medieval and early modern coinage, Barry Cook. The clinking in our pockets begins with the Romans, he says. Indeed, the word *money* derives from Juno Moneta, the leading godess in the Roman pantheon. It's from her name that we also get the word *monitor*. (Money next door to a temple? That sounds familiar.) It seems as if this followed the pattern of Saturn's temple, which likewise had a mint and treasury next door, known as the *aerarium*. The *ases* that were coined here acquired Juno's second name, and the thing we've had to spend ever since has been *money*.

In the antique mahogany cabinets and felt-lined drawers of the British Museum, the array of obsolete coinage is a spectacle. In fact, just as Monty Python sang: 'There is nothing quite as wonderful as money. There is nothing quite as beautiful as cash...' Anyone who wept at the passing of those deliciously English words *shilling, farthing, thruppenny bit, florin, half-crown, ten-bob note* and the like would sob buckets at what has disappeared from previous centuries—not just *sovereigns* and *half-sovereigns*, but *angels* and *half-angels, George nobles, testoons*, and much more, each with its history.

If you've thought that the monarch's presence on your cash was a mite overstated, then the 1500s would have had you overwhelmed. The sovereign was called the sovereign as a way of reminding everyone that Henry VII (not someone with a tremendously clear-cut claim to the throne) was here to stay. The angel, introduced in the 1460s by Edward IV, bore that name because it showed the Archangel Michael attacking a dragon. The name also gave Shakespeare a rich source of puns, as when Richard II rather optimistically weighs up his chances against the usurper Bolingbroke:

> For every man that Bolingbroke hath press'd
> To lift shrewd steel against our golden crown,
> God for his Richard hath in heavenly pay
> A glorious angel: then, if angels fight,
> Weak men must fall, for heaven still guards the right.
> (*Richard II*, III. ii. 60-64)

The testoon was worth a shilling and had that particular name because it was the first coin in Italy to bear a realistic profile portrait (*testa* = head in Italian). This too was a coin that Henry VII introduced to English coinage. The testoons of Henry VIII, though, were described by Barry Cook as 'horrible, green and coppery, disgusting little things'. The copper coming through the silver was an indication of the debasing of the coinage that Good King Harry introduced. Nowadays, with almost valueless materials in our money, there's no point in debasing the coinage. We call it *devaluation*. This is enacted by dint of the computer keyboard. If the singer Woody Guthrie were alive today, he would have to change the words of his lines: 'Some will you rob with a shotgun, and some with a fountain pen.'

What governments do with money—or, more importantly, why—is for most of us a mystery. This is exemplified perfectly by the fact that the linguistic currency of high finance is itself so difficult: *fiscal, overheating, the FTSE, bullish, marginal propensity, creative accounting*. Some words take on an almost mystical quality: like *business confidence*, where commentators talk as if directors of companies start feeling a bit shaky round the knees and give up overnight. There's *the economy*, spoken of as if it's something that goes about doing its business without us being the ones doing it. There are the poetic words *boom* and *slump* that come over as mysterious forces that well up and down. It seems as if booms and slumps are things that are done to business, rather than things that business does to the rest of us.

Some words have no agreed meaning. When we spoke to Lord Lamont, the erstwhile Conservative Chancellor of the Exchequer, he pointed out that there was no agreement on the word *recovery*. Should it, as he wanted, signify that the total of all the country's sales was no longer falling, but was now increasing? Or should it, as Peter Jay, then the BBC's economics editor, wanted, signify the moment when the upturn on the graph reached the same level as the line had reached before it nosedived—rather as the top points of the letter 'u' line up opposite each other?

Lord Lamont was also adamant that there was no agreement about the colour of Wednesday, 16 September 1992. This was the day that the pound was ejected from that most hesitant-sounding of acronyms, the ERM, the European Exchange Rate Mechanism. 'Some called that Wednesday "Black",' said Lamont, 'but if you weren't in favour of us being in the ERM in the first place then it was White.'

Word of Mouth questioned Lord Lamont on the even more mysterious term *the reserves*. Does this really refer to vaults of gold? Are there shelves down there each marked with a country's name? Do men with wheelbarrows cart bricks of bullion from one shelf to the next? He hedged a little, conceded that, yes, some gold would physically be in the vaults but essentially, the changes in the gold reserves were what he described as 'entries in the Bank of England's ledger'. This conjures up the picture of a dried-up Dickensian figure, perhaps slightly hard of hearing, perched on a stool, hunched over a page lit by a candle, scratching the figures in the nation's gigantic ledger. 'One quarter of an ounce from Tanganyika, did you say, Mr Worthington, sir?'

Lamont remembers an occasion at university when the students were lectured to by Richard Crossman, later to serve in the Labour Government of 1964. Crossman was explaining that when Labour came to power they would pretend that there was an economic crisis as a ruse to justify doing whatever they wanted to do. Lamont reports Crossman as saying to them in a grand and gloomy voice: 'We'll go down into the vaults of the Bank of England, and when we come up, we'll tell them that there isn't anything there.'

All this is a far cry from the talk on the street. We visited Mr John Julian, owner of a fruit stall on Ridley Road market in Hackney, London. 'One pound is a *oncer*. And you say three quid is *three ounces*, nine quid, *nine ounces*.' There was a moment of confusion here, as Mr Julian, being a fully fledged speaker of cockney, pronounced 'ounces' as 'ances'. 'Ances? What are they?' we could be heard asking in our best BBC voices. 'Ances. Sixteen ances to the pand.' Of course, of course. A pound is an ounce.

The ten-pound note to him is a 'cockle'. 'Cock an' 'en rhymes wiv ten,' he explained, 'so it's a *cockle*. A *neviss* is seven quid. That's backslang. A fiver, that's a *godiva*. We don't bovver wiv the Lady. A *bullseye* is fifty quid. A *monkey* is five hundred.' Our resident slang lexicographer, Tony Thorne, chirped up at this point and said, 'And five hundred thousand is a *gorilla*.' 'I don't see that sorta cash,' said Mr Julian.

But it wasn't only terms for money that trip off his tongue. What if he saw someone a bit dodgy coming near his stall? 'If I see someone a bit on the slippery side,' he said, 'I'll say, "Watch out for Mr Mustard over there." I might think he's going to dip someone, see? So I say, "Keep your eyes on Mr Mustard." Mustard, it's hot. I'm saying he's red hot. 'My dad, he always had loads a money, he was loaded, so we called him *Billy Bundles*, bundles of cash. But if you got someone who don't buy you a cuppa tea or nothing, you call him *Johnny Longpockets,* 'cos he don't pull his money out. Money, we call *wonga,* or *wads.* Or *wedge* or *dosh.*'

John Julian had more fruit to sell so we bowed out and repaired to a nearby hostelry, where Tony Thorne filled us in a little. Originally a lot of this slang was a secret language, part of the in-group of traders, muttered to each other so that the shoppers couldn't understand what was being said. But now a lot of it, particularly the rhyming slang, has leaked out into TV comedy, school playgrounds, and even the floors of the money markets. Some of it is quite old, nineteenth and eighteenth century, but a couple of words for money that Tony's heard, *pelf* and *rhino,* are medieval. *Dosh,* he says comes from *dash,* an East African word, while *ackers* is from Egypt—loanwords from army days.

Students today seem to be stimulated by something more rhymey. Standing outside the pub, wondering who's got enough for a round, you can hear them asking, 'Are you holding folding?'

And the thing about the poetry of the street is that we'll never know who first coined that phrase. As it were.

" "

Dear Sir, I Wish to Complain . . .

DINER: 'Waiter, waiter, what's this fly doing in my soup?'
WAITER: 'Breast-stroke, sir.'

DINER: 'Waiter, waiter, there's a fly in my soup'.
WAITER: 'Please lower your voice, sir, they'll all be wanting one!'

The jokes about complaining in restaurants are as corny and as familiar as the ubiquitous soup that turns up in them. They are a tradition that reeks of the Donald McGill saucy postcard and has echoes of battle-axe seaside landladies whose notion of service belonged more to Wormwood Scrubs than Scarborough. So ingrained is that tradition that the most famous Monty Python sketch of all featured a complaint—not about soup containing unrequested additional protein but, of course, about a parrot. Michael Palin's pet-shop owner's firm protestations about the qualities of the Norwegian Blue in the face of John Cleese's strident complaints are the stuff of comedy legend. So much so that today, thirty years after the Pythons first brought these British archetypes to the screen, it is a brave person who goes into a shop and addresses the assistant behind the counter with the immortal phrase *I wish to complain*.

The reason why the Parrot Sketch is intrinsically so funny is partly because we British are so reticent about uttering words of complaint. Less so today, perhaps, than when Cleese first expressed his dissatisfaction with the ex-parrot, 'bereft of life, it rests in peace ...', but we still, I think, hesitate. Despite a cultural change which resulted in the linguistic somersaults that turned *passengers* into *customers*, despite decades of critical judgements delivered from the lofty authority of the Consumers' Association, despite the People's Charter and any number of satisfaction-guaranteed-or-your-money-back reassurances, there is still a level of embarrassment when complaints are to be made in public. 'We didn't want to make a fuss' is the explanation too often still forthcoming. Maybe there is some lurking fear that even a mild observation will result in antics like those of Basil Fawlty in the face of the legitimate complaints of virtually every client of his eponymous horror-hotel.

But the tide is rising. The other day, a man missed his footing in front of me on the pavement and went flying headlong to the ground. After enquiring if he was all right, his companions very audibly and immediately encouraged him to 'sue the council—it'd be worth a few bob!' Television advertisements tempting viewers into making legal claims for accidents sustained are daily on our screens. The culture is shifting, slowly, and *Word of Mouth*, with its finger on the *Zeitgeist*, took a look early on in its run at this evolving phenomenon of what has now become a cliché, the 'rising tide of complaint'.

Seated at his swish office desk in the City is Jasper Griegson. He is a man who has found a form of words that has proved almost irresistible to the product manufacturers, service providers, and any other organization or individual with whom he has found a cause to complain, protest, and seek redress. Because Jasper Griegson is a professional complainer. He was even once in his career adopted by the *Sun* newspaper as its official complainer, taking up readers' misfortunes on their behalf.

He says the art of the successful complaint lies in the language. It is not enough to have a good case; what really secures a result is the phraseology and the framing of the letter. And to cut through the thick undergrowth of professional resistance of big corporations, the language needs to be up to the job: 'If you want to get an effective result, it tends to be aggressive,' says Griegson. He leafs through a thick folder of his letters and sheaves of replies and receipts, and extracts one of his complaints about a proprietary window-cleaning product which begins in language that leaves no doubt how he is feeling:

> Excuse me! I understand from the labels on the outside of your bottles of your product that it is made by appointment to Her Majesty Queen Elizabeth the Second. If she has the same

problems that I do with the spray-heads that you have recently introduced, she must be considering abdication...'

Tough-talking, then, but also witty. The Griegson technique of getting through uses a great deal of humour, alongside the aggression. Another key component is linguistic confidence. The effective letter of complaint needs to leave its recipient in no doubt that you know what you are talking about, no matter how insignificant the product or service which has not measured up. 'Ideally, I suppose, for every single complaint from one about a 30p bar of chocolate to a million-pound compensation claim one would like to have a letter from a firm of solicitors. Now, obviously, one can't have that, so what one needs to do if one wants to bring an effective complaint is dress it up in legal style.'

Not that you need to be a lawyer to get the phrasing exactly right; it just has to *sound* convincing. 'The language that I use is a sort of slightly pompous quasi-legalese. One of mine that I tend to end up with for example is "I look to you for a substantial and meaningful gesture of goodwill." I never mention money.' On the other hand, it is no good simply to complain into thin air; the company needs to know that you expect some form of payback. So Griegson recommends a phrase such as 'I look to you for a positive result'. No fobbing off will be acceptable, or so he hopes.

Now, how many times have you eventually overcome your British scruples, put pen to paper, and confronted a firm with the evidence, only to be referred to some apparently invincible minion hiding behind a force-field known as Customer Complaints or Customer Services? Like some invisible screen, they lie in wait for your carefully drafted letters, ready to bounce them off into deep space where nobody can hear you complain.

You only have to read the consumer pages of the national press to disclose ream upon ream of these formulaic responses. 'We have been experiencing temporary difficulties at our factory, for reasons beyond our control ... we regret that our liability does not extend to matters such as the one you raise ... we can assure you that we are doing everything in our power to rectify the situation' and so on and so on. Like the words of skilled politicians, the verbiage is spun, respun, and unravelled in a never-ending stream of usually meaningless expressions. Excuse is piled upon excuse and those weasel words of vacuous pomposity (*everything in our power, as soon as possible, sparing no effort*) pour limitless balm on our frustrations, disappointments and—worse—justifiable claims for financial redress.

I suppose we have almost all read them sometimes in our lives; and who—less cynical perhaps, gullible maybe—has not been momentarily soothed by them? After all, they contain those absolutes which leave us believing action to be on the way—*everything, as soon as possible,* and the rest. The fact is that *everything in the firm's power* may amount strictly to nothing; *as soon as possible* may mean in twenty years' time; and as for *sparing no effort,* who is to say they have any effort available? No. The key is to avoid the honeyed words of customer services. Head straight for the top.

And while you are about it, suggests Jasper Griegson, make it clear that you are not going to put up with being bounced off into complaints hyperspace: 'I try and pre-empt what they are going to say by writing something like "Let me assure you now that a mere two-line apology from your Customer Services Department will not suffice".' Because, of course, the immediate reaction from the managing director who gets my letter is "Let's give it all to the customer services department". So you pre-empt that one and you actually get a letter from the man that matters.' Or at least that is the theory.

Griegson is in his letters a terrific showman, and it is probably unlikely that the average person with a legitimate grievance is going to push the imaginative boat out as far as he has done. It takes quite a bit of chutzpah—and a not particularly significant issue at stake—to go as far as he did in this example about a famous brand of bottled water. 'It was a jokey complaint,' he concedes: 'I put as a heading: "Re: mineral water that tastes like water from the Paris sewers", addressed to the managing director, of course. "To my amazement and horror the standard of the water did not comply either with your normal very high standards or with the requirements of the Water Act (1972) Section 3, subsection 4, sub-subsection A". I don't know what that section says—I made it up—but it sounds rather impressive.' This bit of bluff got a result, as did another famous claim against an airline for lost luggage which, so they say, involved a threat to impound an aircraft were the issue not resolved. If you are Jasper Griegson, the rule has always been: think big.

When selecting your language, it is important to judge how forceful you need to be. Go too far and it can go horribly wrong. 'Abusive tends not to work,' is the verdict, and certainly losing your temper on the telephone and bellowing swear-words at some benighted call centre operative does not seem to produce results. Other, that is, than the termination of the call. Many if not all firms these days have a policy of refusing to deal with abusive callers—however justified the complaint—and operators now routinely state clearly that they are instructed not to deal with people who swear at them. So the rule is—don't yell and don't curse, even if the switchboard has been serenading you with 'Eine Kleine Nachtmusik' or a wobbly rendition of 'Memory' for half an hour, while you were 'held in our queuing system... an operator will deal with your enquiry *as soon as possible*' (that phrase again!).

And that can even extend to Jasper Griegson's favoured format, the written complaint. A particularly strong letter he sent to an airline, with whose food he had taken issue, produced the curt response: 'I am returning herewith your letter dated 24th June which I find unduly impolite and offensive. We are not used to dealing with this kind of correspondence. If you would like to present a formal complaint we should be happy to deal with it.' The knack is to be aggressive, not abusive.

So once you have sorted out the language, what about the overall framing of the grievance? Our official complainer has his golden rules:

> Start off the letter: 'I wish to register a complaint', very much in the style of the Monty Python sketch about the parrot. So straightaway you're making it quite clear what you're after— you're complaining, you're here to complain. Then, go into the history in a concise way of precisely what happened. In the final paragraph: what do you want?'

And, when composing your letter, it is no bad idea to keep somewhere near the top of your mind the image of John Cleese stabbing his finger accusingly at Michael Palin, or—as Basil Fawlty—losing it royally with his hapless guests, for another reason too:

> Control your temper. The people who get nowhere are the ones who never even get to the stage of writing the letter but bang their fists on the counter and shout and scream at somebody who doesn't matter. The golden rule is: don't get mad – get even.

Cut and Thrust

Oh dear. They're still at it. Politicians! Who would credit it? I mean to say, you'd have thought that after all this time they'd have improved a bit, wouldn't you? But no. Same old rubbish, year in year out. Put a political talking head in front of a microphone or a camera or up on a platform and bowl a few questions at it and they get out the *Westminster Thesaurus of Evasion and Devious Language* and bury their brains in it. And it seems that this is a practice that has been with us for centuries. In the 1770s, the Earl of Grafton wrote of honourable members that 'if called upon in Parliament for information which every member in either House has a right to expect, they either give no reply or evade the question'. So that's all right, then. Sanctioned in print and sealed into the soul of every aspiring politician is the ability to use language to avoid answering the question that is being directly posed, whether the arena be the chamber of the House of Commons, the BBC *Today* or *Newsnight* studios, or the calmer atmosphere of a dinner à deux between politico and political correspondent at some little Westminster eaterie.

It is of course everywhere, because every politician needs at some point to avoid giving away the facts, admitting he or she is wrong, saying that he or she has made a mistake or that things are going less than swimmingly. Sometimes they do it by downright untruths. President Nixon of the United States was famous for lying publicly about his involvement in the Watergate scandal ... and paid the price. But usually, the language is rather that of evasion than of untruth. In the bowels of Broadcasting House, in the BBC sound archives, there is a notorious interview that was given many years ago by the then Prime Minister of Malawi, Dr Hastings Banda. The hapless interviewer has a string of questions ready to put to Dr Banda, who responds with such excellent parries to the questioner's thrusts as 'Why should I tell you that?', 'Why do you ask me that question?', or 'I'm not going to tell you that.' At the end of the long list of questions to which not one single concrete answer is given, the interviewer asks, firmly, yet with some despair in his voice, 'Are you going to answer any of these questions?' To which Dr Banda's answer is, inevitably, negative. 'Then this is a singularly pointless interview,' concludes the BBC man. He had done his job.

But, in a strange sort of way, so had Dr Banda. Because, in fact, political discourse often consists of exactly this sort of refusal to play ball; it is just that the form is rather more covert when it is John Humphrys, James Naughtie, or Jeremy Paxman doing the grilling rather than the unfortunate BBC man on the ground at the Prime Minister's residence in Lilongwe. The distinguished political columnist Peter Riddell has heard too many politicians offer the weasel words that belie the truth of what they are meaning to be fooled by them.

Take that favourite and apparently graceful response by politico to inquisitor while on live radio or TV, *with respect*. *With respect* means 'You're an awkward so and so and you put me in a difficult position and this is the only way I can try to get rid of a few seconds before I think up an answer.' Therein lies one of the keys, too, to the linguistic art of the political interview—delaying tactics. Comments Riddell, who has seen literally hundreds of politicians of every party hue come and go: 'It was particularly used at Labour Party conferences by the late John Smith—he used to get up at conference and say *with respect* or *with great respect...*'

The *Observer*'s political columnist and microscopic analyst of Blair's Britain, Andrew Rawnsley, goes further: 'I think *with respect* means I'm just going to be fairly rude to you; *with great respect* means I'm going to be seriously rude to you.' This ubiquitous phrase owes its origins to that other arena of cut-and-thrust where gentlemanly conduct is *de rigueur* yet where intellectual and linguistic fights are as bare-knuckle as they come, the courts of law. Not surprising, given how many professional politicians possess law degrees and have spent the better part of their careers throwing about insults in the most genteel of manners in the Central Criminal Court at the Old Bailey and elsewhere, that it should slide effortlessly across into the politico's lexicon of choice. 'It's a great one used by lawyers—we always hear them doing it in court, don't we? *With great respect, M'lud*, they say, when they're really saying to the judge, "You stupid old duffer, you don't understand the point." And they use it in Parliament in exactly the same way.'

So this little two- or three-word phrase packs a useful punch *and* delays the necessity for a real response. We should not underplay the value of the well-turned (and frequently well-worn, to the point of the springs coming through in some cases) set of words to fend off the urgency of the ticking clock on the studio wall. In the old days, interviewees and interviewers were reminded of the onward rush of time in a radio studio by the regular jerking round of the second hand on a large clock on the wall. There was something ineluctable about that forward movement of the second hand which urged a response. As if, Magnus Magnusson-fashion, it was saying, 'Come on, I'll have to hurry you.' Today's digital equivalents, more discreet, make less of a fuss about it. Yet playing for time remains one of the first rules the political interviewee learns while being schooled for media appearances. With the piranhas of *Today* and *Newsnight* circling to catch one bloodied chunk of revelation, of admission, of U-turn or contradiction, and that clock relentlessly flicking away the seconds on the wall, it is truly hard not to fall back on that much-thumbed *Thesaurus of Evasion*.

Always good, then, to kick off with a confidence-inspiring *Frankly*. Nobody is under the illusion any more that the speaker is seriously intending his or her listeners to believe that he or she is truly being frank, but *frankly* offers that same double-points value-for-utterance, in fractionally delaying the meat of the response and buying a brain-churning second-and-a-half. It also seems to convey a degree of confidentiality. 'I am taking you into my confidence and telling you the truth over this issue. I shall make a clean breast of it and you are fortunate to be sitting opposite me to garner these hallowed truths that I am about to utter.' Useful word. It was said—probably by Mike Yarwood—that one of Harold Wilson's favourite opening gambits was 'to be perfectly frank and honest and reasonable'. I just wonder how many times he had to use that phrase before he was rumbled. Nice and long, though—a great delaying tactic—especially when he had that other most useful prop to hand with which further to delay, punctuate, and indeed theatrically gesture when a point needed underlining, namely his pipe.

If we feel that *frankly* has now lost some of its allure and lustre, how about : *I want to make it perfectly clear*...? Clarity is promised but, as so often with politicians' promises, rarely delivered. But that clock has ticked on by at least two seconds and the cat has still not been let out of the bag.

One of the perils of early morning political interviews is, of course, just that—they are done most often in the early morning. If pre-recorded, that may mean a 4 a.m. start and a phone lifted by a dressing-gowned MP yawning only three hours into his slumbers after some late-night sitting of the House. Playing for time is very important here, then. And if live, it may be that the sole contact between your telling the truth—or not—and the Humphrys elephant trap is a grotty satellite link from the radio car. A sudden tumble onto air with little or no warning can be your undoing. So for early-rising politicians, who *want to make it perfectly clear...* there is the oh-so useful vamp-till-ready extension of that, *precisely where I stand on this matter.* Just run a stopwatch on this concoction: *I want to make it perfectly clear precisely where I stand on this matter.* I reckon that rates a good five seconds of saying precisely nothing, but implying that you are honest and about to utter a real home truth. Great stuff.

There are many variants. We tried this one out on Andrew Rawnsley: *Let me be perfectly clear about this...* 'Well that's much the same as *Let me be perfectly frank,* which means "I'm not going to tell you anything at all about this and in fact I'm going to do my damnedest to cover up whatever you're asking me about".' The evasion can also be less cover-up and more a diversionary tactic. The Conservative minister Michael Heseltine had his own very neat way of turning the question away from perilous areas by openly 'interpreting' the interviewer's question thus: *the question I think you're asking is,* which Peter Riddell decodes as follows: 'That means "the question I want to answer".' Riddell—like all the Westminster veterans—is long skilled in finding turns of phrase that, he hopes, will leave the politician dangling from the noose of his or her own ingenuity. The rules for broadcast interviewing are simple: ask questions that require a *yes* or a *no* and that cannot be fudged. If possible, ask a 'double-bind' question to which either possible answer catches the politico on the hop. That is the holy grail. It rarely works. Peter Riddell: 'It's always particularly humiliating, I find, talking to a politician when he says, *I'm glad you asked me that* or *That's a very helpful question*. Nothing annoys one more—but that's a similar technique to *I think the question you're asking*—you've got on to ground where they want to be.'

Back to that infernal clock. While Jeremy Paxman is deep in hand-to-hand combat with Jack Straw, or whomever, he has one eye on his monitor and one ear on his director in the gallery. He knows that the *I'll have to hurry you* technique has more than one benefit: not only can he come out of the item on schedule and leave himself sufficient time for the news headlines, but also, in pressuring Straw, he may just get him to stop waffling on along the conventional party line and jerk him suddenly into a fit of clear, unspun, from-the-heart words of true wisdom. But Straw has developed a neat line in avoiding this ploy. He sounds rather aggrieved, and says things like *if I may finish my point*. This makes him sound a victim, engages the viewer's sympathy, and allows him the time to do just that. After all, Paxman is hardly going to say *No*, is he? Along with this phrase go similar aggrieved-interrupted utterances like *May I just say*, *As I was saying when I was interrupted*, and even *Do you honestly expect me to answer that question?*

Andrew Rawnsley again:

> The terrible thing is that they do all now come in with their little bits of card before interviews with their bullet point or points. And you can ask them whatever question you like: 'Are you going to resign, Chancellor?' You'll get the same answer. 'What did you have for breakfast this morning, Chancellor?' You'll get the same answer. 'When did you last make love, Chancellor?' You'll get

absolutely the same answer, because they're going in with that one specific answer that they want to give, and whatever question you ask that's the only answer you're going to get.

One thing, therefore, that you can be certain of as a political interviewer is that it is highly unlikely that the person on the other side of the desk from you will say 'Yes, I agree.' Such clear-cut answers are simply hardly part of the lexicon. The delight of the television series *Yes, Minister* and *Yes, Prime Minister* was exactly such evasive language, with Sir Humphrey Appleby's 'Not *exactly*, Prime Minister' offering just such linguistic sleight of hand as true politicians deploy at every opportunity.

So, faced with a searingly straight question from the other side of the microphone, what are the options open to the politician who will say anything but answer the question on offer? Well, he or she can simply ignore it—and answer another question, as Andrew Rawnsley suggests above. Or they can simply decline to answer at all, Hastings Banda style. They can acknowledge the question ('That's a very good question and one which is preoccupying many of us at this time, but may I just say this?') and not answer it. They may criticize the questioner ('That, if I may say so, is a highly inappropriate question at this time') or answer just part of the question, ignoring the difficult bit. They may claim that they have already answered the question ('I think you'll find that I have already dealt with that point') or turn the interviewing tables ('Well, may I ask *you* what *you* consider to be the best option?'). But straight answers? Never. Not even when they say, 'Let me give you a straight answer.'

Many of these phrases ring extremely familiar, and with the rise of so-called 'spin' the non-answering of questions while appearing to answer them has over the past ten years been polished into a fine political art. Add to the brew the rich crop of political clichés that still bulk out the most banal discourse and, as the clock measures out the platitudes second by second we have the ingredients for the sort of political prevarication that gives the whole business a truly bad name.

> I want to make it perfectly clear precisely where I stand on this matter. Frankly, the time has come when we should stand shoulder to shoulder. We should explore every avenue and leave no stone unturned. To be quite honest with you, when all is said and done, I can see light at the end of the tunnel, a just and lasting solution. In all honesty, what it all boils down to at the end of the day and in the last analysis is that each and every one of us—our kith and our kin—should stand up and be counted. Having said that, I think, if I may say so, with the greatest respect, that you're missing the point. The fact of the matter is ... [and so on and so on and so on]

As Peter Sellers declared, in the final words of his famous skit on a speech by Harold Macmillan: 'Finally, in conclusion, let me say just this ...'

Lies, All Lies

It is of course a slippery character, the truth. Just when you think you have it bang to rights, it slides away from under your hand. *Well, it depends what you mean by ..., in a manner of speaking, it depends where you're coming from.* Ah, the caveats and qualifications that chip away at the absoluteness of the truth. And after all, was not the organ of the Soviet Communist Party for generations called *Pravda*—Truth? So which particular truth would you like to hear today, sir ... madam?

That is not to say, on the other hand, that if the truth is in some way qualified or—worse—tainted, the reverse is true (there we go again), i.e. someone is *lying*. Lies are not the automatic flip-side of the truth. The truth is ... that the truth is very grey and very flexible. 'Did you watch the telly when I told you to get on with your homework?' asks the irritated mum of her recalcitrant teenager. The answer is always 'No'. Even if the television was still switched on when the mother entered the room. How come? 'Yeah, right. It was on but ... I wasn't watching it!'

The truth will out. Or will it?

Word of Mouth set out to investigate some of the labyrinthine pathways that wind across the hinterland between truth and untruth, in the company of two expert witnesses whose very lives have over the years been much taken up with these very far-from-absolutes. One is a lawyer, Catherine Bond, who has in her time spent much energy and effort schooling witnesses in how to deliver their evidence and respond to cross-questioning in the witness box with a level of linguistic conviction that honours the truth of their evidence.

Geoffrey Beattie, now Professor of Psychology at the University of Manchester, has spent a number of years analysing the way people behave when they stray from the truth.

> People lie for all kinds of reasons, of course, and they seem to lie every moment of the day. I remember a while ago someone did some research looking at the kinds of lies in a typical day, starting with the lies of advertising. And then I suppose we kind of go through our lives not wanting to hurt other people and often not

being entirely honest about things. And it's just amazing really how lies are kind of part of everyday life.

So alongside the real whoppers, the 'No, m'Lud, I was not in the vicinity of the premises when Burglar Bill and his gang showed up. No sir!', you get the so-called 'little white lies', all innocent and insignificant, where telling an untruth is designed to save someone's face or someone's bacon, or spare someone's blushes. 'Try it as an exercise,' says Geoffrey Beattie, 'when you wake up in the morning and you start off reading the cereal packet, till going to bed at night. I mean, we're just surrounded by lies all the time.'

Washo washes whiter, Guaranteed to remove all known stains, The one and only... Advertisers know few rules of honesty when it comes to truths, and the trade description legislation was enacted precisely to protect consumers from the more fraudulent claims of what used to be known as *Madison Avenue* (after the location of New York's advertising agencies). No longer can a certain brand of tobacco claim—as once it did on enamelled signs outside tobacconists—*does not affect your throat*. Today's cigarette packets are billboards for dire truthful warnings about the perils of smoking.

Yet today, West End theatre proprietors and those touting Hollywood's best are still hard at it picking selective quotations from the debris of disastrous reviews to salvage the one positive phrase from an otherwise damning notice. Lies, all lies. But it goes with the territory.

The territory inhabited by presidents of the United States of America has in the past quarter-century been much raked over by truth-seekers. Bill Clinton famously—or infamously—stated emphatically that he had not had 'sexual relations' with Monica

Lewinsky (all a question of what you mean by 'sexual relations', I guess, your Honor. Fear not, such definitions are not the preoccupation of the present volume.)

But it was a *British* civil servant, Sir Robert Armstrong, who famously explained that he had been 'economical with the truth', and a *British* politician, the Conservative minister Alan Clark, who coined the variation 'economical with the *actualité*' to describe his own statements. And lies lay at the heart of the scandal that actually brought down a president—Watergate, named after the building where the first crimes were committed in 1972 (and linguistic mother-lode for all the *-gate* formations created wherever the reek of political scandal has been detected since then). It was President Richard Milhous Nixon who famously adapted the truth to his own purposes:

> I had no prior knowledge of the Watergate break-in. I neither took part in nor knew about any of the subsequent cover-up activities. I neither authorized nor encouraged subordinates to engage in illegal or improper campaign tactics. That was and that is the simple truth.

It was as flagrant a lie as politician ever uttered; Geoffrey Beattie, a specialist in discourse analysis confirms:

> Almost every psychologist in the world now has studied videotapes of Richard Nixon during his classic period in order to watch his behaviour, and you can say that his pause patterns were distinctly odd. Much more recently I've spent a lot of time studying politicians talking about the *green shoots of recovery* from recession, metaphorically and in terms of their pause-patterns, and also in terms of their body language. Because I can certainly detect some behaviours here which would normally be associated with lying!

So the maxim that poiticians always lie may not be so far removed from ... the truth! This is how a pause-laden, hesitant, and untruthful former President Nixon revealed his true colours to analysts such as Beattie: 'Let me say... as far as what my motive was concerned and that's the important thing my motive was ... in everything I was saying ... or certainly thinking at the time ... er ... er ... was not ... er ... to try to cover up ... er ... a criminal action ...'

In a court of law, rather than in the court of public opinion, lawyers like Catherine Bond watch their clients—and their adversary's clients—like a hawk for telltale signs of untruth: 'I have once seen a woman social worker lie appallingly, and I have been sure. But it was more the *content* of what she was saying; there was no pattern to her *language*.' The words, then, are not the clues one might imagine them to be. A convincing liar does not deploy a specific lexicon of untruth. 'The only language thing I can come up with is if there's any inconsistency.' By which she means language which appears inappropriate to the condition of the user.

Geoffrey Beattie agrees, but has observed what he reckons to be tiny signs of wobble: 'One thing to look out for is expressions like "you know" or "well" and so on. Again there's a lot of evidence that they increase generally with anxiety and of course when people are lying they're often anxious so ... Another thing to look out for of course is the *pitch* of speech, because in about 70 per cent of the people who have been tested the pitch rises when people are lying.' But this is only the case, observes Beattie, when they are nervous. The confident liar can maintain a level tone, no problem.

> People always think that cues to lying will be easier than they actually are. And the reason they're so complicated is that there's a whole set of emotions which are normally associated with

lying—some negative and some positive. They may feel a kind of pleasure in putting one over on the person they're lying to—American psychologists tend to call that 'duping delight'—it's a nice expression—it's the kind of positive emotion that people feel when they're getting away with it, basically.

It is not hard to imagine Nixon and Clinton, proffering their whoppers to the world's media, live on television, indulging in a veritable orgy of duping delight.

Standing up in court, the expert witness—the forensic scientist, for example—must not only 'tell the truth, the whole truth and nothing but the truth' but (and this is where Catherine Bond's skills are deployed) *appear* to be telling the truth. It is no good trying to convince a jury of twelve average citizens of the strength and veracity of your evidence if it sounds as though you are—shall we say—unsure of the certainty of the truths to which you are attesting. It's a linguistic pressure cooker, the central criminal court of the Old Bailey.

'They certainly fall over their words more than they would usually do. We train some very talented scientists, scientists who deal with murder cases, forensic scientists, who have thirty years experience and PhDs and they will crack under just about ten minutes' cross-examination by me.' And to this end, of course, a skilled lawyer like Bond is ready to invoke the darkest language ploys at her disposal: 'I will interrupt them when they're in full flow, ask them to answer a question *Yes* or *No*, and stop them from giving as full an answer as they would like—I will even question their qualifications and experience. And even just questioning them about it, without putting any sort of nastiness, can make them crack.'

In this game of legal catch-as-catch-can, the evidence being offered by the forensic scientist—and over which the lawyer for the other side may, as we have seen, be trying to cast an appearance of doubt or even untruth—can sometimes itself be linguistic proof of lying. Geoffrey Beattie comments:

> What gives people away in terms of language when they're lying are the pause patterns in language. Whenever we speak spontaneously there are many micropauses which accompany speech. These are pauses which are quite brief—200 to about 500 milliseconds—and they're found all over language. Whenever we listen to speech we don't notice them particularly, but we can tell when they're *not* there, if you know what I mean. You can't actually tell which way the pauses are going to be, but you *can* tell that they do differ from when people are talking *without* lying.

One instance Geoffrey was called in to examine involved hoax 999 calls to the fire service.

> What was fascinating about that was that operators sometimes showed signs that they really didn't believe that they'd got a genuine call on the line. One thing they seemed to be particularly sensitive to was what psychologists called 'false starts' in speech. The call would go something like 'There's a fire in um ...', then the construction would stop and they'd start the phrasing again: 'I want to report that there's a fire in Lakemore Street ...' And that's the kind of index that the operators seemed incredibly sensitive to.

It is commonplace in fiction—on the page or on the screen—that the cleverclogs investigator can somehow divine, by intuition, guesswork or simple cunning that his or her interlocutor is not being wholly straight with the facts. 'You're lying!' flies the accusation. 'Dammit you're right! but how the devil, inspector, did you know?' The fact is, according to Geoffrey Beattie, it is extremely difficult to know when someone is lying. The pointers are certainly not lexical, but—as we have seen—may be a matter of millisecond differences in patterns of speech, between what is normal and what is rehearsed or made up.

An academic's careful distinction, but also, perhaps, the expert witness's equally careful avoidance of absolutes. Catherine Bond knows all about avoiding 'words like *always* and *never*, because witnesses can get caught out with those. So—again going back to a forensic scientist—if they say, "this particular test *always* has such-and-such result", there is a danger that they could get caught out on that particular point. So I like them not to use those words. They're too absolute.'

The courtroom is, then, a theatre of justice where words may be twisted and turned inside out, where rock-solid evidence may be convincingly portrayed as doubtful or even false by skilful cross-examination, and where the linguistic black arts of both barrister and witness are given full rein. Yet sometimes that most complex matter, the truth, may be resolved by a simple monosyllable, *Yes* or *No*. 'They're extremely powerful,' comments Bond,

> and far be it from me to teach a technique to disconcert a barrister, but certainly at the end of a very long, rambling question, if a witness just answers *Yes*, that can really get the barrister bamboozled, flummoxed. I would again train my witnesses—they have to speak the truth, the whole truth and nothing but the truth, but if that can be encapsulated within a *Yes* or *No*—go for it!

'I can tell you're lying,' says the teenager's mother, 'it's written all over your face!' Maybe so. Maybe the youngster's blushes are giving her away as she fumbles the fibs. Geoffrey Beattie certainly maintains that body language is an indicator, and many believe in the reliability of the polygraph—the so-called 'lie-detector'.

But words alone? Can the trained ear detect that famous 'ring of truth'? Lawyer Catherine Bond has concluded:

> I find that there is no language of truthfulness. In fact, if you had two experts of exactly the same professional standing, giving exactly the same evidence, and you trained one of them in speaking clearly and confidently and looking at the jury, and you had two juries listening to them, the person who'd been trained to communicate properly would literally be believed as more truthful. It's the messenger that's believed, not the message.

Chapter 2
Persuasion

BODIES BUFFED AND BEAUTIFUL, ready to take on all comers in clubland, twenty-first-century city kids know better than ever before what's cool and what's not. Whatever the idiom, they are across it: croptop and pavement-sweeping elephant-feet jeans, the must-listen band on the portable CD, the latest pore-enhancing, wrinkle-resistant slap applied with the care of an Old Master at his easel, the sensational new novel tucked into the top of the shoulder bag—trendy sports label, natch. They are the ultimate in today's persuadable public. What's new is what's cool and *Word of Mouth* calls upon an adman to dish the dirt on the way the 'hidden persuaders' (in Vance Packard's memorable phrase) pitch to their punters. But if you wanna really be cool you gotta shape up. Get down to the gym with *Word of Mouth* and *pump those pecs*—or if you prefer, take a stroll through the sweet-smelling pharmaceutical paradise which is the cosmetics counter of your local department store and sort the hype from the hypo-allergenics.

Ready for the fray now—so what's your type? Tall, dark and handsome . . . petite, blonde and bubbly? GSOH essential? *Word of Mouth* decodes the classic lonely-hearts ad. And if all that sounds more like the setting for some trashy just-published paperback, how are you going to convince the reading public to shell out their £6.99 for it? We blow the cover on blurb-speak.

The N-Word

It is perhaps the most abused word in the language, certainly in the language of buying and selling, and, they say it is the single most powerful word that advertisers have in their lexical quivers. It is a bare three letters long and begins with 'n'. It is, of course, the word *new*. Our word comes from a Teutonic root, but that flows out from the great Indo-European river of language that is the source of so many of our words; so in Greek it appeared as *neos*, in Latin as *novus*, and in Welsh as *newydd*. Compare *nuovo*, *neu*, *nuevo*, and (going one better) the French *nouveau* and *neuf*, to reach for only a handful of our nearest neighbours' versions; the n-word has a ubiquity rarely found elsewhere in language.

Not surprising really, when you think how fundamental the n-word is to our lives. It is the gatekeeper of history, the high priest of the present, standing as it does in contra-distinction to *old*, its doughty comrade-in-arms in the sweep of *then* into *now*. Therefore when marketing people get involved and advertising copy is being dreamed, it is the word that delimits the past and emphasizes innovation, renewal, and the excitement of the hitherto unknown. In fact, as far as fashion is concerned, if it is not new, you can say it is no good, or almost. Tom Bussmann has worked in advertising and writes for the *Guardian* newspaper. *Word of Mouth* invited him to offer his thoughts on the chic of the new.

Look up *new* in the Oxford Dictionary and you come across fourteen pages devoted to the word. That of course is the current

Oxford Dictionary, which was quite new when it came out (and was called the *New English Dictionary* in fact). So they immediately started working on a newer one. This, when it appears, will give every underfunded library another £1,500 or more to spend on a full set for the shelf, which is very often the point of something being *new*. Basically what the dictionary and common sense seem to be saying is that something is *new* if it's never been around before, [something] which is rare or new in relation to something *old*, which is more common.

Think of *York* or *Zealand* or *Testament* or *Labour*. *New*, however tattered and torn, remains the marketing man's or woman's favourite three-letter word, preferably with an exclamation mark attached. But does *new* have a sell-by date?

When does *new* officially become *old*? You'll be pleased to hear that *new* in the world of advertising is generally allowed one year of shelf life. Incidentally, the New Labour government is already five to six years old. As a product, that means it has already outlived its natural shelf life by a couple of years and it's high time the advertising authorities demanded a significant reformulation of the product. It is in severe danger of turning by default into Old Labour, and that would never do.

To reassure the faithful, *new* is religiously qualified with *improved*. To go back to an earlier example, take *Testament— New* as opposed to *Old*—even though the new one was written on Dead Sea scrolls. This suggests that, if you, as a marketing hot-shot, won the New Testament account, you might have some trouble getting the product past the advertising watchdogs without some additional justification, which gives you *New Improved Testament*. Sounds good. But you can't leave it there. Why is it *New and Improved*? Are you implying the old one was less than ace? No way, guv! It's *New and Improved* because of ... And then you have to hunt around a bit, do some research, put together a focus group. Let's see now ... *New Improved Testament! Now with added Compassion!*—Love it!

You may well wonder is it possible to use *new* without being suspected of hucksterism. The wise consumer, on hearing the word, will, as a conditioned reflex, move his wallet to an inside pocket. Perhaps marketing could learn something from journalism; it wouldn't be the first time that hucksters nicked ideas from hacks. *New* on its own has been banished from those middleweight think-pieces you find in the middleweight press. Instead, *new* is bolstered, refurbished even, by a simple yet deadly three-letter prefix, *the*. Somehow, this combination, *the new,* pre-empts argument and mysteriously defies and deflects rational cries of 'Cobblers!' Thus you will find portentous articles on 'The New Drunkenness of December', 'The New Sobriety of January', 'The New Finality of Death', 'The New Health Benefits of Heroin'—though not in the *Guardian*, which would have as headline: 'Can Heroin Have New Health Benefits? And Is It Too Early To Ask?'

" "

Heart to Heart

Let's face it, we are not always completely honest about ourselves. Big nose? No. Sticky-out ears? Of course not. Bald patch? You're seeing things. So when we set out on an advertising campaign on our own behalf, the basic rules of the ad-biz pertain.

Don't lie; just don't tell the whole truth. Mention your USP (unique selling proposition) and emphasize the positive.

What used once to be called newspaper *lonely hearts* columns, now go under more catchy and zeitgeisty titles like *Soulmates* and *Meeting Point*. But the objective is the same: make yourself sound as attractive as possible while keeping a close eye on the wordage. Because, in the idiosyncratic linguistic world of the small ad, letters and words are all a question of numbers. Hence those mysterious strings of letters that today litter the ads—maximum information at minimal cost. If you have not got a *GSOH*, or less frequently a *VGSOH* (very good sense of humour), you have hardly started. The other essential small-ad contraction is a verbal phrase squashed into four vital letters, as in *Attractive M 30 GSOH, WLTM warm, creative F. WLTM*, short of course for 'would like to meet'. If you are not into acronyms, *WLTM* invariably becomes *seeks* (how often in the real world, beyond small ads, do you find yourself using that word in the third person singular?). The other essential abbreviation, the thing everyone is after (or indeed *seeking*), is an *r'ship*, or perhaps an *r/ship*, possibly even (with luck) a *l/term r/ship*. People seeking *r'ships* (or *poss r/ship*) are often really after a *1-2-1*, but start off with a little gentle *f/ship*. A hint of a hoped-for More, without spelling it out too explicitly (and still keeping the letter count minimal), is *f'ship +*.

The vocabulary—like the abbreviations—is often standardized. If you like a good laugh, not only do you have a *GSOH*, but you are *bubbly*. Lookers are usually *attract* or *curvy* or maybe simply *sexy*. If you don't want to live your life in a fug of fagsmoke, be sure to indicate you are a *n/s*. Brains are usually *intellig* people. And if the partner of your dreams is *intellig* like you, then don't waste words: *intellig F seeks sim M*. *Sim* is the heartfelt abbreviation that stalks these ads. We are all looking, it seems, for our equal in intelligence, looks, and interests.

So much for Ldn. In India, personal small ads have a different flavour, and are driven by different social concerns. Open any English-language newspaper in the subcontinent and somewhere you will find a page of densely printed boxes advertising not for l/term r/ships but for marriage. This is the famed matrimonial advertising that carpets the inside pages of India's English-language newspapers.

Professor Raja Ram Mehrotra was in charge of English language at Banaras Hindu University for many years and he has made a study of the very special language deployed by those—as Jane Austen put it—'in want of a wife'—or indeed husband.

> I came across a phrase in the matrimonial pages, *Wanted a suitable match for a university professor boy*. To an outsider that would look funny. The boy and the university professor may not go together. But in the Indian context of matrimony—marriage—every bridegroom, irrespective of his age, is called a boy. So the groom may be fifty years of age. Thus you get *university professor boy*.

Likewise, in his standard guide to Indian English (*Indian English: Texts and Interpretation*, John Benjamins Publishing, 1998), Professor Mehrotra quotes the following: *Suitable match for respectable Melhotra family, businessman boy.* While another reassures readers of an ad seeking a partner for *pretty girl, 24, undergraduate, knowing shorthand* that the *boy's merits only consideration.* That's a relief, then.

Professional qualifications and the contents of the aspirant's bank balance tend to be major plus points, rather than a VGSOH, in the sub-continental school of lonely hearts advertising: *match for graduate boy, 31, employed Nationalized Bank* ... And this same ad throws up another interesting linguistic original, which Professor Mehrotra has identified as unique in contemporary Indian English (though it has a certain pedigree in the mainstream English of 400 years and more ago, after which it disappeared until now). The ad continues: ... *and his teacheress sister, 26* ...

> The word *teacheress*, has more than 90 per cent occurrence in preference to *woman teacher* in matrimonial advertisements—*wanted a suitable match for a teacheress* of such and such description—in spite of the fact that the word *teacheress* does not occur in any current English dictionary. It's pure Indian English.

" "

From Soap to Serum

> The wrinkles which thy glass will truly show,
> Of mouthed graves will give thee memory;
> Thou by thy dial's shady stealth may know
> Time's thievish progress to eternity.
>   (Shakespeare, Sonnet LXXVII)

Rather more sonorous than your average television cosmetics ad, yet the thought in Shakespeare's mind was little different from that of the high-street purchaser of anti-wrinkle cream or any product that makes you look younger. Because the inevitable and ineffable decline that the human frame undergoes—'Time's thievish progress to eternity'—is what so many products of the so-called beauty industry are hell-bent on disguising.

With the Bard's lines ringing in its ears and fashion-conscious as ever, *Word of Mouth* set about finding out how the language of beautifying has evolved, and what latter-day word-spinning is going on behind the face pack and the skin toner.

On High Street, UK, the cosmetics counters define the art of the department store. Have you ever walked into the ground floor of any of the major names—and most of the smaller, locally owned ones too—*without* being overwhelmed by a fog of sickly smells, blended as in some infernal perfume lab to emphasize the most reeky, bottom-of-the-range contents of the atomizer? And all those white coats! Helena Rubinstein, it is said, was the first cosmetics manufacturer to make all her sales staff look as though they had just emerged from researching the human genome. It is all part of the marketing, of course. And as we have seen elsewhere in this chapter, the language which interprets these smells, these creams, balms, lotions, scrubs, serums, and the rest, is as carefully selected, tested and adjusted to catch the passing breeze of fashion as any segment of contemporary marketing. These product names and the phraseology used to describe them on the packets and in the advertising copy is very definitely tested on animals, human ones ... and tested to destruction. After all, there is nothing more out of date than last season's—last month's—fashions than the cosmetics that are designed to enhance them.

Human beings have been titivating themselves for millennia, and the Romans went in for a considerable range of unguents (cream preparations for anointing the skin, from the Latin *unguentum*, derived from the verb *unguere*, meaning simply 'to anoint'). But cosmetics died out with the fall of the Roman empire. Crusaders returning to Europe from the Middle East in medieval times reintroduced the tradition, and by the Renaissance, *cosmetics* (the dictionary dates the term in this sense as long ago as 1650) were an accepted part of social behaviour in the West.

Kohl, the Arabic word imported along with the preparation of antimony which Eastern women used to darken their eyelids, is reported in English writing by 1799, and *rouge* was the name descriptively borrowed (from the French for 'red') to describe a product for heightening cheek colour. Rouge—the word is recorded in English in the cosmetic sense from 1753 ('to lay on a great deal of *rouge*, in English called paint')—is made from the petals of the plant safflower, cultivated specifically because of the red dye that could be extracted from it.

But it is with the application of scientific manufacturing techniques by the French in the nineteenth century that the birth of today's exotic laboratory language of beauty products really begins. Victorian Britain frowned, such matters being seen as frivolous, if not downright sinful. The First World War put an end to the moral crusade against makeup and the flood of products that were aimed at women (unless you were an actor, it was still really only women who cared—or dared—to try to make themselves look more beautiful). But the language of these cosmetics of the Victorian era emerging into the twentieth century emphasized—how shall I put it?—their clinical efficacity. 'Our White Lily Facewash', states an American advertisement dating from around 1899, 'the ladies' favorite toilet preparation. This product removes pimples, freckles, swollen, rough skin, wrinkles and tans, blackheads and just plain old imperfect skin.' Not much romance or fashion-consciousness about the language there, but then what can you expect for thirty-seven cents?

These were cosmetics which owed as much to the great tradition of quack medicine as to engaging the emotions and promising visions of loveliness. And the names emphasized the natural: *Cream of Pond Lilies, Almond Lotion,* or *Cucumber Lotion* sound more kitchen-garden than boudoir. (Though how terribly postmodern it is to read this advertisement from spring 2002 which offers a *Soothing and Calming Eye Base* containing 'liquorice and horse chestnut to soothe skin and reduce puffiness' or *Eye Colour* with 'apple to protect and coconut to moisturise'. This so-called *Botanics* range 'uses modern science to harness the pure power of plants ...' *Plus ça change?* No pimples, wrinkles, blackheads or *plain old imperfect skin* these days, however.)

By the end of the First World War, new techniques and new words were joining the lexicon of English. In 1919 the worthy British medical magazine *The Lancet* referred to *cosmetic* surgery, and by 1926 that term had gained sufficiently widespread acceptance for the *Encyclopaedia Britannica* to record that 'cosmetic and plastic surgery, especially of the face, has undergone considerable improvement following our large experience in the war'. (It is interesting to record that *plastic* surgery is ninety years older, noted as far back as 1839.)

In the 1920s, cosmetic terminology was—not unlike one of its own preparations—still fairly fluid. So by 1922 we can find *face-lifting* (or indeed *face-raising*), but not yet *face-lift*. According to lexicographer John Ayto, it is the writer Rose Macaulay who gets the credit for the first use of the now standard term when she wrote: 'What I needed ... was a face-lift ... I should have a new, young, tight face ...'

And so we come to *toiletries*. This all-purpose word fairly breathes that particular smell that still greets you in certain old-fashioned chemists' shops (the ones that don't also sell you sandwiches and calorie-counting juices). *Women's toiletries* ... it is redolent of an innocent generation when the simply titled *vanishing cream* (Pond's Vanishing Cream is advertised from 1916) and *cold cream* (from more than a hundred years earlier) seemed to be the essential beauty products available for women. It has connections with *toilet preparations,* and with an era when painters could catch Venus at her *toilette. Toiletries* is a twentieth-century word (1927), another of those creations of the 1920s vogue for cosmetics.

On the other hand, *toilette—toilet—*(and we are *not* referring to lavatories here) goes back several hundred years and contains an interesting little etymological history. As you might guess, the word is French originally, and in the seventeenth century referred to a little *toile,* or cloth, used to wrap up linen, and subsequently to the cloth spread on a lady's dressing table. As is so often the way with language, the word was then transferred again to the *contents* of the dressing table, i.e. the implements required for a lady's *toilette.*

With the application of science to the manufacture of beauty products, and of the twentieth century's marketing techniques to the business of selling them, the names and the words used to persuade customers to buy begin to take on a different tone. Romantic *beauty* and *loveliness* become the aspiration dominating advertising copy. *Lip-gloss* arrives—as a variant of *lipstick,* a late Victorian term—on the brink of war in 1939, but with the outbreak of hostilities, it was all change once more. For women in the vanguard of war work, looking lovely while 'looking lively' on the war front were dual goals.

The phraseology of a wartime advertisement by Yardley expresses this succinctly: now the rather clever slogan is *Put Your Best Face Forward,* beneath the image of a woman in battledress, gazing intently, purposefully, her badged cap firmly set on tightly controlled locks of hair. No swirling, slow-motion, luxuriant tresses like those served up endlessly by today's TV ads; this is beauty—wartime economy style.

Under the headline *No Surrender*, the text is pregnant with coded messages.

> War gives us a chance to show our mettle. We wanted equal rights with men; they took us at our word. We are proud to work for victory beside them ... Above all, we must guard against surrender to personal carelessness. Never must we consider careful grooming a quisling gesture. With leisure and beauty aids so rare, looking our best is specially creditable. Let us face the future bravely and honour the subtle bond between good looks and good morale ...

Oh, the copywriter did have fun. Spot the careful planting of key words—*no surrender, victory, guard against surrender, carelessness, careful* grooming, *quisling* gesture. You only have to remember how important the adjectives *careless* and *careful* were when you recall that this was the era of that famous admonitory cartoon captioned 'Careless Talk Costs Lives'. This was cosmetic language fully adapted to war work.

By 1944 supplies were scarce, and *Good Housekeeping* magazine's 'Emergency Beauty' column was not mincing its words: 'For the morning after a sleepless night—I recommend the three-S treatment—salts, stimulation and suggestion ...' The same year, Susan Drake, in her column 'Kitchen Beauty Calendar', was listing such useful cosmetic hints as 'A few minutes to spare and half a pound of prunes in the cupboard? Then make this Swedish complexion drink...' or: 'Sour milk may be a domestic tragedy, but it is also a beauty find...' and then again, 'A paste of flour and water will discipline unruly eyebrows...'

Make do and mend was the cosmetic order of the day—and in language too—until peace broke out. But with the slow rolling back of wartime austerity and the new-found prosperity and social role models arriving from across the Atlantic, by the 1960s cosmetic language was back to full-swing, lovely-as-she-goes mode. Try this example from the American monthly the *New Yorker* from the mid-1960s:

> Next to 'I love you', nothing thrills a woman more than 'How lovely you are'. These are words said to a woman who is warm and alive, young and exciting in her outlook, her looks. For such a woman Frances Denney created Source of Beauty, the cream that stands alone in its excellence, and a coordinated collection of Source of Beauty make-up. How lovely do you want to be?

Yet today this rather glutinous prose that links sentiment and *loveliness* seems completely dated. Now, together with our friendly assistants in their white coats, we are back in the laboratory... or is it the *clinique*?

'I think the language the beauty industry uses has changed a lot in the last twenty years,' says Lesley Kenton, an American writer on beauty and cosmetic issues. *Word of Mouth* travelled to her home in the far west of Wales to find out what she made of the way we speak—or are spoken to—about cosmetics:

> Twenty years ago people were using the kind of fantasizing words that built dreams for women in selling face creams, the kind of words they used in 1940s movies: 'This will soften your skin', 'This will make you feel more feminine', 'This will enrich the quality of your beauty'. Nowadays they're talking about free-radical damage, and liposomes...

Just listen to the wording of this product's pitch to women in 2002: 'The Science behind Flawless Skin,' headlines the brochure. 'Choose the colour and the texture that you like and experience Advanced Luminous Technology in action.' (This is make-up, remember, not some new piece of gadgetry to bring you digital pictures from space.) And it goes on. This company's *Cream Foundation* is 'rich with emollients, yet lightweight and easy to wear. This luxurious foundation moisturizes and hydrates skin as it conceals pores, fine lines and other imperfections.' Not so very far, curiously enough, from that American product of a hundred years ago with its claims to remove 'pimples, freckles, swollen, rough skin, wrinkles and tans, blackheads and just plain old imperfect skin'.

Back to Lesley Kenton:

> I think the beauty industry has moved into this quasi-scientific way of saying things for two reasons. First because from a very genuine point of view the sorts of things that can be done with cosmetics and skin care now could not have been done twenty years ago. So there is some justification to it. And second, because we live in a world which is increasingly technospeak. And I think that, selling anything, you sell it to people speaking the language that they are most comfortable with. As far as the beauty industry is concerned, the language of science at the moment is the language that most people are most comfortable with. It attempts to overcome the cynicism and the lack of belief that may affect people when they buy a face cream that is worth £75 and wonder whether it is really going to be worthwhile and do something valid for them.

But where science, language, and fashion really get going is in the *eco*-sphere. In a world where *biodiversity* is on the lips of your average shopper-in-the-street, and *eco-friendly* products (the expression dates from 1989) are to be found everywhere, it is not surprising that language has undergone some bio-cosmetic surgery in the last few years.

Examine the following piece of twenty-first-century promotional material for a new range of cosmetic preparations in its linguistic artfulness: 'Dynamic Homeostasis ... seeks to restore balance to every layer of the skin. As a powerful response to rough, dry skin, Shiseido developed Super Bio-Hyaluronic Acid...' On and on it goes, cajoling customers who just want something to stop them looking quite so grim. And note the neologism in the next phrase: 'creating vibrance—Optimizing Beauty.'

Having intrigued customers with the mysterious *vibrance*, we are back to science once more: 'The performance of Advanced Super Revitalizer N' (oh, the mystery of *N*) 'is further enhanced by two potent energizers, Bio-EPO and HKC, which work in synergy to diminish signs of environmental damage.' You would think that they were at least working to protect the ozone layer; but, no, this is aimed at your skin. Time, now, for the copywriter to bring on the marines as they embark on 'Mission: Whitening' and 'Mission: Clarifying', as if to say: 'Let the SAS go in to nip those zits and splat those blackheads.'

'In the beauty industry you've got two sorts of scientific language or jargon.' The speaker offering a cool head in this linguistic whirlwind is Tony Chu, a consultant dermatologist at the Hammersmith Hospital in West London.

> You've got the scientific language, which is appropriate, because if a product contains an alpha hydroxy acid you should know about it and you should therefore know what it could potentially do to you. There's also the jargon that is there to baffle the customer. When you get down to the rather nebulous terms like 'this cream contains collagen' or 'this contains liposomes that feed the roots of your hair' you're into pseudo-science. Liposomes are a real entity and we use them in science, but do they actually get down to the hair roots? And once you get to the hair roots what

are you feeding? Because you're not watering a plant and feeding a seed. The hair root is fed by the blood stream. And nothing that you slap on hair will actually feed it.

It is as though cosmetic manufacturers have entirely forgotten the hucksters of the eighteenth century who stood on street corners to claim medical wonders for their bottles of coloured water.

Sometimes, the quasi-scientific language strays from the lab to the doctor's surgery. Try this claim from a French company that 'draws on the work of the C.E.R.I.E.S. (Epidermal and Sensory Research and Investigation Centre)... The Précision Diagnosis is a true reflection of these scientific findings.' Note the language selection here—and remember, this is marketing, straight from the product brochure. We have *Précision* for the impression of technological exactness; then there is *diagnosis*, which comes straight from the physician's lexicon. And that acronym *C.E.R.I.E.S.* is presumably meant to conjure up a secret research centre buried deep in the countryside, working on hush-hush formulas... And, oh yes, here they are, a little further down the brochure: four *formulas*, 'all of which respect the balance of the skin's ecosystem'.

So have we completely lost the notion of beauty in this whirlwind of sort-of-science, real words that have been used across hundreds of years to suggest human grace and physical perfection? Romantic words like *bloom* and *blossom* and the *sheen* of the skin: to dermatologist Tony Chu,

> The *bloom* on a cheek is like the bloom on a ripe peach. There's something very tangible about it and something very physical—something that everybody understands. You don't hear about it these days in cosmetic advertising. You hear a lot about rejuvenation and ironing out the wrinkles and things like that.

So at the start of the twenty-first century, sentiment is out, precision is in. A famous company's range now limits ambitions for its skincare range to making 'any skin great skin. Even. Smooth. Healthy-looking. Radiant'. *Great, even, smooth?* Not a lot of romance there.

Let us leave the last words to beauty consultant and writer Lesley Kenton:

> The language that is used to sell beauty is largely *denotative*. It's language that describes very accurately—or purports to describe very accurately—what something will do and why it will do it. The language that we use to describe a sunset or a painting or a beautiful woman is very much a *connotative* language. It's a language of poetry, where a word is used not for its denotative meaning but for the echoes of feeling—it's the language of the soul that is sent out from the words.
>
> I have to say in all the welter of hydroxy-this and ethyl-that, I miss the romance of '"How lovely you are". These are words said to a woman who is warm and alive, young and exciting in her outlook, her looks...'

Cover Story

Not so long ago, a colleague stopped me in the corridor and asked what I called that little strip of detachable cellophane that you pull to open a packet of cigarettes, CD wrapper, or cassette cover.

Not a little thought later, I could still produce no definitive response, though I was in no doubt that the manufacturers of cellophane wrappings for the packaging business had a precise way of describing it. (*Pull n' tear tab? Seal-strip?*)

This is a difficult one, because it is neither a *fastening* (after one has managed to rip it open, there is no refastening possible) nor a *seal*, as it is designed purely to *open* the package, not close it. And the indication on the wrapper is no help either, as it usually merely has some instruction like *Tear here* rather than calling it by its name. In fact, after some considerable searching it turns out to be known rather prosaically and predictably as the *tear-tape* (though most people I know seem only to call it by mostly unprintable names, owing to its propensity for not working efficiently!)

However, there is clearly a wonderful opportunity for someone of an inventive disposition to come up with a really effective and sharp new name for this doofer, thingummyjig, or whatsitsname. Which is, I guess, the sort of non-specific definition that book publishers used to have to resort to on a daily basis back at the beginning of the twentieth century, until clever Mr Gelett Burgess came along. Because Gelett Burgess was of a very inventive turn of mind, and he coined one of the twentieth century's really useful little words.

In 1914 it was that this American humorist and illustrator, little known today beyond this feat of invention, wrote of what he found on the new books section in the bookshop: 'On the "jacket" of the latest "fiction" we find the blurb; abounding in agile adjectives and adverbs, attesting that this book is the "sensation of the year". *Blurb*. It is such a satisfying word. It seems to wrap up in those five letters both the size and shape of that text you find on the back covers of books, and at the same time a sense of unstoppable promotional nonsense (*blurbing* on and on ...).

In fact, according to the reference books, Gelett's coinage reputedly dates from seven years earlier, when as a joke he dubbed a beautiful woman in an illustration adorning a comic book jacket Miss Blinda *Blurb*. Whatever the precise origins of the word, publishers have been advertising the virtues of their products for many a long year, and—as with the frustrating cellophane strip—presumably had to resort to approximations until Gelett's great invention came along.

The past hundred years has been, amongst many other things, the century of the advertisement. Books, once a relatively discreet and polite corner of the merchandising machine, have for thirty years at least now been hyped and hawked almost like potato crisps and washing powder. So the downright usefulness of the blurb itself to the marketing departments of today's aggressive publishing empires (the dictionary definition is 'a publisher's brief, usually eulogistic, description of a book, printed on its jacket or in advertisements') has meant that *blurb*—the word—has stuck fast.

Good blurb copy is therefore an essential ingredient of today's book. So much so that in our disposable age, when books are sold in *dump-bins* (big boxes filled with volumes, and I wonder who invented *that* unlovely word) and on *spinners* (rotating display shelves) in the supermarket, the need is overwhelming for a basic digestible notion of what a book is about before you grab it and cart it off to the checkout along with the loo-freshener and freshly baked ciabatta (and some annoyingly packaged un-unwrappable CDs, for all I know).

'A wonderful new collection of words that define the twentieth century,' shouts a handsome volume published at the end of the second millennium. Yes, but what is it? That is where the art of the blurb writer begins. The appetizing first line is designed to get the intellectual juices flowing and the mind engaged, so that the next bit of text can draw you yet further into what the book is about. It is classic advertising technique, of course—the slogan followed by the body of text that elucidates and whets the mind's appetite for more.

That blurb, incidentally, is not from a seminal novel of the last century, though the text's ambiguity could lead you to think it, but from that most useful guide to the neologisms of the last hundred years, John Ayto's *Twentieth-Century Words* (*blurb* is on page 73).

So how, then, about this one? '... a byword in its own time. It is a novel of enormous richness and art. It is deeply serious, yet at the same time, brilliantly funny. It is mentally gymnastic. It is without question one of the great novels of the century.' Today, this book would be dubbed a *modern classic*, but that blurb was written before it had quite achieved that canonical status, in 1975, twenty years after its first appearance. Would that do the trick in today's dump-bin? I somehow think not, but then *Catch-22* by Joseph Heller needs very little to promote it to its readers. It is what they call a 'steady seller' that has achieved a permanence in the canon of modern satirical novels. Come to think of it, claiming—and in some cases over-claiming—almost mythical status for the volume in question is almost automatic for any book that is up to its—say—twentieth impression. Take this endorsement for J. G. Ballard's fine *Empire of the Sun*: 'it is one of that small and select group of novels by which the Twentieth Century will not only be remembered but judged.'

Or this rather more hooting set of claims for ... well what? 'The novel for every woman who ever thought she knew herself, and for every man who ever thought he knew a woman ... This is perhaps the most important novel yet written about the realities of life experienced by today's women ... a landmark not only of literature but of our developing consciousness.' Big claims, big bestseller in the 1970s, but how many still recognize amid the hyperbole *The Women's Room* by Marilyn French? Old blurbs recollected in tranquillity have an uncanny knack of sounding like overblown trumpets.

So where do blurbs come from? Are there armies of highly trained blurb writers, ready to condense the essential literary oils of the latest piece of fiction into five lines of tempting copy that will sway you at the supermarket spinner? In fact, the editorial departments of most publishers do have staff whose brief it is to compose the text for the jackets of their publications. At Penguin Books, *Word of Mouth* spoke to Sue Miles, the managing editor of the publisher's cover editorial department. Holding in her hand a copy of Laurie Lee's classic account of a Gloucestershire childhood, *Cider With Rosie*, adorned with linguistic temptations like *wonderfully vivid, tangibly real, now-distant, fresh, full of joy, marvellous morning freshness*, Sue observed:

> Somebody came up with a list once of a hundred adjectives and said, 'This is all you need for blurb-writing', which is not at all true. I think the thing about the adjectives is that you do not want to overdo them at all. I mean, the whole process of writing a blurb starts off with quite a long draft, and then you begin honing it down to the essentials.

Which may mean that you end up with a big heap of adjectives, of course, but let that pass. The current vogue seems as much to seek the endorsement of others as to do the pushing yourself, so carefully selected quotes from suitable endorsers or publications are *de rigueur*. For example, you would not in normal circumstances think that a word or three from the Bishop of Edinburgh would be a big selling point for your average novel, yet Michael Arditti's well-regarded book *Easter*, set in the parish of St Mary-in-the-Vale, shows, according to Bishop Holloway, 'the truth about the Church and does it with wit and power'. Sue Miles says:

> We usually read all the novels, if we can, and if we can't—if we don't have time to read them—then we'll skim-read the whole thing so that we get a very good working knowledge. I mean you need to do that because you need the information to write the blurb; you've also got to be careful that you're going to be accurate because, you know, you may think you've got the story-line and then it could have a sudden switch ten pages later and you'll be totally inaccurate and make the author very upset when you send them the blurb.

Another favourite blurb style is the pastiche. Try this for style: 'Here, *meine Damen und Herren*, is Christopher Isherwood's brilliant farewell to a city which was also a state of mind which will never come again.' *Goodbye to Berlin* inspired the musical *Cabaret,* and the 'master of ceremonies' approach obviously inspired the blurb-writer. 'The flow of the blurb is very important,' observes Sue Miles. 'You don't want anything that jars; I mean the whole thing is consciously constructed really from start to finish,' and she produces a contemporary thriller that Penguin have recently published. The blurb is again pastiche—Raymond Chandler-cum-hard-boiled cop, this time: 'He gives $200 to a beautiful woman in a red dress ... a scar at the edge of her mouth ... and a body like a knife ... wakes up in a bath full of melting ice ... fresh blood on his fingers and staples in his side. Now she haunts his dreams and his days ... she's got his kidney on ice and her teeth in his heart.'

As with the Isherwood, the blurb text is fashioned after, though not extracted from, the book: 'The ideas are from the text in the sense that it follows it—a lot of this happens in the first twenty pages or so. It's got quite a fast pace to it with staccato sentences. A lot of blurb-writing is I think subconscious because we are so used to doing it actually that it becomes second nature,' adds Sue.

One of the problems that soon becomes apparent is repetition. I imagine no one would be so foolish as to sit down and tot up all the novels whose blurbs claim them to be 'possibly the twentieth century's most important work on the subject' or 'arguably the most significant statement on [supply your own subject] to date...' And while we are about it, note the weasel words that are a feature of such hyperbolic claims: *possibly*, *arguably* or even, more ambitiously, *indisputably*. Then there are the Big Nouns: *landmark* is always good, while *classic* confers timeless authority. But it is above all in the adjective department that repetition becomes tiresome—and ultimately diminishing. Here is a brief list of some of the evergreen epithets: *dazzling* (and blinded to the overused adjective), *funny and touching* (both at once), *original* (though not in the blurb-writing department), *ingenious*, *brilliant* (you can do better than that), *astonishing* (that's better), *elegant* (a classy one) ... In the adjectival glare of all these over-the-top claims, I wonder whether David Lodge was enthralled to have the following endorsement for *Therapy* from the Boston Globe quoted on the back cover: 'a fairly dazzling comedy'. (But then perhaps it depends how you accent *fairly*—a difficult business, selective quotes.)

But, according to Sue Miles of Penguin, it is factual texts that cause the biggest headaches: 'We repeat ourselves lots of times actually. I mean, reference books can be a problem with that where you're trying to say it's "comprehensive", "detailed"—whatever—you can find other words but often you find you've slipped into using the same word three times.' With the *Penguin Dictionary of Language*, the tack is more to puzzle and intrigue: don't be put off by long words, technical terminology and -isms. Come on in, the linguistics is lovely. 'What precisely are Structuralism, semiotics and sociolinguistics? What distinguishes "pidgins" from "creoles", gerunds from gerundives and the hard palate from the soft palate?' Sue's department was responsible for that blurb and she is proud of it: 'Again this is a new approach on our reference blurbs, and we've gone for a short paragraph which will attract the reader's attention, hopefully.'

Finally, the classics. The real classics, rather than those the publisher has elevated to the podium. Here, the blurb-writer can appeal to a broader knowledge and use adjectives like *Hogarthian* or invoke the names of Dr Johnson and Coleridge (all on the back cover of a now vintage Penguin edition of Fielding's *Tom Jones*).

> We have to be much more serious with the classics, but also you do have to be entertaining at the same time—you don't want to make the thing sound boring. And I think again with the classics—it's one of these things with blurbs—we always have to be terribly careful not to give away too much of the story. It's a bit of a fine line, really. You know if ever there's a complaint about a blurb, it is that 'you've completely ruined this book for me because you've given away what happens'.

No fear of that in what I think is, as blurbs go, itself a bit of a classic. In fact, I'd say it was *sharp, intriguing,* and *indisputably ingenious*. In three lines of bold, red, type, Philip Kerr's *Gridiron* has the following come-on:

> They designed the perfect building.
> They gave it a mind of its own.
> Now it's going to use it.

That should get Mr Kerr's novel out of the dump-bin and into the trolley in Tesco's all right.

" "

Working It Out

What is failure? Seems perfectly clear to me. Failure is ... well, not succeeding. And in the fashion-conscious world of gyms and gym culture, *complete failure* is an everyday occurrence. In fact, that's what you're actually aiming for. Because *failure* is, as you will have realized, a technical term. It is the point at which the would-be toned and honed muscle-fashion victim just cannot perform any more repetitions of a particular exercise. *Repetitions*. That is another bit of jargon, incidentally, though always shortened to a much more macho *reps*. As we have so often seen in these up-to-the-minute, drop-dead fashionable lingos, talking the talk is an integral part of walking the walk.

This is a world where narcissism and legend collide, a world of steroids and stamina, of vanity and hip talk. Go to a sports shop and look at the racks of dumb-bells and weights, the exercise machines and ergos, and you are not so very far removed from the whiffy memories of cold school gymnasiums and tatty pommel-horses. But in the world of the serious, fashionable *workout*, the mood is very different.

Here, physical perfection and image, self-love and superman are the order of the day. And the language is trimmed to fit. There is something distinctly psychosexual about the acts and the way the gym freaks describe them. *Freak* is, by the way, a term of approbation. An award-winning British bodybuilder, Ernie Taylor, explained for *Word of Mouth*'s enquiry into this twenty-first-century craze: 'A *muscle-bound freak* is a bodybuilder who's got ridiculously large muscles. It's a compliment!' When asked whether he considered himself to be one, Ernie replied without hesitation: 'Yes, definitely!'

So in California's legendary Muscle Beach Gym (known as *the Dungeon*), as throughout the world of weights and workouts, the dark and suggestive language is exchanged and honed. Technical, physiological terminology is crumped and crimped to shape. Deltoid (muscles) become *delts*, hamstrings, *hams*, and the well-known pectoral muscles of the chest are *pecs*. *Abs* are the abdominal muscles that help give the would-be Mr Universe his *six-pack*—back to the sweaty world of male bonding where guys chill out downing a half-dozen cans of beer. Here too you find *glutes*, *guns*, *lats*, and *quads*. In the gym, tough-talking monosyllables disguise the florid Latinate terminology of the anatomist.

As bodybuilders admit, the sport has its own special language. Dial up the gym-culture websites and they all have their glossaries and vocabularies. To do your stuff in the gym you have to know your linguistic stuff first. In fact, without one of these guides to hand, the uninitiated may just begin to think they have gone loopy, with all the talk of *flat-bench flies* and *hack squats*. To quote one instruction manual: 'perform one straight set to complete failure—congratulations! You've completed your shoulders. They should be pumped and fried.'

Says Ernie Taylor: 'You'll find a lot of men do tend to focus on their upper body, on the showy muscle ... the biceps, the chest, the pecs and it's at the expense of their legs.' So gym-talk is merciless when it comes to those whose lower-limb physique is found wanting—a *Bambi*, with *drainpipes* or *chicken-legs*...

And another quality pervades all this bodytalk, a certain sloganeering feel for assonance and rhyme. So, as writer Paul Burston told *Word of Mouth*, in the world of the gay gym, the rule is *No pecs—No sex*. developing your leg muscles becomes *fry your thighs*, and the bench where pectorals are developed becomes the *pec-deck*. The words have resonance and rhythm—while getting *shredded* (the lean and hungry look), *muscle-marys* seek *definition* and *vascularity*, though probably not *bitch tits* (highly developed chest muscles).

'Biceps and triceps are called *guns*,' says Ernie Taylor;

> big legs are called *big wheels*. A *Christmas tree* is that sort of shape in your back. And if you're in very good condition you'll have a *star on top*. We don't talk about *washboard abs* or *ripped abs* any more—that's in the old 'pumping iron' books. As for *six-packs*—like meself I've got an *eight-pack* plus a *cooler-box* below so ... Where you get all those little muscles showing up that's called *shredded*, *ripped* or *striated*. *Vascularity* is having a lot of veins, where your veins are showing up like a road-map.

But Sally Gunnell, the British Olympian who has done her fair share of workouts in her time, dismisses all this self-referential, narcissistic talk as so much macho nonsense: 'All this language like *I'll spot you* that comes out, and then when you get down to lifting the weight they seem to just want to grunt and shout—you know, the straining *Aaargh* and *Come on, you can do it, get out there—push that iron!*'

Chapter 3
Homework

A S A SNOTTY SCHOOLBOY, I well remember sniggering at the line in that Victorian hymn we used to sing that spoke of 'intercourse at hearth and board'. Being typical foul-minded teenagers, we would always misconstrue the hymn-writer's intended notion of conversation in the home to mean something quite else (the original lines ran *Praise in the common words I speak, / Life's common looks and tones, / In intercourse at hearth and board / With my beloved ones*). But that exchange of domestic politenesses—'would you be an angel and stop hogging the remote all the time?'—the way we address our hearth-occupying quadruped companions and an itsy bitsy little thought-ette on the dozens of diminutives that we use daily are the subject of the following few pages.
To round off this domestic diversion, some linguistic thoughts on how to speak of the great unspeakable, the limitless unknowable 'from whose bourn no traveller returns', death.

Toujours la Politesse

Someone once told me, with real anguish in his heart and voice, the story of his builders. They had taken over, as builders from time to time are wont to do, and he found himself, with his wife and children, held captive for weeks by hordes of structural engineers, masonry experts, brickies and plasterers. Their lives were controlled by them, parties hijacked, space utterly invaded. But my friend's real angst was reserved for how he should *speak* to them. How could he express his horror at being so overwhelmed? He was a polite fellow, nicely spoken as the phrase goes, and not given to throwing his weight about linguistically. Yet what he dearly longed to say to this army of professional invaders that he himself had invited into the fastness of his home, was 'Get out! Leave me alone! How dare you take over like this?'

But he could not. He simply could not. The idea of an honest expression of how he felt was beyond him. And so, meekly, he subsided into platitudes and the gentlest of inoffensive enquiries like 'Making progress, then?', or 'I wouldn't want to hold you up, but would you by any chance care for a cup of tea?', or 'Is there any chance that we might be able to have a corner of the bedroom back to sleep in at some point next week?' Decoded, what my friend meant was 'For God's sake, when are you going to get this job finished? I've never seen such a bunch of lazy layabouts.' 'I'll bribe you with tea, but only if you'll just get on with the job a bit faster.' And finally: 'We're sick of sleeping on campbeds in the utility room and we want our bed back NOW.'

This predilection for circumlocution seems to be a national habit in Britain. Hugh Grant has built a whole career round playing characters who can never ask a straight question. And from another, gentler age many will recall the linguistic tangles that Leslie Phillips used to get into in the 1960s radio series *The Navy Lark*, where his character could never, but never, give a command outright. So where does this come from, and who does it?

It is, of course, not just builders for whom we reserve this. Traffic wardens, the police, librarians about to fine you fifty pence for an overdue book ... anyone, in fact. But those from whom we seek a favour, especially when they have some power to wield over us, are particularly likely to get the round-the-houses treatment. We avoid giving orders at all costs and seek to achieve instant compliance only by a coded polite insistence. Yet the same scenario can also be seen played out across the kitchen sinks and hearthrugs of the nation as the finer points of domestic transaction are traded in a delicate linguistic dance. *Word of Mouth* invited the writer Fiona Walker to reflect on this theatre-of-the-absurdly-polite:

> If I want something, I ask for it. Or do I? As a child it was simply a matter of adding the verb to the object. 'Want sweets!' Later, I introduced a little sophistication, with a subject, a determiner ... and occasional sycophancy: 'I want a pony, Mummy. Pleeease!' My questions— or demands—remained direct and to the point, and being a lowly child, I received similarly direct requests in return. 'Tidy your room!', 'Turn that music down!', 'Don't talk to your mother like that!' It was only when the complexities of early adulthood arrived that I learned to manipulate my language for best effect. 'Can I have a pair of six-inch snakeskin boots' would get me nowhere, but 'Do you realise that I will be ridiculed at

school and fail my A-Levels if I don't have snakeskin boots *and* driving lessons?' immediately got me into the L-plated Cavalier en route to Stead and Simpson.

And so I had graduated into the adult world of asking for what you want the British way, a way so magical and roundabout that Zebedee and Ermintrude are on board. The British question is usually about as direct as a flight to Rio via Vancouver. In a family situation, the direct request is seen as a power-gauge. The husband who says: 'This house is a tip! Clean it up!' is, traditionally, a tyrant. The wife who demands: 'Will you get your feet off the coffee-table and mow the lawn, you great lardbucket!' is a good old-fashioned nag. But the couple who are *polite* appear to have the Mills and Boon of marriages: 'Darling, would you mind *terribly* clearing up your dropped underpants this evening?' 'Not at all, darling. Could you possibly just empty the dishwasher while I'm doing that?'

And upon meeting a stranger, particularly an antagonistic one, asking for something is nigh on impossible: 'Excuse me ... I wonder ... would it inconvenience you very much ... that is, if you're not too busy ... Would you mind not pulling the wing-mirrors off my car like that?'

To which there is really only one reply: 'But mate, you're just *asking* for it!'

So why do we do it? Why are couples driven to these apparently eccentric circumlocutions to achieve the simplest of domestic chores? And what possesses an otherwise mature and forthright man to indulge in roundabout ways of asking for a service from a team of builders, whom, after all, he is paying to do work for him. *Word of Mouth* consulted two experienced observers of the sociolinguistic scene, the novelist Lisa Appignanesi and the Rupert Murdoch Professor of Language and Communication at Oxford University, Jean Aitchison.

Professor Aitchison attributes the phenomenon to a sequence of factors which are fundamental to us as social human beings: we are social animals, we like to talk with one another, and there is a relatively formal ritual of turn-taking that we observe within such exchanges. To this is added a natural disinclination to impose on and criticize one another. 'So you add on the turn-taking to the "Don't boss people around, don't impose" and "Don't tell them they're an idiot" by having these roundabout ways of saying things.'

From the social observation on which she draws for her novels, Lisa Appignanesi concludes that there are other factors at play which have to do with class and age. Citing the hesitant character incarnated by Hugh Grant and for which he became famous in such films as *Four Weddings and a Funeral* and *Notting Hill*, she believes that this stereotypical British tongue-tiedness is possibly a middle-class, middle-aged phenomenon: 'I'm not sure this is the case across society and certainly my children don't speak like this—they have no problem at all about asking for what they want!'

Fundamentally, according to Jean Aitchison, these linguistic ploys are an indication of power relationships. This explains the householder's tongue-tied rage when confronted with a chisel-and-plumbline army—he is reduced de facto to being a humble servant in his own castle—and to the awkward interaction with the traffic warden, police officer, and accusatory librarian. 'There are power relationships going on throughout language,' observes Professor Aitchison, 'so when a mother addresses her child she says "Shut the door!" to them because pretty obviously you are in a situation of power over this child.' But she would never use that form of expression, for example, to someone whom she had only just met, and with whom she was 'still negotiating our power structure—so we wouldn't boss each other around. We'd assume we were equals.'

How then would she address, for example, Michael Rosen in those circumstances? 'If I did want you to shut the door, I would say "I wonder if it would be possible to shut the door, please?"' There is an expression of desire involved in the request, but no compulsion on Michael's part to carry it out: 'I don't imply that *you*'re going to do it, but that there might be some sort of lackey round the back who's going to jump up and shut the door. So I don't have to say to *you*, "Shut the door!"' Nonetheless, though she expresses it politely and by inference, Professor Aitchison has thereby made it abundantly clear that she is uncomfortable and would like the door closed.

It is, thus, all a matter of delicate negotiation of the boundaries of human space, negotiation in which self-deprecation and a desire not to impose may even result in personal inconvenience. So to achieve the object of getting the door shut without appearing excessively rude, Jean Aitchison might possibly feel constrained to say, 'I wonder if *I* might shut the door, please?' And if the context were even more sensitive, she might simply observe 'It's a bit chilly in here', hoping to elicit the response, 'Oh yes, you're right. I'll shut the door.'

This dance of language is hugely sensitive to milieu and context. It plays on social expectations and norms, on discretion and coded behaviour, as well as on politeness and power. As a writer, Lisa Appignanesi appreciates them as a key to character and setting: 'You need the circumlocutions because they're much more alert to context, much more alert to other people's desires and wishes and ... I rather like them!' They are part, she says, of an extended structure of socially sensitive euphemistic language, 'helping social communication along: I think sometimes the *I'm sorry but...* or *Might I be so bold as to presume...* is quite useful.' This embraces the politician's less than subtle politeness prefix, *with due respect*, uttered before a stinging criticism, the professional diplomat's code that speaks of *constructive and meaningful* dialogues (when maybe less has been achieved than was hoped), and the academic's dance of intellectual disagreement: *I don't know if I've understood you altogether correctly but it seemed to me that A equals B*, when, says Lisa Appignanesi, 'really what they are saying is that the other person's completely barmy.'

And, it appears, all this euphemistic talk is nothing new. Professor Aitchison comments: 'With recent work, we're finding this kind of interaction goes back to the beginning of humankind, and so we must look at how we interact with others as part of our ape heritage.'

" "

Of Mogs and Dogs

We share our hearthrugs with them, they sleep on our beds, curl up on the sofa, provide endless companionship and amusement. Their late-night *walkies* can be the bane of people's existence or a blessed excuse to get out of the house. And that's just the dogs. Cats play a different role in our lives, as those who have encountered Rudyard Kipling's 'Cat that Walked by Himself' from the *Just So Stories* will remember: 'for I am the Cat that walks by himself and all places are alike to me.' This is the cat-king, the lordly, super-independent feline that roams the world, nose in air.

The way we look at the animals that share our lives and our landscape has been since the beginning of time a potent source of linguistic inspiration. *A dog's life, dog eat dog, man's best friend, going to the dogs, dogging someone's footsteps, putting a cat amongst the pigeons, playing cat and mouse,* being *catty* or *bitchy*, and so on.

And what do you call your dog or cat? Are you a *Tiddles* fan or a *Rover* raver, or do you go for a name that is altogether more exotic? *Word of Mouth* went in search of things canine and feline, in the company of a veterinarian, Ken Thompson, the distinguished writer on dogs Beverley Cuddy, zoo vet David Taylor, and the etymologist and lexicographer Dr Tania Styles.

To start with the words *cat* and *dog* themselves, *cat* is extremely old, its origins lost way back before Latin and Greek, in which languages the animal was respectively *cattus* and *kattos* or *katta*. Since the cat was first domesticated by the ancient Egyptians, Tania Styles suggests that the word may derive from them too. *Dog*, on the other hand, is Old English, with no trace earlier.

As for the common or garden *moggie*, used somewhat disparagingly to describe felines that are not destined to be Best in Show and that do not boast long certificates of pedigree, the actual word on the other hand has a decent lineage that Tania Styles traces back to the seventeenth century. She says the term was first used in Scots and in dialects of northern England to describe scruffily dressed or sluttish young women and which was thence applied to alley cats of undistinguished appearance. *Moggie* is probably a corruption of *maggie*, likewise a seventeenth-century Scots word, meaning a young girl.

But whether a moggie or a pure-bred Manx, what you call your cat, or your dog for that matter, is of course a matter of personal taste. And anything goes. When veterinarian Ken Thompson suggested on Radio 4 that *Rommel* was not a likely or appropriate cat name, his affirmation prompted a minor storm of letters contradicting him.

However, he says, an unscientific survey in his consulting room indicates that the majority of names derive from the colour of the cat's coat and its length—hence classics like *Blackie* and *Sooty*—or from its behavioural habits; so names like *Reckless* and *Gentle* are common. 'I have come across a *Spit* and even a *Toshack* (because, like John Toshack, the celebrated 1970s Liverpool footballer, he dribbles balls well!).' A big fat chocolate-coloured kitten was called *Plummet* by its owners because it was always dropping on people ...

Kipling's *Just So Stories* cat has no name: he is simply 'the Cat'. In a beautiful early edition of the tales 'for little children', with illustrations by Kipling himself, the Cat that Walked by Himself is depicted in a severe and elegant woodcut, striding out haughtily. Kipling's black cat catches exactly the fierce independence that he describes in the story, and which has been part of the linguistic pedigree of felines since the dawn of time.

Just So Stories uses alliteration and assonance to great effect throughout (remember 'the Great Grey Green Greasy Limpopo River'?) and the Cat is no exception. In the illustration, he walks alone down a long avenue between bare winter trees—'This is the Cat that Walked by Himself,' Kipling has written next to it, 'walking by his wild lone through the Wet Wild Woods and waving his wild tail. There is nothing else in the picture except some toadstools. They had to grow there because the woods were so wet.'

Kipling's Cat—and the dog who also features in the prehistoric fable—inevitably end up scrapping and dogs and cats have rarely been congenial companions of the fireside since. But as our favourite household companions, they often also crop up together in phrases and proverbs.

A cat may look at a king goes the expression, again capturing that feline haughtiness of Kipling's Cat. And this expression, or a close equivalent is found, reports Tania Styles, in German, Dutch, and Italian. Yet, she says, for the French, it is the dog that can out-stare authority, as expressed in the formation found on the other side of the Channel, *A dog may look at a Bishop*. What that says about French dogs—or bishops for that matter—is open to speculation. In any event, the proverbial use of the cat and king encounter has, as it were, a pedigree worthy of Crufts, since it is quoted as a recommended idiom for writers in John Heywood's poetic *Dialogue Conteinyng the Nomber in Effect of All the Prouerbes in the Englishe Tongue*, which was first published in 1546 and which became a bestseller, going through ten editions in the course of the sixteenth century.

Cats and dogs are together again in the altogether rougher world of street hucksters. *To let the cat out of the bag* is recorded in the *London Magazine* in 1760, describing the unmasking of cheating traders in the capital's markets when, instead of a fine suckling pig sold in a bag (or *poke*), a street moggie was hidden in the bag in its place. To *let the cat out of the bag* was literally to lay bare the fraud. 'I'm not sure how many customers would have been taken in,' comments lexicographer Tania Styles, 'by being sold a fierce scratching cat in place of a docile piglet, but in any case the image of a trapped cat emerging spitting and scratching from a sack is quite a nice analogy for the shock, pain and chaos that can ensue when a dark secret comes out.'

(This practice must have been widespread, because another well-known expression that belies similar fraud is *to buy a pig in a poke*, i.e. sight unseen, and still synonymous at the start of the twenty-first century with securing a bad deal.) And those dogs? Well, they are likewise not what they are cracked up to be by the vendor, whose fraudulent trading is known as selling someone *a pup.*

Far more recent is a trio of originally American phrases that soon became popular on this side of the Atlantic, *the cat's pyjamas, the cat's whiskers,* and—less familiar—*the cat's miaow.* All meant more or less the same, i.e. the acme, top-notch. The show business bible, *Variety* magazine, in November 1921 reported an order issued to vaudeville houses 'barring the use of current phrases *that's the cat's pyjamas, that's the cat's miaow* and *hot cat* ...' Why this feline phraseology was on the blacklist is not clear, though double meanings are suspected.

In Rudyard Kipling's *Just So* caveman menagerie, the cat proves itself by far the cleverest of all the animals, outsmarting even the human beings and leaving the dog hot with indignation and ready to chase it up the nearest tree. But how smart are animals in reality? Just how much can they actually understand when being spoken to by their mistresses and masters? In other words, *Word of Mouth* wondered, are—say —dogs any good at learning English?

We asked Beverley Cuddy, a distinguished writer on dogs and the editor of *Dogs Today* magazine, about canine IQ. She considers that even the dimmest dog usually recognizes a few words, 'but there are some superintelligent ones that have really learned a couple of hundred words—really bright dogs. These dogs learn just like children do when they're growing up.' But this can be a hazard for their hapless owners, as a number of weary dog-owners confided, having lost all semblance of linguistic places to hide in the face of super-pooch. Comments Beverley: 'They go on adding to their portfolio of words and symbols till it gets to the stage when, if you've got a really really super-bright dog it will become impossible to hide what you're thinking or planning to do.'

The idea that dogs can actually understand English is quite a striking one. David Taylor, the internationally renowned zoo vet and author of many books about animals (including *Is There a Doctor in the Zoo?* and *Zoo Vet*) believes that certain animals, notably primates, can respond to actual words, but that when it comes to dogs, the language abilities are limited to sound recognition only. 'It's the repetition of certain sounds. You may say that *Walkies!* signifies the actual movement of the legs outside in the park and all that goes with it. But of course it's just that they know the sound *Walkies* is always uttered by Homo sapiens when you're about to get your coat on and go out of the door!'

David Taylor says you can test this by using words which resemble the trigger sounds and yet differ, say, by one phonological component (phoneme) and the dog will still respond in the same way. It is as if you offered someone some *cake* and then changed the word to *hake* instead. A normal user of English would discriminate between the two food items. A dog, according to Taylor, would not: 'For example if, instead of *Walkies* you said *'Warmies* or *warbies*, they will start wagging their tail and leap for the door. So it's got to be distinctive and it's got to be repeated. But I don't think you're having a real conversation.'

Beverley Cuddy, I think, would not entirely agree, as she claims even to be able to 'understand' doggy-talk when taking an urgent call on the—erm—dog and bone (which, for the uninitiated, is Cockney rhyming slang for 'phone'). Believe that if you like, but Beverley insists she knows of some really first-class doggy-linguists: 'I met somebody who can just say to her dog *go upstairs and get this* and *this* could be one of twenty or thirty objects and the dog will go upstairs and look in all the rooms till it finds that object. That's getting close to understanding complete sentences.'

History does not record what this particular graduate of the University of Barking was actually called, but you would hope it was at least Einstein or Leonardo. What's the betting it was Fido or Spot?

" "

Icky Bitty Babytalk

It was the TV dog expert Barbara Woodhouse who famously turned a one-word exclamation into a national catchphrase that passed into British popular culture for a generation. 'Walkies!' she would cry imperiously to her pooch, and a nation of dogs would start pawing at the front door in search of their daily constitutional. *Walkies.* Not, of course, *walkie-talkies* which are something completely different. Which are, as we all know, completely separate from the *talkies* (a term, interestingly, conceived of and coined back in 1913, long before Al Jolson ushered in the reality in 1927 with *The Jazz Singer*).

A simple string of words interconnected by form, though not by meaning, all illustrate a common feature which in the home is known as baby talk, is sometimes thought of simply as a diminutive, and is referred to by sociolinguists as 'hypocoristic features'. Hypocoristics is just a fancy term for these slangy, affectionate forms of words, modified to express familiarity or endearment.

You get them at the heart of every family. How often have you received a *prezzie* for your birthday from someone you love? When were you last offered a *chocky bickie* at a particularly cosy teatime? And then there was that essential adjunct to the Thatcher 80s, the country-loving *green wellie brigade*... But it is not just a recent phenomenon. We have been being familiar with our word endings for generations. Take the *hanky*, for example (not *hanky-panky*, though, which is quite different). As a familiar diminutive of *handkerchief* it has a pedigree that goes back to a book by J. Davison in 1895 ('and the schoolmaster's wife used her *handky*'. *Hanky-panky*, on the other hand, is fifty years older, dating from 1841, when it turns up in *Punch* magazine.)

These are parts of our routine linguistic currency, these so-called baby talk terms, lurking in the heart of day-to-day usage: Barbara Woodhouse's dog might well also be called a good *doggie* ('How much is that *doggie* in the window?'); your American *aunty* might well enjoy *cookies* (from the Dutch *koekje* 'little cake') and might have done so since the early eighteenth century, while a British *bobby* (named after Sir *Robert* Peel, whose new Police Act became law in 1828) might like to compare notes with his newly appointed Canadian counterpart who is a *rookie Mountie*.

But the most familiar application for these hypocoristic words is as an expression of affection, especially at the heart of the family. Children (indeed *kiddies*, and especially *babies*) adore their *teddy* bears (*teddies*) almost as much as their *mummy*, *daddy*, and *granny*. Milly Molly Mandy and Andy Pandy were often the companions of childhood and in the 1930s, 'Our *Gracie*' (Gracie Fields) made her name singing of '*Sally, Sally*, pride of our alley...', while round the piano in days gone by families would chorus folk songs like 'Where have you been all the day, *Billy* boy, *Billy* boy?'.

It is as if these *-ie* (and, just as commonly, *-y*) endings are so deeply entrenched in British culture that we not only take them for granted but hardly notice that we are using them. *Word of Mouth* asked the American writer and film-maker Jane Walmsley, who has lived in the UK for a number of years and has published a guide to the differences between the way Americans and the British express themselves, what she made of this familial baby speak.

> I guess I noticed it slowly. There were a lot of words that I didn't understand. I mean, for example, when I first got here grown men would talk about betting on the *gee-gees*. And I thought, 'How odd. What are those?' And what's a *sarnie?* [sandwich] I mean, I thought it was some sort of bath! You talk about wearing your *cossie* while watching the *telly* wearing your *wellies*, having your *chocky bickies* while wearing your *cardie*. At Christmas time you get *prezzies*—you might get *smellies* or *chockies* or whatever and it's all very safe and it's terribly twee. And of course it takes you a while to get used to things like that!

On a historical note, the *gee-gees* that so flummoxed Jane Walmsley come from Victorian children's usage, being a version of the word *gee*, which has been used of horses since the beginning of the seventeenth century. Indeed, W. S. Gilbert, in the famous Gilbert and Sullivan opera *The Pirates of Penzance*, memorably lends it to the Major-General for his great patter-song, in the excruciating rhyme:

> In short, when I've a smattering of elemental strategy,
> You'll say a better Major-General has never sat a *gee*.

As for the perplexing *sarnie*, that is far more recent, Eric Partridge first noting it in the early 1960s.

As often as not, we British use this sort of infantilizing word without self-consciousness, and it seems to be that— and the fact that they crop up everywhere—which Americans find so striking. Not, however, that the *-ie* endings do not exist in American English. We saw that *cookie* has a pedigree on the other side of the Atlantic of hundreds of years, and it was of course Americans who exported to us the term *movie* (which, today, some British commentators are lamenting as beginning to overwhelm the more native *film*). Then again, one has only to remember the success on both sides of the pond of Bryan Hyland's 1960 rock 'n' roll hit with its chorus of 'She wore an *itsy bitsy teeny weeny* yellow polka dot bikini'.

But it is often the casual use by adult British *males* of these baby talk terms which outsiders find, to say the least, surprising. Jane Walmsley thinks: 'On the lips of a man it's very odd. I used to think it was slightly effeminate, and that impression was borne out by the fact that those words seemed to be used by people who were camp, the Kenneth Williams type of entertainer.'

But certainly not exclusively so. *Wellie*, observes Walmsley, is widely used by both men and women, though sometimes with different meanings and applications. *Wellies*, as an affectionate abbreviation of *wellington boots*, she maintains, tends to be more usually used by women, 'but a man might say I'm going to give it *a bit of wellie*' as he slams his foot down on a car's accelerator.

So what is going on here? Why are we always trying to make friends with our policemen and turn them into *bobbies* on the beat, or cosy up to the man in the betting shop, who is forever the local *bookie*? We turned for enlightenment to Randolph Quirk— Lord Quirk—one of the world's most distinguished figures in the academic study of the English language. 'Pet forms of one kind or another', he says, 'seem to be universal in language and they respond to the simple mammalian need to show affection.' But we should, he says, take care not to confuse how these non-standard formations are being used. 'Because, although we think of pet forms as being largely diminutives, it's not diminutives in a dismissive or pejorative sense, but diminutives in the affectionate sense.'

Many languages have formations which modify standard words and turn them into the sorts of friendlier language you might be happier with at home, he says. And any student of Italian learns early on that the addition of different endings can express both affection (as with *-ino*) and dislike (*-accio*). Sometimes this can be very elaborate indeed, especially where names are concerned. So the name *Giuseppe* can affectionately extend to *Giuseppino*, which may then jocularly abbreviate to simple *Pino* and thence stretch once again to the equally familiar *Pinuccio*. Surely that does not happen to English names?

It may not be quite so systematic as in Italian, but English first names are routinely abbreviated, and the *-y* and *-ie* endings are familiar to everyone (*Johnny, Bobby, Billy, Tommy, Robbie, Jilly, Kenny, Minnie*, and the rest). But in his *Encyclopedia of the English Language*, Professor David Crystal shows just how distant from the original name some pet forms can sometimes get. He cites the case of the classic English Christian name *Elizabeth*, which can evolve diminutives that range from the familiar (*Lizzie*) via the less obvious (*Elsie, Libby*, and *Betsy*) to the downright obscure (*Lilibet* and *Tetty*).

Randolph Quirk agrees: '*Bobby*, for example, is a long way from *Robert* and *Betsy* is a long way from *Elizabeth*. In both cases, the baby form is used at the front (*B-Betsy* and *B-Bobby*), and you have in the case of *Betsy* changed the consonant in the middle from *th* to *t*; then you've added the *s* (as in *Babs*—and *Wills*) and finally you've added the -*y* at the end. So that *Betsy* is a quite complicated way of getting around to "I like you Elizabeth"!'

But the place to find these pet forms in real profusion is neither the UK nor the US. It is Down Under. The frequency with which Australians refer to the *arvo* rather than *afternoon* or drinking a *tinnie* at the *barbie* has become fairly familiar through soaps and comics like Barry Humphries. But the complex lexicon of Australian shortenings contains hundreds of examples which have little to do with affection or even simple diminutives.

The Salvation Army, for example, becomes the *Salvos* when patrolling the streets of Sydney (compare the British equivalent, *the Sally Army*), and Dr Kate Burridge of La Trobe University in Melbourne told us that she thinks this love of abbreviations is, apart from the accent, the most distinctive feature of Australian English. 'So you might say in a jokey example, "*Robbo*, the *weirdo journo* from *Freo*, ended up a *derro* and *metho*" ['derelict' and 'meths-drinker']. Or "I took some *speccy piccies* of us opening our *Chrissie prezzies* at *brekkie*." You find these endings in other varieties of English but they have quite different meanings, I think. People wrongly call them diminutives, which are endings that you put on something that you have a warm affectionate feeling towards.'

According to Kate (or, as she is sometimes known, *Kato*), these modified forms are an expression more of Australian informality. 'When you get someone who works on the wharf being called a *wharfie*, or a musician a *muso*, there's something else going on there. I mean, I don't call a politician a *pollie* because I think of the politician as a warm, endearing creature!'

This 'cult of informality' that linguists like Kate Burridge use to explain the Australian penchant for abbreviation is "a sort of casual, laid-back toughness; good humour, with a hefty dollop of anti-intellectualism thrown in'. But like Jane Walmsley, Dr Burridge has noticed a careful gender-related code when it comes to who says what: 'So you'd get great hulking Australian blokes talking about *mozzie* for a mosquito or a *maggie* for a magpie, but you wouldn't get them saying *birdie* or *doggie*, so they're clearly very different from these so-called diminutive endings, or nursery talk.'

One view of why in certain cases Australians say *-ie* and in others *-o* is that the former are more routine terms (*brekkie*, *Chrissie*) while the latter are rarer words, made familiar by 'familiarizing' them (*compo* for compensation or *ambo* from ambulance, *metho*, methylated spirits and so on). But in truth there are as many exceptions as there is strong evidence for the rule.

What is certain is that despite the existence of a wide variety of pet forms, the *-ie* ending stretches worldwide, and well beyond even the bounds of the English language. Randolph Quirk comments: 'We have some that are a bit long in the tooth like *-kin* and *-kins* (as in *babykins* and *Jenniferkins* and so on). But our chief affix for hypocoristic purposes is chiefly *-ie* as an ending. And the *-ie* is a classic instance, probably the nearest to being universal as a "sound symbol".'

Sound symbols are cases where certain affective values are attributed to particular word sounds, also known as 'synaesthesia' (*sn-* words, for instance, are said to suggest unpleasantness—*snarl*, *snatch*, *sneak*, for instance). So, in the case of the *-ie* sound, says Randolph Quirk, 'it represents "small" because we squeeze our mouths small in order to say *-ie*. So the word *tiny* is not as small as *teeny*, and *teeny-weeny* is even smaller than *teeny*. Now that sound symbolism of *-ie* is very widespread. Even in Swahili, I'm told, there is a prefix *ki-* (pronounced like *key*) which you can stick in front of any word and it means "nice little".'

One thing is for sure: it is a very long way from Barbara Woodhouse, her *doggies*, and their afternoon *Walkies*.

" "

Never Say *Die*?

A telephone call interrupts a happy family scene. The voice at the other end is unfamiliar, yet gentle and kind. Who? Why? The scenario is familiar, yet happily not usually visited upon us often in a lifetime. Because that friendly yet unfamiliar voice turns out to be that of a doctor, and the message is that someone close, perhaps very close, has died.

Shocking, yes, devastating, probably. But does the *bearer* of the message make the terrible news easier or more difficult to accept, the loss less or more acute? The way we as ordinary members of the public refer to death is often circumlocutory or even downright dishonest. We talk of people *passing away*, of *being lost*, of *going to meet their maker*, and use a host of other euphemisms for the simple yet irrevocable fact of death.

In these first years of the twenty-first century, we in the West at least rarely live with the day-to-day presence of death, of loss, in the way that our fathers and mothers—certainly our grandfathers and grandmothers—were compelled to. With greatly enhanced life expectancy, of spectacular advances in neonatal care for babies who would in previous generations simply not have survived the perhaps premature passage into the world, death is not for most people an everyday reality. So has this affected the way we talk about the great truth? Dr Robert Buckman once made us laugh as one of the most brilliant young Cambridge comics of the 1960s. Since then he has gone on to a distinguished career in cancer research both in Britain, where he worked at the Royal Marsden Hospital, and in North America. His work with terminally ill patients has given him rare insights into the difficult process of articulating the reality of death, which he has written about in his book *I Don't Know What to Say*.

> A hundred years ago we didn't have any difficulty talking about death, and people were able to say, 'Your soul will be with its maker by the ebb-tide' or something like that. Since really the end of the Second World War, we have had a phase of true 'death denial'. This has been partly because religion has changed its role and become much more personal instead of being social and monolithic, and partly also because the expectations of health have increased dramatically from the end of the Second World War onwards. I think that continued until maybe the late 1970s or early 1980s when we began to accept that we should be considering *death*, because the process of dying is actually married to, and irretrievably fixed to the business of, living. And in some respects language can actually help us with that process of marrying up again.

If most of us these days, then, encounter death only rarely, for doctors and nurses, particularly those who care for the chronically or terminally ill, it is a daily reality. For these carers, familiarity can on occasion lead to a certain casualness with the way they impart the news.

There was the true story of the daughter who telephoned the hospital to learn news of her mother's routine tests who was brutally told: 'Oh, she died.' The daughter, a timid and solitary woman, calling from a damp phone-box nearly 400 miles away, had no close relative or friends to turn to. Powerless in the face of this brutal loss, she threatened suicide. The news—unexpected and shocking in its own right—had been made infinitely worse by the ruthlessly uncaring manner of its delivery.

This was an appalling case, yet I suspect less uncommon than 'health-care professionals' (that contemporary rather glib chip of jargon) would like.

So how best to convey the news of death? The linguistic judgement that doctors and nurses make is a fine one and an individual one. A cursory glance at those outpourings of public grief that accompany the sudden death of a child perhaps shockingly knocked down in a busy high street—the bouquets of flowers, cards, and teddy bears left to dampen in the rain, dangling from lamp-posts and piled up against fences—reveals the huge range of the language of loss. Do you want to have the sad news wrapped up in those elaborate euphemisms to be found there—*breathe one's last, be taken, expire, fall asleep, pass over* and the rest—or would you prefer the terrible news straight?

The latter is generally the preferred form these days. But was it not exactly 'giving it straight' that the hospital did to the poor woman in her dismal phone box? *Word of Mouth* interviewed some of the recently bereaved and some doctors to find out:

A newly widowed woman recalled:

> I think they said, 'I'm sorry to have to tell you that your husband died earlier this morning.' I think that was all—it was something very brief like that, which I appreciated. You don't want a lot of rigmarole do you? It was a telephone voice, anonymous. I just said 'thank you' and put down the phone.

A junior doctor told of the difficulties she had had when for the first time she had to put the reality into words:

I went in and told her that I was very sorry but I had some bad news and that her husband had died. And she was very composed. She didn't cry. She just looked at me and said, 'I've got nobody else in the world; he was the only person that I had.' I think one of the hardest things is that they always say, 'Thank you very much, doctor', and you always wonder what on earth they are thanking you for.

This recently bereaved mother found that while she and her partner had been able to cope with the fact that their daughter had died, the linguistic reality was too much for others to bear:

We rang everybody up and said that Harriet had died. But some people just don't want to hear that word. It frightens them because it means human beings are not immortal as most people like to think they are.

For this mother, whose baby daughter was stillborn, the reverse was true. The maternity staff were not only apparently unfeeling, but also unwilling in her case to use the one word which was the inescapable truth:

No one ever said to us, 'Your baby has died.' It didn't even matter that they didn't say that they were sorry, it was the fact that nobody articulated those words. They would use words like 'You know, it looks bad', or 'It doesn't look very good at all', or 'We'll do everything we can to look after you, but it's not very good at all'. I was desperately trying to come to terms with the fact Victoria had died, but because nobody actually said that, I think it made it all so much more difficult.

One midwife did, however, break down the barrier of formality and euphemism, through a *personal* linguistic response to this mother's distress: 'Because Victoria had died inside me, I thought I'd created some sort of freak. And to hear somebody tell me that my daughter looked pretty was just wonderful. I will always treasure the words that midwife spoke.'

For this doctor, specializing in terminal cases, language often seems completely inadequate. In one case, the news he was imparting was not to relatives but to the patient himself. Words literally failed him:

> I remember specifically there was a 32-year-old man—he was recently married and he had a young eighteen-month-old child, a guy I identified with although he was a couple of years older than me at the time, and we were investigating him for a condition called motor neurone disease. It was quite clear that he had motor neurone disease of the worst sort, and that his prognosis would not be more than two years and that it would be an appalling two years. I just felt completely powerless in the face of the situation. And I looked at him and he looked at me and we both just burst into tears. I just didn't know what to do, and though I suppose my contribution could be seen as rather negative I think it was honest. But that is what being a doctor's all about, I think.

Dr Robert Buckman articulates this need to be linguistically on the same wavelength as your interlocutor, whether it is the terminal patient or the bereaved relatives:

> First of all, listen to the words that the other person is using. Those are the words that person is comfortable with at this particular moment, and those are very good words. So, if the person says, 'I'm afraid of dying' you don't say, 'Oh you're not going to *pass away* through this.' You say, 'Tell me what you feel about *dying*.' As it were, use their own stage of acceptance and consciousness of what's going on as a listening device to get you to hear more accurately what they say. So my message is, don't get hung up on script. Stick to your friend's agenda and talk about the things that he or she wants to talk about, not the things that you feel you should import in to cheer them up or get them over this.

And, above all, be honest and avoid those dreaded circumlocutions:

> I personally have led a campaign for the last ten years for actually using the words *dead* and *dying* and *died* because they can't be misunderstood. A houseman recently told me about when he said to somebody, 'Your husband has passed on.' The wife, who came from a different culture, said, 'I see, and when will he be back?' And there was an awful pause, and then the resident, obviously feeling even worse, said, 'No, I don't mean *passed on*, I mean *passed out*.' In the end, he did actually eventually say, 'What I mean to say is that your husband has *died*.'

Clarity of language, Dr Buckman says, is vital: 'There have been some terrible stories, like the woman who was told: "Your son's heart has stopped—we did our best. Can we have permission for an autopsy?" Two hours later she finds the doctor and asks "did the autopsy work? Is he all right?"' Above all, the key when talking about death is honesty: 'If you are terribly embarrassed and you don't know what to say, you are *allowed* to say to the other person, "I don't know what to say." The more direct and honest you are, the less embarrassed and tripped-up you'll be later on.'

Chapter 4
Minding Your Speak

IN THE NEXT FEW PAGES, words to soothe and smooth, as well as to insult and injure. *Word of Mouth* has explored the way language can be used to mollify and assuage, to assault and aggress, and here investigates extreme forms of both—the ultra-sweet, excessively polite pleasantries invading Britain from North America, and the long tradition of public insults that in recent years have had a very public profile in parliamentary debates Down Under and once were one of the highest forms of poetic achievement north of the border.

In the early twentieth century, as the days of the horse gave way to the era of horsepower and the internal combustion engine, so the special vocabulary of the bridle and bit which has contributed so much to the imagery and metaphor of English was overtaken—quite literally—by the vroom-vroom vocabulary of the car.

Vroom-vroom ... wham-bam ... ding-dong ... They are all forms of onomatopoeia, those imitative words that strain to resemble the sound of what they describe, and just part of the armoury of daily conversation for most of us. But for the comic-book writer, *Zap!* and *Kersplatt!* represent the heavy punches of sound symbolism on the page.

In this chapter, too, a dip into that linguistic emergency kit we call on when all else fails: you know, um, the ... er ... thingummy of whatsitsname ... no ... of course you know ... it's the whatdyoumaycallit. Erm ... the doofer that whatsits the doobry!

Nicely Spoken

There was a time, I seem to recall, not so very long ago when a British satirist visiting the United States for the first time reported to the British masses on his return of the extraordinary antics that went on across the pond. Conventioneers (what a word!) all wore enormous identity badges on their lapels the size of car number-plates (he reported). They all said, 'Have a nice day' and—in his book, the worst sin of all— drank best malt whisky out of paper cups. Ah, those quaint, innocent days when such goings-on were deemed exotic. Now we all do it... and much more. The huge growth of what is glibly known as the *service sector*—from restaurants and hotels to call centres and answering services—has brought with it a tidal wave of fixed smiles and sunny, smiley language.

Now *Have a nice day*, *You're welcome*, *Enjoy your meal* are no longer rare in British shops and restaurants. But do they mean anything? The fact is these routine utterances have almost always been bled quite dry of any real meaning or genuine enthusiasm, and Deborah Cameron, Professor of Linguistics at the Institute of Education in London, has had enough. She has been monitoring the apparently unstoppable advance of this surge of niceness and reported for *Word of Mouth*:

> In 1990 I came back to Britain after two years away, and discovered I no longer spoke the language. English was still my native tongue, but as I went about my business I was constantly bewildered by strange new ways of speaking and writing it. From

Marks & Spencer to the local sub-post office, every organization had acquired a *mission statement* or a *customer charter*, proclaiming its commitment to my happiness and satisfaction. Bank clerks greeted me by name and thanked me for my valuable custom. I bought half a pint of milk at a fast food outlet, and the assistant handed it over with a cheery *Enjoy your meal.*

Eventually I came up with a name for this phenomenon: Nicespeak. Nicespeak is when you wrap up an irrelevant, unhelpful or vacuous message in a language of sincere concern for the person on the receiving end. It's the notice on the door of a shop that says, *In order to better serve you, we have moved from this location.* It's the recorded voice you hear on the phone when you've just been put on hold, saying, *Your call is very important to us* at thirty-second intervals. It's the announcement that your train has been cancelled, followed by a formulaic apology *for any inconvenience caused.*

Like many other things that started in the 1980s, Nicespeak was invented by management consultants. The *mission statement*, for instance (first recorded in the *Oxford English Dictionary* in 1971), and its shorter, pithier relative the *vision statement*, were popularized by the management guru Tom Peters. According to Peters, the most successful companies proclaimed their goals and values to the world in clear, inspirational words. In fact, most company mission and vision statements are neither informative nor inspiring. They rely heavily on vague platitudes like *pursuing excellence*, or *quality, service and value*; in many cases you can't even tell from them what business the company's in. But that's not the point: the mission statement belongs to a time when the purpose of most large companies is not making things, but branding things. Like the designer logo on a T-shirt, the language in a mission statement is part of the brand—designer words, chosen to communicate image, not substance.

Linguistic image-making goes beyond the mission statement.

One of the things I found disconcerting in 1990 was the proliferation of scripted formulas in service encounters—the standard phone salutations delivered with standard perky intonation, the replacement of traditional British courtesies by Americanisms like *How may I help you?* and *Enjoy!* This way of speaking didn't just evolve naturally. It was imposed on service workers by companies that wanted to control every detail of their customers' experience. Only if every employee said the same thing in the same way could customers get what one company's manual called 'a consistent experience of the brand'.

Not so long ago, western audiences were astonished by reports of a call centre in Bangalore dealing with customers in the United States, whose Indian employees had to impersonate Americans. Operators invented American names and personal histories to go with them, watched episodes of *Friends* to keep their colloquialisms current, and perfected their Midwestern accents. But you don't have to go to India to find workers adopting prescribed forms of language remote from their ordinary ways of speaking. Next time you phone Directory Inquiries, spare a thought for the operator who answers your call. In the thirty-two seconds your inquiry is meant to take, the operator is supposed to give you an impression of excitement, courtesy, friendliness and helpfulness. One company's instruction manual goes so far as to tell the operators: 'Your phone manner should sound to the customer as if you've been waiting for that particular call all day.'

Managing other people's language has become a business in its own right, complete with its own fads and gimmicks. The *New York Times* recently reported on a new trend in training computer helpdesk workers. Rather than being trained to diagnose the caller's computer problem, workers are being taught to assess the caller's personality type, and then select the right words to appeal to that type of person. That way, so the theory goes, the customer hangs up satisfied whether or not their computer works.

In politics, too, there's a belief in the power of managed language to distract us from unpleasant realities. In 1999, officers of the New York Police Department shot and killed Amadou Diallo, an unarmed West African they mistook for a dangerous criminal. More than a thousand people were arrested in public protests. Mayor Rudolph Giuliani decided to try to defuse the tension by giving police officers little cards with instructions on how to speak politely to members of the public. Faced with a serious political problem, he adopted the customer care approach—speak nicely, and all will be forgiven. It may be inane, but precisely because of its caring, sharing quality, it's hard for anyone to object to. Who would be against the pursuit of excellence, or polite police officers, or service with a smile? It's not that these things are objectionable in themselves; the trouble is that all too often, they're used to avoid confronting more serious problems—from poor quality service to institutional racism.

In 1990 I was baffled by Nicespeak; today, like most of Britain's working population, I'm fluent in it myself. Now, though, I've made a resolution: I'm going to pursue excellence in the use of the English language. I'm going to make it my mission to avoid vacuous jargon, to resist fake sincerity, to judge the service behind the smile. I'm going to close my ears to the chorus of voices saying that every problem is a communication problem, to be solved by a generous application of Nicespeak. That's like spreading butter on a burn: just because a lot of people swear by it doesn't make it an effective remedy. We might stand a better chance of solving our problems if we stopped wrapping them up in linguistic cotton wool.

To Er ... Er is Human

One of the not so well-kept secrets of radio broadcasters is the fact that recorded interviews are almost always subjected to the ritual removal—together with redundant comments— of unnecessary hesitations, clearings of throat, coughs and pause noises. This technique is officially known as 'de-umming' (really). In the days when all interviews were recorded on magnetic tape, it was a real hard-graft practical skill that involved a fine ear for an *um* and a good eye, steady hand and sharp razor blade. Each snip of tape—they could be a metre or a millimetre in length, depending on the fluency of the speaker—represented a removed *um*, *er*, *erm*, *uh*, or other unwanted utterance. These days, such edits are usually made on computer, dispensing with the blade and the physical scraps of plastic on the floor beneath the tape machine. But the trained ear for what constitutes a 'necessary' or 'redundant' *um* is as essential as ever.

Why go to all this trouble? Certainly it does allow the broadcaster to cram a little more real material into a limited time slot—with some particularly hesitant speakers, reductions of up to 30 per cent are possible. But the real reason for spending so much time cutting out people's natural hesitations is because they tend to get in the way of smooth and easily listened-to broadcasting. Too much 'umming' and 'erring', the theory goes, and the ear of the listener goes walkabout, so to speak, the attention wanders and the mind stops taking in what the speaker is saying. And this is true, at least up to a point.

So why—conversely—do speakers hesitate in the first place? Surely communication would be enhanced if people spoke—as the character Monsieur Jourdain realizes, to his amazement, that *he* does, in Molière's famous play of 1670, *Le Bourgeois Gentilhomme* – in prose? Smooth, flawless prose. 'The general view is that this is because you're under some kind of a pressure and it's a reaction to being under pressure,' says John Wells, Professor of Phonetics and Phonology at University College, London.

> Though the most recent research I read suggests that this is not actually supported by research findings. A more sophisticated view is that you need extra processing time for some linguistic decisions you've got to make in sentence structure or in finding some word in your vocabulary. So as not to lose the turn in the conversation—which might be indicated if you did nothing at all—you 'um' while you're doing this extra mental processing till you come up with the word or construction that you're looking for.

So 'umming' and 'erring' are actually vital to being able to find the right word at the right time. Maybe this is why politicians are so prone to falling back on a small lexicon of terms and expressions that they can deliver with confidence and without hesitation, when faced with the darts of a John Humphrys or a Jeremy Paxman. Safety first, use a cliché. Never be heard to hesitate, felt to falter. 'If there are a lot of hesitation noises from a speaker, we tend not to view them as being terribly competent, not as being terribly dynamic, not as being as dominant as we would if they spoke confidently and without hesitation noises,' says John Wells.

And there is living proof of this—if proof were needed. The BBC Archive has preserved a recording of a meeting dating, as I recall, from the 1964 general election campaign, in which Sir Alec Douglas-Home, the Conservative Prime Minister, is speaking out of doors to a largely unsympathetic crowd. Not only does the unfortunate speaker have to contend with heckles from the mob, but as the rally appears to have been taking place directly under the flight-path from Heathrow airport, he has somehow to make himself heard above the roar of departing aircraft. Sir Alec always had, even under the most favourable circumstances, a tendency to pause, to reach for a word and not deliver a completely ringing, assured performance. On the soapbox, however, fighting the planes *and* the crowd, his delivery suffered badly. In 1964 the media age of the televisual performer and the confidently delivered soundbite was beginning to dawn. Sir Alec belonged to an earlier, less scrutinized era, and it was in part because of these handicaps that the election was lost by the Tories. 'These days, they'd make a clip out of it and replay it a hundred times, wouldn't they, and poke fun at you' observes Professor Wells.

For the politician, therefore, hesitancy is a distinct handicap. But for most of us it is a most useful verbal prop, a pause point where we can select the appropriate word, fish for a missing word, frame the exact shape of what we want to say, so as not (for example) to give offence, annoy or hurt the person to whom we are speaking by rushing in with an ill-thought-through phrase. 'Umming', then, can be a vital part of the diplomatic toolkit. Humour, too, makes use of man's willingness to *er*, as a famous *Two Ronnies* sketch proved, where Corbett repeatedly filled in Barker's *um*-filled pauses only to be contradicted to hilarious effect when the right word was eventually located. And—if you are old enough—who can fail to remember *The Navy Lark*'s Sub-Lieutenant Leslie Phillips's drawling *er... m* before his classic punchline, 'Left hand down a bit'?

Leslie Phillips's *er... m* was gormless but rather charming, full of the sort of suave seductiveness which is his trademark. But one man's suggestive *er* is another's admission of a guilty secret: the way you hesitate—the way the *ums* and *ers* are distributed in the sentence—varies from person to person. As the skilled BBC 'de-ummer' will tell you, there are dozens of ways to deliver an *um*—mid-pause, drawling out of the last syllable of the previous word, providing a little auditory ramp into the next word. Sometimes even mid-word. Some are easy to remove, others so difficult that if an impossibly jerky effect is to be avoided, to leave well alone is the only practical policy. Edit out *all* the *ums* and the result is frequently an almost unlistenable gabble of phrases and clauses, tumbling out higgledy-piggledy without the natural dynamics of speech. Thus, as every experienced audio-editor will tell you, *ums* are very definitely a structural part of our speech *patterns*—cut them all out and the pattern becomes broken, the sense almost unreadable.

'Umming' becomes far more pronounced when the speaker is not using his or her native language. This can be a real barrier to smooth and unambiguous communication. The French speaker's *euh*, dropped in mid-phrase with great regularity, becomes irritating when repeated at length to an ear attuned to English patterns of 'umming'. A case of the wrong sound in the wrong place.

So although *um* has no direct semantic status, no actual meaning (though, as in the Leslie Phillips example above, I would contend that it has tone and mood and thus can convey a *feeling* or *intent*), it does carry a recognition factor. The speaker is identifiable as an English user by the correct insertion of the correct pause sounds (like *um, er, erm* and *mm*) in the correct places in the utterance. 'It depends what we mean by *English*,' points out John Wells; 'that's what we say in *English* English. But Scottish people tend to say *eeh* rather than *er*, and that's because they don't really have an *er* sound.' To demonstrate this he points to the words *nurse* and *serve* as voiced in standard English Received Pronunciation (RP) and in standard Scots pronunciation. 'Scottish people will typically say *nuhrrrss* and *sairrrve*, with other vowels and a (rolled) "r" sound after it.'

Americans do not go for the same pause sounds either: so the British person trying to fake an American accent and saying something like *errrm* (with a strongly voiced US-style 'r') will immediately sound wrong: 'They don't do that at all,' Wells points out; 'they say *ah* or *ahm*, using a somewhat opener vowel.' Likewise, our English-speaking Frenchman may have near-perfect pronunciation and complete command of English vocabulary but be tripped up by that telltale, indisputably Gallic *euh* inserted between words.

So why does RP choose *er* rather than *euh*, *eeh*, or *ahm*? It is, says Professor Wells, simply a matter of how we use our mouths in British English: 'I think what it is is a sort of "neutral position" for the organs of speech. You can think of all the other vowels as being some kind of an excursion from this "rest" position, and if you have a basic vowel position, for us it's *er*.'

And for the French, presumably, it's *euh*. So *now* we know why French faces look the way they do ...

" "

Rude!

High Street, UK, some time in the early years of the twenty-first century. Heavy traffic blocks all the lanes, cars jostle for advantage. A cyclist is nearly upended by a bus drawing into the stop across his bows in the specially reserved cycle lane. Nothing particularly unusual in any of this. Nor in the result, as the cyclist hammers furiously on the side panel of the bus as he slips past with a string of oaths. Which, in turn, provokes an equal stream of abuse from the bus driver leaning out of his cab to shout at the cyclist. Abuse—verbal abuse—is now a fixture on our streets and in our lives.

Time was when an outpouring of verbal abuse would be enough certainly to turn heads, draw a crowd, even maybe occasion the arrival of the law. Rarely today. 'Rage' in its various formulations (road, air, and, heaven help us, surf rage) is a modern phenomenon, and abusive language is how it is most commonly expressed. This is not the same— not quite the same, anyway—as swearing. Swearing is the use of strong or offensive language in order to reinforce a verbal point. Abuse, obloquy, or invective may contain such terminology, but swearing does not necessarily imply being abusive to someone. As Dr Johnson wrote: 'The difference between coarse and refined abuse is as the difference between being bruised by a club and wounded by a poisoned arrow.'

However, as Feargal Murphy of University College, Dublin explained to *Word of Mouth*, the need to be rude and use gross language openly to someone satisfies a deep need in many of us: 'For a lot of people it's a particular type of language and they love using it.' For many, it seems to be a primary emotional and linguistic building-block. When a well-known writer recently suffered a serious stroke at a frighteningly young age, the first and only word he was able to articulate was the 'f-word', which he kept repeating. 'I mean, we know it's special,' comments Murphy, 'because it's things like—if someone has had a stroke, obscene language is the kind of language that returns quickly. So it must be very expressive. And people would be attracted by the ability then to generate a good insult because it actually says something you feel deeply—but say it in a civilized way.'

So we are already moving beyond the sphere of the road-rage incident into the world of the calculated piece of invective. Public obloquy is, of course, bound by the rules that protect us from defamation and slander, so the would-be abuser must be careful to wrap his or her invective in the safety blanket of 'fair comment' or of lawyers' advice. Most newspapers and broadcasters have a legal department on more or less twenty-four-hour notice to offer advice on the potential legal problems that a particular piece of copy may offer. The invective that was unleashed upon the character and behaviour of Lord Archer following his conviction on perjury charges was astonishing. He was known before his trial to be extremely litigious, and had threatened court action over a number of years for abusive or malicious claims in the press about his character or dealings. Once he was jailed, the press knew that no court of law would entertain his charges and so it was open season.

Likewise in Parliament, where, although unparliamentary language is closely regulated—it is not permitted to claim in the Chamber that a member had *lied*, for example—claims of alleged misdeeds and potentially damaging observations are protected by the rule of parliamentary privilege. Despite this, the Mother of Parliaments remains a relatively polite institution. In parliament in Canberra, in Australia, few such niceties are observed. Try this little exchange, captured verbatim by the house microphones:

> The Honourable Member is a galah! Lunatic!
> Order!
> That fellow down there is mad!
> Order!
> That fellow down there is mad!
> Order! The honourable minister will withdraw that remark! Can I say he's certifiable...
> The minister will withdraw both those...
> ...unbalanced...
> ...will withdraw the remarks—The minister will withdraw...
> I will withdraw and just say that he's got a couple of kangaroos loose in the top paddock...!

and so on. Now wouldn't Question Time at Westminster be fun if insults were traded with that sort of Antipodean verve!

In the world of journalistic criticism, too, being rude about a performance in a play, film, or whatever is considered fair game. I know of one popular broadcaster whose reputation was ruined by the repeated crucifying copy published on a weekly basis over many months. He left the programme and went back to his old job, battered and demoralized. Yet there was little to be done about it: the sort of repeated abusive criticism is normal practice in newspaper reviewing.

One man whose columns in the London daily newspaper, the *Evening Standard*, are frequently a confection of rudery and invective is the art critic Brian Sewell. Not content with pouring regular bile over the capital's art establishment, Sewell has a number of favourite targets whom he goes for with unstinting glee. And yet, he says he hardly recognizes the author from the copy that he writes:

> I get up early in the morning and take the dogs out and come home, have a bath and sit down and write. At that point I am convinced somebody else takes over. Because when I reread the thing after bashing it through the typewriter, I very often say to myself, 'Good Lord, how could I have said that?' And I roar with laughter at my own copy because it is so insulting and so full of invective and so to the point. And if I thought about it when I wrote it I would never write it. It is somebody else.

The advantage that Brian Sewell and his fellow newspaper critics have is a guaranteed audience. So too do MPs as they rain down insults on the hapless minister whose 'staggering incompetence' they have come to highlight. 'Insulting in general often does need an audience,' observes Feargal Murphy;

> You know, the Oscar Wilde, Whistler, George Bernard Shaw kind of thing. And that the cleverness of my insult is what wins through. And if I can ridicule you in front of the audience, that's how I insult you. A famous beauty, Lillian Russell, suggested to George Bernard Shaw that as he had the greatest brain in the world and she the most beautiful body, they ought to produce the most perfect child. Shaw is said to have replied, 'What if the child inherits *my* body and *your* brains?' In effect, he admitted—yes, I'm ugly, but you're stupid.

Famously, in similar vein, when Sir Winston Churchill was accused by the far from slimline MP Bessie Braddock of being drunk, he is said to have responded: 'And Bessie, you're ugly. But tomorrow I shall be sober.'

The use of abuse to raise a smile is a tradition that many have traded on: Groucho Marx's rudery became his trademark comic turn and the ritual verbal humiliation of Margaret Dumont in such films as *Duck Soup* are the hilarious linguistic set pieces that beautifully counterbalance the slapstick. Take the following exchange between Rufus T. Firefly (Marx) and Mrs Teasdale (Dumont):

> MRS TEASDALE: You are the most able statesman in all Freedonia.
>
> FIREFLY: Well, that covers a lot of ground. Say, you cover a lot of ground yourself. You better beat it. I hear they're going to tear you down and put up an office building where you're standing ... You know you haven't stopped talking since I came here? You must have been vaccinated with a phonograph needle ...

Marx's heyday was the 1930s. Seventy years later the tradition of public rudery is still being kept alive in the United States. There, it is known as *snapping*. Snapping is competitive, loud, and incredibly fast-moving. It consists of a sort of verbal duel in which two snappers fling insults at each other, with each constantly attempting to cap the outrageousness of the opponent. Less known than rapping, snapping similarly delights in verbal word-play and audacious gags. In a special edition of the programme from New York in 1996, *Word of Mouth* met two of the stars of snap, James Perclay and Monteria Ivey, who gave a virtuoso display of the genre—outrageous, offensive, blasphemous, and hilarious—of which this is a reasonably publishable extract:

> Your sister is so fat, she can use a circus tent for a miniskirt.
>
> Your girlfriend is so fat, when I got on top of her I burned my ass on the light bulb.
>
> Your mother is so fat, she puts on lipstick with a paint-roller.

There are rules, Perclay says, such as: 'Don't touch your opponent, use a referee, snap in front of a crowd ... and don't spit.' The art of the snap is to find words and images that in a 'snapshot' moment are both funny and outrageously insulting.

Back in the more sophisticated world inhabited by the art critic Brian Sewell, rudery offers a greater level of linguistic precision. His preferred technique is to undermine his victims' authority or reputation: 'I don't think there's any single word that wipes people out,' he says, 'but I don't think they like to be described as "ineffectual" or "feeble"—it's words like that that get under their skins—describing them as a "wretched imitator" or "pasticheur" of some other greater artist'.

The interesting thing about this ritualized form of abuse, whether in a British newspaper or in the clubs of Manhattan, is that it has a long and distinguished pedigree. Five hundred or more years, no less. In sixteenth-century Scotland lived a poet one of whose great claims for posterity is to have penned a classic piece of ritual abuse. He was William Dunbar, and amongst his works is a long piece written in low, vulgar Scots and described by one critic as 'scurrilous and colloquial'. 'The Flyting of Dunbar and Kennedie' is a brilliant example of the Scots tradition of *Flyting*, a tradition in which two poets match their skills in 'a contest of poetical invective' according to the dictionary—in other words, a sort of literary slagging match.

And here we pause for a little *flyting* etymological moment (no abuse, please). Nothing to do with *fight* or *flight*, or getting 'aerated' in argument, the word *flyte* (meaning 'argue noisily') derives from an Old English term *flitan* 'to contend'.

'The Flyting of Dunbar and Kennedie' is difficult to make out today as a continuous narrative, wrapped as it is in period terminology, a highly regional form of the language, and some pretty non-standard spelling. Yet some of Dunbar's punch-packing effect still comes through:

> For to be fylde wyth sik a fruteles face
> Cum hame and hyng on oure gallowis of aire
> To erd the vnder it I sall purchas grace
> To ete thy flesch. the doggis sall haue na space
> The ravyns sall ryve na thing bot thy tong rutis
> For thou sik malice of thy maister mutis
> It is wele sett y^t thou sik barat brace
> Small fynance / amang thy frendis thou beggit
> To stanch the storme wyth haly muldis thou loste
> Thou sailit to get a dowcare for to dreg it ...

'I think these Dunbar flytings are absolutely eye-watering,' comments Dr Katie Lowe, an Old English specialist from the University of Glasgow. 'I mean, reading them, you really catch your breath—they are staggeringly rude. You might think that we wouldn't be shocked by something which was written after all in the sixteenth century. Just under fifty years after this was composed, the Scots moved first to legislate against profanity.'

The flyting tradition that saw its high-water mark in the work of William Dunbar actually has its roots even earlier, in Norse times. As Geoffrey Hughes, a former Professor of English at Witwatersrand University in South Africa and the author of a study of swearing and other forms of coarse language, explained: 'We have a Middle English poem called "The Owl and the Nightingale", a thirteenth-century poem which is clearly built on a flyting format.' But the most striking examples, he says, come from the early sixteenth century: 'These are really quite remarkable because it's really the fine art of savage insult. It would seem impossible that people could really have produced these works, extemporarily. They obviously move from being oral forms into having quite a lot of "polish", shall we say.'

For that polish really to shine and to make its point, the choice of words is essential. Shakespeare has some wonderfully constructed verbal duels where insults are traded—*The Taming of the Shrew* and *Much Ado About Nothing* are constructed round such ritualized exchanges as this famous one, between Beatrice and Benedick:

BENEDICK: What, my dear lady Disdain! Are you yet living?

BEATRICE: Is it possible disdain should die while she hath such meet food to feed it as Signior Benedick? Courtesy itself must convert to disdain if you come in her presence.

BENEDICK: Then is courtesy a turn-coat.—But it is certain I am loved of all ladies, only you excepted: and I would I could find in my heart that I had not a hard heart: for, truly, I love none.

BEATRICE: A dear happiness to women; they would else have been troubled with a pernicious suitor.

The choice of the most effective-sounding words to hurl at someone is a matter as much of form as of meaning. So short, sharp monosyllables work best, and—so the theory goes— certain sounds have more negative or 'abusive' characteristics than others. 'Some people have this belief in sound symbolism or "phonaesthetics" that there are certain sounds that are best suited to express certain meanings,' says Feargal Murphy. 'That *sl*, for instance, in *slug* and *slime* and *slush* somehow better expresses some kind of meaning; and then people try to extend this to say that the letters *p*, *t*, and *g* would be better in curses. But the trouble is that it doesn't always work that way.'

Then again, you do not always want what Feargal Murphy calls a 'full-on sledgehammer effect'. Unexpectedly, however, Brian

Sewell found himself using far from sledgehammer language when confronted with an incident in the street, when he spotted a young black man being kicked on the pavement by a gang of white youths. Yet his words had the required effect:

> I stopped the car about twenty yards up and leaped out and dashed back and said: 'Pack it in!', which was what I'd have said when I was fourteen at school: 'Pack it in!' And it worked. And I don't know whether it was the 'Pack it in!' or the presence of somebody who was obviously angry and feeling authoritative or what, but that clearly did work.

Somehow, I cannot quite imagine the road-rage victim having much effect on his persecutor with a gentle 'Pack it in!', can you? Mind you, one should never underestimate the power of laughter.

" "

Crack the Whip and Put Your Foot Down

Chafe at the bit, crack the whip, hold your horses! They are a bit like ghosts, these expressions from a past age, redolent of a time when city streets were clogged with the clattering hooves of horses rather than with rows of beached automobiles. It was a time when doom merchants predicted that London would be submerged under a vast tide of horse dung were the horse population to continue to expand unchecked. But it *was* checked, of course, and this heyday of the city horse, of streets filled with carts and carriages, of city ostlers and farriers, of stable-lads and municipal water troughs, has almost entirely disappeared. Only the occasional stone basin at a street corner, the high-arched entrances to courtyards and now much sought-after converted stable blocks, remain. Together, that is, with a veritable *cavalcade* of equine expressions and vocabulary.

Of course, the Sport of Kings preserves many horsey words and phrases, and renews daily in the racing pages of our daily newspapers the particular range of equine vocabulary that derives strictly from the turf. But those cart-loads of expressions—that one hundred years ago were lugged hourly through our lives at the pace of a shambling dray or rag-and-bone man's nag—they are no longer replenished.

Who now remembers, for instance, that a *cavalcade* was originally in the late sixteenth century 'a ride or raid on *horse*back', a French word formed from the Italian *cavalcata* and a whole family of 'riding' words derived from the Latin *caballus*, 'horse'? Less than a hundred years later a *cavalcade* had become 'a company or procession of riders and carriages, especially on a festive or solemn occasion'. And as literal procession gave way to a figurative one—Noël Coward called one of his musicals *Cavalcade*—so horsepower gave way to the internal combustion engine. And in America at the beginning of the twentieth century drove that wonderfully clunky linguistic coining, *motorcade*.

Not surprising, then, that when horses filled our streets, the words and phrases that were used about them likewise crowded our vocabulary. Now when a burglar *bolts* from the scene of the crime, we no longer have the image of a horse out of control, in which sense the word dates from 1820.

When the ambitious young executive says he or she is *chafing at the bit* to get promotion, the eager horse pulling at its harness is long forgotten. And the worker who complains at the end of a hard day's labour that he's *knackered* surely has no idea that he is comparing himself to a dead-beat horse. 'It's taking a horse down the knacker's yard,' says wordsmith and comedian Arthur Smith, 'and you don't get much more knackered than being ground up for glue, I suppose, do you?' The sports journalist Simon Barnes prefers to refine the definition: 'If you're *knackered* it means you're ready to be taken off for glue; if you say that horse is *completely knackered*, he's got to go.' In fact, the dictionary refines the definition even further, suggesting that a *knackered* horse may have been one who had been castrated (from *knackers*, slang for testicles).

The profusion of these horse-drawn metaphors, now all but completely severed from their roots, is staggering: on *Word of Mouth*, Michael Rosen pointed out a long list of perfectly day-to-day expressions that we are happy to use, for the most part blissfully unaware of where they come from: to *chafe at the bit, have the whip hand, kick over the traces, rein in one's feelings, have the bit between one's teeth, bridle* at something, to be *saddled* with it, to have a *blinkered* reaction, do something *at a gallop*, or simply to *take life at a canter*, not to mention the classically comical image of *putting the cart before the horse*.

Today the tossing head and flying mane of a brewer's dray-horse is rarely seen along the streets of the capital. Yet say that someone is *headstrong*, and for those like Simon Barnes who know their horse-speak, the whiff of warm straw is immediately in his nostrils.

> If a horse is *headstrong* it's literally strong in the head. You're trying to ride it and the horse is leaning on the bit, is pulling your arms out, is trying to do what *he* wants rather than what *you* want. And it's your job to cajole and persuade him to do otherwise, so a

headstrong person is too determined to go his own way, is unwilling to make a cooperative deal of it all.

Typical of these hidden horsey metaphors is the expression *to put someone's back up*. It is a perfectly current phrase meaning to irritate or to cause someone to *bridle* (*bridle*: 'to throw up the head and draw in the chin as a horse does when reined in, expressing ... resentment', according to the dictionary and itself a very old verb, attested since the mid fifteenth century). But back to *putting someone's back up*. Simon Barnes offers one explanation:

> If you *put a horse's back up* before you get on it, you're going to find a horse that's standing very stiff and tall and proud and uncooperative. It also means that his mind is not with you, he's looking—as it were—to 'take offence'. So you have a stiff and difficult and problematic horse. And people will often say 'I'll get on him for ten minutes and *bring his back down* for you.' So if you *put a horse's back up*, you've upset him.

Interestingly, as so often with matters of etymology, picking a single true pathway through the maze of misleading tracks of language is tricky. And this expression proves no exception, since most lexicographers will tell you that to *put someone's back up* in fact originates in the typical behaviour of an angry cat that arches its back. But since riders certainly do use it of their mounts, both, it would seem, are right, though the feline usage appears to pre-date Simon Barnes's horsey one.

Although I can still remember from the 1950s a sound that I now realize to be almost Victorian in its antiquity—the slow clop of hooves on a suburban street and that strangled yell of 'Rag an' bone!' echoing along the houses—today we only have the roar of cars, or the fuming anger (now known as *road rage* first recorded in 1988) provoked by that feature of twenty-first-century cities: *gridlock*. By the start of the new millennium, the fertile source for new transport-based expressions had its horsepower under the bonnet rather than between the shafts. So *gridlock* is a metaphor dating from America in 1981 as the cars stacked up along the typical grid pattern of US cities, their intersections marshalled by traffic lights but locked solid by the sheer volume of motor vehicles. *Bumper to bumper*, as the expression (also now used figuratively too) goes.

Gridlock is in fact meaningless in the context of British cities, which are rarely constructed on the grid pattern and which, though often *congested*, can almost never be said literally to be *gridlocked*. More effective is the expression in its metaphorical application. A 1985 edition of the *British Medical Journal* states: 'the National Health Service is trapped in *gridlock* and lacks the incentives to break out.'

To avoid *gridlock*, the best solution is to *park*—and ideas too these days can be safely *parked* while they are not being called upon, or indeed may be being consigned to non-implementation. *Parking a problem*, on the other hand, can be a useful strategy when attempting to resolve a knotty dispute.

Being *at* or *behind the wheel* is pretty much the same as *holding the reins*, but as far as I can tell it has only been possible to *make a U-turn* in politics—or anywhere for that matter—since cars started losing their way and had to swing round in the opposite direction. Come to think of it, such a manoeuvre in horse and cart—were it practicable at all—would rather more resemble a W-turn...

Changing up a gear is a vivid and clear metaphor for 'upping the pace', constantly renewed by the driver's routine of shifting the gear lever (or, as Americans call it, the *stick shift*) in order to go faster. Sometimes, of course, at particularly hyperactive moments, people have even been known to *go into overdrive* (originally an extra gear that offered additional speed, but now almost entirely used in this figurative sense). And here is an interesting sociolinguistic footnote: in jokey American slang, *Mexican overdrive* is coasting downhill in a car in neutral.

Comments comedian Arthur Smith, 'I think where metaphors for cars come into play is more to do with speed— like *living life in the fast lane* or *revving up*.' *Overtaking*, while clearly something that athletes do as well as drivers, has absorbed Arthur Smith's thrill of speeding. In fact one might, without too much imagination-stretching, conceive of a young executive, say, a *self-starter* (the automotive mechanism and the words to describe it date from the 1890s, the metaphor from the 1960s) *living life in the fast lane* whose career has been *changing up a gear* as he *overtakes* his colleagues by *stepping on the gas* in the career stakes.

Until, that is, he *crashes*. Planes were the first machines to be said to do this as they plummeted to earth, back in 1910, but ten years later, the word was being applied to cars. It is, I think, an interesting micro-shift of meaning that occurs by 1972 when computers which fail are said to *crash*. Whereas the crashing vehicle usually strikes something untoward and ends up in a heap of twisted steel, the computer suffers an internal failure, and the program breaks down. And as your average AA or RAC man will tell you, there is every difference between a *breakdown* and a *crash*.

Back in the days of horse and cart, the problem seemed more likely to belong to a gentler order, like *putting the cart before the horse* or, at its most racy, *locking the stable door after the horse has bolted*. But despite the fact that the horses have all but disappeared from our daily lives, no one ever *puts the trailer before the cab* or *locks the garage door after the car's been stolen*. These miniature horse-drawn narratives still speak for themselves, holding their own against the motorized tide, long after the rich source of metaphorical language has gone, with the animals, to the knacker's yard.

" "

All-Purpose Filler

Have you ever noticed? They're like flying ants on a calm summer's afternoon. One day, there is nothing but a normal existence, full of meaningful communication and conversation. Next moment they're everywhere, you're treading them underfoot and you've got them flying in your face and you can't make head nor tail of anything. And that's just the words. *Thingummybob, thingummyjig, doofer, dooda, doobree* ... Where do they come from, these all-purpose filler words that suddenly break into conversations?

Many years ago, a friend of the family got a bad attack of the doofers. As a child, I used to overhear him chatting to my parents about how his wife had 'got the doofer for the so-and-so, but the dratted doofer didn't fit and she'd had to take it back and get another one'—from the doofer-shop, I supposed. Perplexity reigned—but then, I was not supposed to be earwigging the grown-up conversation, anyway. Far worse was to come. The next and more serious outbreak of flying thingies actually came with a very Gallic flavour. Pity the poor exchange student trying to get to grips at age fourteen with the ins and outs of idiomatic teenage French slang, only to be greeted by a swarm of French doobrees. Only, of course, had they actually been called 'doobrees', I might have stood a chance. But these were French doobrees and they were called *trucs*. I can still recall my penfriend explaining to his sister how 'J'ai laissé le truc pour le truc sur le truc dans mon truc' ('I left the thingy for the thingummy on the doobree in my whatjamacallit'). Nightmare. And I was still trying to work out how you spelled *truc*.

And when they had finished with *truc*, they simply moved on to *machin*—another Gallic thingy word. 'It's a kind of nervous tic really,' observes Professor David Crystal, author of some of the most authoritative contemporary guides to the English language.

> All languages as far as we know—all the common ones that people have studied—have got words like this. It's a convenience, it's a kind of basic form. A word like *thing* is empty of meaning essentially. There aren't many words that are so empty of meaning in that way. It is a nice sort of neutral placeholder. And therefore it has generated a whole wide range of words—*thingy, thingummyjig, thingummybob* and so on—there are usually half a dozen surrounding the base-form. French has *truc* and other languages have similar words.

These essential space-fillers clearly fulfil a useful function— sometimes, as in the two examples I quoted, too useful. They offer the opportunity for the speaker to pause and reach for a word— or at least maintain the structure of his or her discourse without blundering into silence or using an inappropriate or inaccurate term. They are, in David Crystal's words, 'neutral placeholders'. Sometimes, though, they clearly become simple linguistic laziness. In the case of the serious outbreak of *truc*s amongst the French family, there was no question that they could have found the appropriate word if they had bothered to think for a moment. But on this occasion, *truc* did the trick—and that was all they needed. Understanding—at least between those taking part in the conversation—was not affected: *they* knew what they were talking about, even if their unfortunate young visitor from Angleterre didn't (and he didn't matter, anyway).

The alternatives to using one of these neutral words are two: either one simply pauses (at which point conversational advantage is lost, and one's interlocutor is likely to zip in with some thoughts of their own) or one uses one of those other vital conversational pause points like *um, er,* and *erm* (and we all know by now that these very definitely have an individual national accent—by his *euh*s shall ye know your Frenchman!). 'You cannot have just silence in a conversation and get away with it,' affirms David Crystal, 'especially on the radio. So, second option: you can hesitate verbally—out loud. Now other people hesitate by doing strange noises—I have a friend who hesitates by putting his tongue between his lips and going *blublublblublublublubl* as his way of showing that he is delaying, but most people opt for a word.'

Here are a few of the favourites: *Thing, thingy, thingummy, thingummyjig, thingummybob, oojamaflop, oojamaflip, whatsit, whatitsname, whatjamacallit, whathaveyou, whatchacallem, whatchacallit, whatever, whatnot.*

'Different people have different favourite forms in their safety net.' David Crystal says that his favourite is *whatdyoumacallit* which, he points out, is almost unspellable, at least in any standardizable form, and so dictionaries do not list it. 'You can actually write it *what-you-may-call-it* but that isn't exactly what it means.' Many people use forms based on *thing*, and for that reason it is not surprising that there is such a rich cluster surrounding the *thing* base word. Interestingly, this very undefinedness of *thing* has proved its linguistic usefulness over many centuries, reaching back to ancient Rome, where the word *res* (Latin for 'thing') performed the neutral base-word trick for Latin speakers: *res publica* (literally, a 'public thing') was the origin of one of the central concepts of Roman society—the *Republic*.

But if *thing* is the most commonly used and has the longest pedigree, others possess greater snap, crackle, and colour. 'Americans very often have favourites like *oojamaflop*,' comments David Crystal, 'or *hootenanny*, which is another common American one. And an uncle of mine who was in the RAF during the war had *dooda* as his favourite, which is very out of date now. I don't know anybody who says *dooda* these days.'

Nor does one find, I think, many *whatnots* around these days. *Whatnot* is another of these wonderful all-purpose filler terms. Two hundred years ago, however, a *whatnot* was also a common sight in drawing rooms across the country, stacked with *knick-knacks*. Because *whatnot* was the name given to 'a stand with shelves, used for keeping or displaying small objects'. (Just think of it—a whatnot filled with knick-knacks!)

This particular object—the whatnot—illustrates a further interesting linguistic phenomenon, the coining. Elsewhere in this book, we investigate book-blurb writing, and show how the word *blurb* came into existence from out of a blue sky. Someone just made it up. Sometimes, however, such coinings come simply from the very *inability* to invent a name for something. Hence, one presumes, the *whatnot*. Ditto the little opening window to be found high up in the walls of many French buildings. Its name? A *vasistas*. And what is that? Well may you ask. Try it with a German accent: 'Was ist das?' ("What is that?")—Precisely!

A few years ago, a snack-food manufacturer wanted to come up with a name for a new product to compete in the crisp and cracker market. What did those inventive marketing chaps come up with? Another clever version of the *whatnot* and the *vasistas*: Wotsits!

And when a beer manufacturer not so long ago invented a device to make the liquid foam when a can was opened, they called it a *widget*, and based an extensive advertising campaign around the term. In fact, *widget* is yet another of these fill-in terms, with a surprisingly long pedigree, being first recorded in the United States in 1931, where it meant a manufactured *gadget*, of which it is suggested *widget* is possibly a corruption. By the end of the twentieth century, the very anonymity of the product suggested by the word *widget* gave rise to a widely used image for the mindlessness of old-fashioned production line methods: 'What does he do all day? Sit in a factory making widgets.' A brave ad person indeed, then, who decided to use a term with that sort of pedigree to sell something breathtakingly clever and up-to-the-minute!

A word which today has almost taken on real substance but which, like all of these space-fillers, started with no meaning other than yet another synonym for *thingummijig* also started in the United States during the Second World War. It is that so-useful term for a cutting-edge technical device that will solve all known problems, the *gizmo*. Its roots lie in the American navy, 'but', the dictionary opines, 'beyond that its origins are a mystery.'

A *gizmo* is, of course, a form of *gadget*, and, in this strange business of space-filling language, we discover that we are here in one of those mirror worlds where everything comes full circle. A *gadget*, says the dictionary, is 'an accessory, an adjunct, a knick-knack or a gewgaw', and a *gewgaw* is 'a worthless plaything'. What goes around comes around where whatsitsnames are concerned.

Whatever you call them, we love to use them. And the range is enormous: just try this set of terms that David Crystal lists in his *Encyclopaedia of the English Language*: *deeleebob, deeleebobber, diddleebob, diddleydo, diddleything, diddleythingy, dingus, dingdong, dingy, dooda, doodad, doohickey* (and those are only the *d*s). 'And it is, I think, because they have been so ingrained into our consciousness from a relatively early age,' Crystal observes, 'not the most early of ages—young children don't use these forms; you don't usually start using them till you're in your teens—but then they become part of your consciousness. Remember conversation is *the* normal way of talking and therefore we are aways forgetting, we are always groping for words.'

The other contribution that such words offer a sentence is flavour and rhythm. The four syllables of *thingummybob*, the three of *diddleything*, the two of *dingdong* and the assonance that goes with them (we have already noticed how we relish forms like *knick-knack* and *gewgaw*) make them irresistible and flesh out a sentence with a touch of colour—and a slight smile too: who can take a word like *oojamaflop* or *oojamaflip* entirely seriously, after all?

Hootenanny certainly qualifies for a space-filler with attitude, so much so that its early twentieth-century American usage as an alternative to *thingummy* soon becomes supplanted by its now usual meaning of 'a party, especially with folk music'. The *doofer*, on the other hand, that I overheard so annoyingly frequently on the lips of our family friend, is less alluring, showing its origins somewhat as something that will *do for now*.

Finally, a late twentieth-century contribution to the canon, and one which appears so far to have evaded most listings— perhaps because its spelling is not clearly defined—but which is very widespread. *Doobree* is a close transcription, and is thus as accurate an orthography as I can offer. As to the meaning, well, in common with so many of these coinages—*gadget, gizmo, widget*, and the rest—it is the sort of space-filler that has a particular resonance for those who affect it. '*Doobree*'s quite common,' comments Professor Crystal. 'All my children say *doobree* as their favourite one. But *doobree* usually has a kind of technical loose end to it: the *doobree* for the television—what d'you call it? The thing that you press—the *doobree*. So there's often a technical ring to that particular empty word.'

Whatever you prefer to say, and whatever you choose to say it for, the field of invention is vast and spacious. A quick sampling trip along the streets of Britain produced simple notions like *that thing*, nonsense noises like *rarara*, and the colourful *heckythumpers*. So when next you are stuck for a word, avoid the banal—don't say *thingummybob* but invent a new word, offer it up, repeat it, spread it around, encourage others to use it. Who knows, one fine day it may end up listed in all the big dictionaries of the English language with the etymological footnote: 'Beyond that, its origins are a mystery.' Only, this time, you will *know*.

Just don't use it with a French exchange student, though.

Kersplatt!

It was at school that I first encountered them. They were passed with a *Shhh!* of warning under the desk. And woe betide the *Thwack!* of the teacher's board-rubber, brought down heavily on the soon-to-be chalky hair of the victim discovered in the act of surreptitious reading behind a pile of biology textbooks. They were, of course, those strange teenage fantasies that started in the early years of the twentieth century and still sell in their millions across the world, the *Marvel* comics and their imitators. Imported from America, they still bore the US price circled at the top of the page— such exotica, they seemed to me at age eleven, I who had been reared on the altogether cosier British world of the *Beano, Dandy, Topper,* and *Beezer.*

Here was bright red Spiderman, luridly clambering across the world, *Daily Planet* reporter Clark Kent transmogrifying into Superman in a phone kiosk, the lovely Lois Lane, and strangely inseparable Batman and Robin. But much as the grown-upness of the stories fascinated me—could comics be like this too?—it was the words that caught my eye. Dialogue balloons and 'Thinks' bubbles I recognized, but here, also, was an altogether more vivid language than I was used to. These were 'words'—were they actually words?—full of consonants. Hard consonants—Ks and Zs, Ps and Ts.

When Batman brought the Batmobile to a screeching halt, the tyres were enveloped in formations like *SKRREETCHHH…* And as Superman bested his particular enemy-for-today with a series of hefty punches to the solar plexus, each fist landed with a ZAP!, a POW! and a WHUMPPPPHHHH!, the victim's head jerking back against a wall—KERSPLATT!

That's not to say that our British comics never used what in the trade are known as 'sound effects', or FX for short. Minnie the Minx could land a fair old *THWACK* over some poor victim's head, and even Dennis the Menace could *ZZZZZZZ* quietly in class. And the *Eagle*'s famous science fiction strip 'Dan Dare—pilot of the Future' had its own range of FX; Michael Rosen remembers Our Hero socking one to the evil Mekon's chest with a hefty *GRUNKLE!* But these American comics were something else again. They felt so different, and the exotic sterotyped heroes and villains that have since become Hollywood staples captured our minds and filled our ears with a vast new vocabulary to interpret them.

Baddies being *zapped*, however, was in fact nothing new: the comics were only drawing on a rich vein of linguistic form that has been around since the earliest days of the English language. It is called 'onomatopoeia', and it has been found throughout language since the caveman went *Ug*. Crash, bang, wallop ... *clap* your hands, *snap* a twig, hear the *clip-clop* of horses ... they are all listed by the dictionary as having their origins wholly or partly in the sounds they are setting out to describe. They are so useful, they pop up everywhere. As Judy Garland memorably sang in the famous Trolley Song from *Meet Me in Saint Louis*: '*Clang, clang, clang* went the trolley; *ding, ding, ding* went the bell. *Zing, zing, zing* went my heartstrings ... From the moment I saw him I fell.'

Word of Mouth turned for enlightenment to Betty Kirkpatrick, a lexicographer who for many years was editor of one of Britain's most distinguished dictionaries.

Onomatopoeia is the use of a word whose sound resembles the sounds referred to—for example 'sausages *sizzling* in the pan'. This is what the word has come to mean, but if you go back to its origins in Greek it really means 'making a name', because it comes from the Greek word 'to name' and the Greek word 'to make'. So really in its derivation there's nothing suggestive of *sound*.

Since the late sixteenth century, though, the meaning has firmly embraced the notion of those sound effects so beloved of the writers and illustrators of the *Marvel* comics—'the formation of a word by an imitation of the sound associated with the thing or action designated; the principle or practice of forming words by this process' is the formal dictionary definition. 'We are to an extent still inventing imitative or onomatopoeic words,' observes Kirkpatrick. 'I mean you think, for example, of the word *Yuck*, which people will say when looking at something disgusting—that's quite modern' (as the dictionary says: 'imitative of the sound of vomiting') 'and the word *zap*—*zap* is one of those economical words that can mean a lot of things but it's also onomatopoeic.' *Zap* dates from 1929 and, as John Ayto memorably writes in his *Dictionary of Twentieth-Century Words*, is 'a key representative of the iconic onomatopoeic language of US comic book fiction which has entered partially into the mainstream of twentieth-century English ... used to represent the sound of a ray gun, laser, bullet, etc.'. By way of example, Ayto gives a classic citation from a 1929 comic: 'Ahead of me was one of those golden dragon Mongols, with a deadly disintegrator ray ... Br-r-rr-r-z-zzz-zap...'

Seventy or more years ago, such sequences of consonants must have in themselves made quite a visual splash. But at the turn of the second millennium, our visual culture is so dramatic—

television, DVD, Internet, screaming electronic hoardings, mammoth posters, and the rest—that the impact of a string of unlikely consonants hits home less surely. In today's more visually sophisticated environment, the comic book's FX must do more than simply onomatopoeically convey the sound. That's the authoritative view of one of Britain's leading graphic creators, Dan Abnett, who has been responsible for a slew of leading character-strips, including the famous *Judge Dredd*:

> They are onomatopoeic words; but they're also visually onomatopoeic if you see what I mean. They have to look as much like the sound as they sound like the sound. They provide the soundtrack to the way a comic works, from the simplest to the most complicated. And not only are they there for emphasis when a dramatic moment happens but they are also there for the purposes of actually conveying the story when it's the sound alone that's letting you know what's going on. For example footsteps, doors opening, this kind of thing.

Dan Abnett's sound world is one where the word shape is subtly varied to suit the effect he is looking for. And as in the best radio drama, getting the FX right is all part of the illusion.

> It really varies: sound effects are never the same twice. There isn't a 'footstep sound'—footsteps depend on the size and the weight of the person walking: CLICK-CLACK would be for someone in hard shoes and THWUMP-THWUMP if they were a heavy, more lumbering person. That's quite menacing and I would probably use it for Frankenstein's monster or something like that.

A world away from the heavy-typed strings of consonants adorning the *Judge Dredd* strips of Dan Abnett is the altogether more delicate sound environment of the poet. Helen Dunmore made her name as the writer of some of the late twentieth century's most subtly flavoured verse, an art she has more recently adapted to her finely observed award-winning novels. As a writer with an ear tuned to the intricacies of sound—resonance, assonance, alliteration, and onomatopoeia—she has long been aware of its power for the wordsmith:

> My earliest experience of onomatopoeia was when I was about eight years old and I remember being asked to write a poem about a cat. I wrote this beautifully rhyming, adjectival poem about a cat. But another little boy wrote a wonderful onomatopoeic poem, with lines like 'her claws *scrizzed* down my sleeves'. And I remember the teacher saying 'Your poem is *about* a cat; his really *is* a cat.' And that was really one of the first things that I learned about using sound in poetry.

Helen Dunmore feels that this relish for the almost tactile quality of words—not just within a poem but throughout all aspects of our lives—means that we enjoy using them— inventing them, even—whenever we feel the need:

> People themselves very often naturally use onomatopoeic words. I think when we're trying to describe sounds for example—squeaks and squeals and that kind of noise—we naturally use onomatopoeic words, and often we make them up. Think of all those words like *squidgy*. Think of the word *squidge* and *squiggle* and *squirk* and *squirm*. They're all very evocative words that enrich your writing. *Squidge*—I imagine mud *squidging* up through the fingers—a very tactile kind of word.

Word of Mouth had the idea of trying out the inventiveness of the public for creating new sound-words by asking people on London's teeming Oxford Street how they would describe the sound of scissors cutting through paper. After a spluttering of various imitations, some quite audibly like that very distinctive noise, the shoppers were asked to put the noises into words. How would they spell them, these new-found pieces of onomatopoeia?

'*H-H-H-LICK*,' said one man; '*HRASP*,' offered his female companion; 'It's a sort of rasping sound: *CCS*,' proposed a third. 'It sounds sharp: "*SSHHHH*,"' rejoined another. Little doubt, judging by those spellings, that the influence of those graphic realizations in the comic books have a lot to answer for. Writer Dan Abnett remarks:

> A lot of words that I find that I'm inventing I don't think you could really read aloud because they lack vowels or they have far too many consonants threaded together. I go for fairly obscure combinations of letters, as I said, really as much to make them *look* like the sound as *sound* like the sound. So a growling dog, for instance, might have far too many Ls in the sound to be easily pronounced. But you can have a lot of fun if you're reading it out loud just approximating it. *GRRRRRLLLLL*... And if that was a threatening growl it would end in an exclamation mark, and if it was a more subdued warning, it might end in dot-dot-dot so that we knew that there was more to come afterwards.

One of the other facets we noted earlier about these sound effects is the preponderance of consonants and lack of vowels. No accident, this, according to Dan Abnett:

> I have a rule of thumb which is that I very seldom use vowels unless vowels are absolutely essential to conveying the words. Again, it's something to do with the visual side. For instance, a simple word like *click* I would first of all spell phonetically with *k*s rather than *c*s and I would remove the *i*. So that it was a *KLK noise* rather than a *CLICK word*.

And even the quiet environment of a poet like Helen Dunmore deploys the power of consonants. Her poem about a baby orang-utan evokes the sound of its mother's heartbeat, 'using the word *yes* not for its meaning but to convey the kind of *shusshing* sound of the blood in the mother orang-utan's heart: "He listens to her heartbeat going *yes, yes, yes*..."'

Judge Dredd's world is an altogether punchier affair—quite literally—one of goodies and baddies, of fist-fights and pistol-shots. Dan Abnett says:

> So many of the sounds that I'm forced to describe are violent, active sounds—they're impact sounds and things like that—where really you could never really spell them, but where we're blessed with lots of lovely letters like K and T and S and P—all the plosive letters—which do the action for you even if it's not actually coming up with a sound that is real.

So what would the sound of that legendary uppercut to the villain's solar plexus sound like when realized in heavily inked capital letters straddling the comic-book frame? Abnett suggests something like WHUMPH or WHUMPFF. 'I'd put the vowel into that word simply because you're also conveying the idea that the breath's being knocked out of him, so you need to kind of vocalize that as the same time as suggesting the impact.'

On the other hand, a less crunchy, more sustained sound such as that of a kettle coming to the boil (and just as in old radio plays, comic-book kettles are always the old-fashioned whistling variety) would be full of long strings of vowels: 'a very simple word like PHWEEEEE', Abnett suggests, adding, 'and you would show that the pitch was rising by literally raising the lettering up through the panel so that it started by the spout of the kettle and rose to the top of the panel, to show that the note was increasing as it went along.'

You can sense the relish with which Abnett describes the craft he displays in working with onomatopoeia on the page, and Helen Dunmore too in the very different sound idiom in which she works. 'A lot of poetry', she concludes, 'does bypass your purely intellectual response and it's a mixture of giving you sensory pleasure—the kind of sensory pleasure you get from sound—and intellectual pleasure.' Powerful stuff, these words.

Chapter 5
Muscular Language

AND ... STRETCH! A little gentle workout for the linguistic muscles over the next few pages—nothing too arduous, mind you: it's wordpower that needs exercising rather than anything more physical. So a quick jog round the Football League with Rogan Taylor in search of the histories behind those mysterious names that pepper the Saturday afternoon classified results, from the *Arsenal* to *Hamilton Academicals*. And while we are north of the border, an excursion onto the fairways of language with an investigation of the terminology of the tee—can *you* tell your birdie from your eagle?

Down Under, the surfers' paradise of Maroubra Beach near Sydney is a linguist's nightmare as we try to pick our way amongst the *lids*, while avoiding the *bluebottles*, to go *out the back* to catch *a tube* ... which has nothing to do with a form of metropolitan transportation.

A final flourish on horseback, all flashing blades, lances at the ready as *Word of Mouth*, chivalrous to the last, limbers up for a bit of medieval jousting. A knight to remember!

" "

Football United

It's early evening on a Saturday in winter—not long before 5 o'clock. It's time to draw the curtains, and with the smell of toast in your nostrils it's almost impossible to escape a very English sound: the formal recitation of the football results. With its distinctive rhythms, cadence, and modulated pitch, it could almost be a poem, couldn't it? To pursue this further, isn't there something poetic about the way the reader takes us on a trip round England, Scotland, and Wales, from Exeter to Aberdeen, from Cardiff to Lincoln? There's a touch of mystery with an unlocated name like Arsenal—which arsenal? Whose arsenal? And there's the curious, inexplicable range of appendages, each one conjuring up a different image: the *rovers, wanderers*, and *rangers* evoking countrymen and outlaws striding over the moors; the stolid *uniteds* implying something corporate; the *counties* taking us back to the shires; the *cities* and *towns* keeping us municipal; while a stream of the idiosyncratic confirms our eccentricity: *Hotspur, Albion, Academicals, Villa* and *Alexandra*.

As with place names and family names, this most ordinary of nomenclatures is pregnant with social history. Take that innocent sounding *county* as in, say, *Derby County*. More often than not, it reminds us that the clubs we see today weren't born as football clubs. Derby County was formed in 1884 by members of the Derbyshire County Cricket Club, though Notts County (who claim to be the oldest football club in the world) seem to have acquired the *County* simply by playing on county cricket grounds.

The *rovers, wanderers,* and *rangers* arrived by a different route. Rogan Taylor, Director of the Football Research Unit at Liverpool University, enjoys the emergence of Bolton Wanderers. There's nothing romantic about such a name. More often than not, he says, it tells the story of a club that didn't have a home. In Bolton's case it was a church team (Christ Church, Bolton), but after some kind of bust-up with the vicar they ... wandered off. Meanwhile, Blackburn Rovers was genuinely homeless and in its year of foundation in 1875 played all its games away. The most famous of the various rangers, Rangers from Glasgow, began life in 1872 as a group of youths kicking a ball round Fleshers' Haugh on Glasgow Green.

'The uninitiated have to be careful,' Taylor warns, 'if they assume that the word preceding the *rangers* or *rovers* is a place. After a great Raith Rovers victory, one famous commentator roared out: "They'll be dancing on the streets of Raith tonight."' Slight problem: the Raith in question was the local laird of Raith at the time of the club's foundation in 1883. If they were going to be dancing anywhere, it would be in Raith Rovers' home town of Kirkcaldy.

Another club with an aristocratic link is Tottenham Hotspur, a team founded in 1882 as Hotspur FC. Anyone familiar with Shakespeare's *Henry IV* part I will have pricked up their ears at that—and they would be right to do so. The earls of Northumberland (amongst whom Harry Hotspur was a famously feisty sprog) owned large stretches of land around Tottenham in north London. In fact Spurs, as they are colloquially known, had their first enclosed ground at Northumberland Park.

A much humbler club but with an even grander name is Leyton Orient. Situated in east London, you might be forgiven for imagining that the *Orient* owes its origins to a bit of over-striving on the part of the club's owners, looking to turn the down-at-heel east side of the metropolis into something exotic. Not so—the *Orient* in question was the Orient Steam Navigation Company. One of the players at what was then the Eagle Cricket Club worked for the shipping line and suggested it. Prosaic but true, says Taylor, though this still leaves the possibility that the *Orient* stuck because of the flavour it lent to the East End.

As you might expect, there isn't always agreement about exactly how these suffixes are derived. Take Crewe Alexandra. John Ballard and Paul Suff, authors of *The Dictionary of Football* (London 1999), would have us believe that there's a royal link. The football club had been formed as the footballing section of the Alexandra Athletic Club in 1877. The *Alexandra*, say Ballard and Suff, was adopted in honour of Princess Alexandra, who married the future Edward VII. No way, says Taylor. Club members met at the Alexandra, a nearby hotel that served as their local.

So what of this country's most famous club, Manchester United, and all the other uniteds? Once again, history is involved. The 1880s saw a massive expansion of football. Tens of thousands of clubs sprang into existence, frequently off the backs of other sporting associations—athletics and cricket usually, but also from groups of workers at a factory or old boys from a school—thus the intriguing Hamilton Academicals. But rather like the over-reaching we are witnessing with the football league's struggle with television fees, football had a crisis of overproduction. There was nothing for it but to unite. Inauspiciously, the great Man U began life as the Newton Heath Lancashire and Yorkshire Cricket and Football Club, founded in 1878 by the workers at the Lancashire and Yorkshire Railway Company. Newton Heath went bust in 1902, but a local brewer pulled together the remnants and formed Manchester United.

These days, the social origins of the clubs, whether it was working class or ex-public school, are only discernible from the kind of unpicking we are doing here. Arsenal, with no suffix, began life as the works team of the Royal Arsenal in Woolwich, and supporters claim that it is the only football team in the world to have given its name to a locality and to a railway station—scant compensation for spending most of the 1990s coming second to Manchester United.

One old, peculiarly named club, but not in the professional league, is Corinthian Casuals. Rogan Taylor is particularly fond of the story here.

> Football had been midwifed by the posh folks in their public schools, but it got mugged by the English working class particularly in the west Midlands and Lancashire. The name *Corinthian Casuals* harks back to the public school era. The whole history of the game is in that name. It was a team made up of ex-Public School boys with a classical education—thus the allusion to the Corinthian tradition. And by saying they were the Casuals, they showed that gentlemen didn't ever take the game seriously. Winning wasn't important. They even refused to take penalties. The idea of gentlemen committing a foul on purpose was more or less unthinkable.

With the kinds of accusation flying round the commentary boxes in today's game, perhaps any new team wanting to typify the more 'professional' approach to penalties could call itself, say, *Blanksville Divers*.

Surfin' NSW

'The cams show what's happening down this beach right now, and we're getting more people coming down here. So again the poor little locals are going to have to share some waves.'

The speaker is nut-brown from the sun, hair tied back. Difficult to gauge her age, but she is no longer a teenager. We are sitting sipping cappuccino at the Maroubra Beach Café on a glorious autumn morning, in April. Yes, autumn, because this is New South Wales, Australia, and Maroubra Beach is where *Word of Mouth* visited to learn some of the linguistic riches of Australian surf-talk. Sitting on the other side of the table is Susan Moore, who has been running the tongue-twisting Sydney Safe Surfing School for the past five years. She is half-lamenting, half-delighted that her beach, here at Maroubra, is attracting a crowd of newcomers. The Internet site that allows virtual surfers and real ones alike to assess the quality of the waves at any particular beach—the *cams* or *web-cams*—are bringing in a new breed of water-babies.

'It's on surf-cams, and you can pick up how Maroubra's looking. We're getting a lot of people that we don't know down here and I'm getting blamed for every man and his dog who's coming down here and having a surf. "How come you're letting all these people come down? What are you doing sending them *out the back?*"' By this, Susan means locals are accusing her of introducing novice surfers from outwith Maroubra to the toughest stretches for surfing *out the back* of the waves, closer to the open ocean.

There is a brisk wind, but not enough to bring on the goose pimples; and dotted out in the pure blue-green waters of the Pacific, off the south-eastern suburbs of Sydney a few miles down the coast from Bondi, are twenty or more pin-figures of surfers. 'Right now, we've got offshore winds, so we've got westerlies blowing. We've got quite a huge *crashing* area, and there's a few lulls, but we've got *body-boarders* or guys on *lids* just out the front here trying to break their neck!' *Lids*, Susan patiently explains to me, are what she also calls *boogie-boards*: 'they're where the effort is mainly from the waist down, so that's *kick*, whereas surfboard-riding is from the waist up, which is *paddle.*'

Crashing area, *boogie*-boards, *lids* ... I realized almost immediately that my visit to Maroubra Beach was going to be an initiation into a completely new linguistic culture. Here were guys *cracking a few waves, catching waves*, doing *lefts* and *rights*, taking turns—there are strict rules of surfing etiquette to be observed to avoid bursts of that twenty-first-century phenomenon *surf rage*. Susan studies the water carefully and declares there are 'about six rips running'. A *rip* is standard terminology in surfing for 'a stretch of rough water in the sea, caused by the meeting of currents' (as in the expression *rip-tide*) and is a meaning that long precedes the sport of surfing, dating from the end of the eighteenth century. In nineteenth-century America it was applied to rough water in a river as well as the ocean.

In surfing, rips are the motor for the sport and so have a number of different descriptions, as Susan explains: 'rips are *tow-lines* which are *trams* or *trains*; they're a passage out the back, and it's a quick trip out the back.' She says rips are always to be found on a beach where rocks and sand meet, 'and always on a big open beach there are more and more rips'. The trains, trams, and tow-lines are rips that surfers use to take them to the take-off point for the manoeuvre: 'That means that I only have to paddle, or kick a couple of kicks and I'm being taken out by the natural movement of the water.'

Susan is a passionate enthusiast for the surf, spending hours every day throughout the year—winter and summer— in wetsuit in the water, instructing her pupils of the SSSS in the ways and the words of practising the sport with security. Sometimes, though, she gets a little carried away: 'I went for about twenty minutes and this guy said to me, "I've got no idea what you're talking about". And I said, "What?" And he said, "I don't understand," and the first thing was, "I don't know what a *rip* is, I don't know what a *bluebottle* is ..."' (A bluebottle is not, on this occasion, a species of housefly, 'but what some people call a jellyfish—it's a stinger, a marine stinger, that hits you with about a hundred little stings at a time running down your arm. We advise people pull the damn thing off, don't just run around with it attached to you, and get up to the beach and get some ice on it!')

At this point, joining Susan from the changing rooms were an English couple whom she had just been instructing *out the back*. Helen seemed to have got the hand of what she was talking about, but Neil said very little, somewhat browbeaten, maybe, by Susan's stream of consciousness that flows on like the tide itself. 'We just talk a jargon that we don't really understand sometimes what we're saying,' admitted Susan, 'or if that's kind of a word that's set in a dictionary, we just kind of just spill out *different* kinds of words. Or we have people *speaking to the hand* a lot, in surfing, where they're angry or carrying on. We put our hand up and say, *Speak to the hand.*' When someone *speaks to the hand*, it means that no response will be forthcoming (as in the similar expression *Talk to the hand, because the face isn't listening*). It is a form of verbal stop signal, as executed by traffic policemen—

from New South Wales to old south Wales. Thus angry surfers, instead of indulging in surf rage (and it appears that on the Sydney beaches, that is all too common), should *speak to the hand*—and shut up!

Word of Mouth asked Susan for some more examples of baffling jargon. How about *front slide*, she suggested.

> Oh yeah, a *front slide* on your beach, where you can just say that she slips away. What I mean is there's a bit of a slide of the waves as they're sucking back. And if you're a young kid who didn't like a *boogie board* too much, or your *lid*, or *speed humps*, you shimmy along and you jump on and then you go along the slide in the foreshore where it's all nice and flat and you see how far you can go along and how many waves you can more or less pop over and go in on the way out.

Susan Moore's stream of talk sums her up. She is all action, always moving—dodging the bad waves, picking the good ones. In the driving seat of her pick-up, she swings about the winding little coast road giving a non-stop commentary on the iniquities of the local council, on incomers, and on the way surfing ain't like it used to be.

Finally, we wanted to know about one of the legendary surfing terms, from Bondi to California—the *tube*. Not, you understand, anything to do with the London Underground, nor American TV (what we refer to as *the box* for Americans conventionally is *the tube*). No. These *tubes* are waves. Does Susan Moore talk about tubes? You bet she does.

Here she is on the big-eyed expectations of some of the novices she takes into Maroubra's rips.

> A lot of people expect to be able to ride on their tube on their first lesson. Well, you wouldn't want to ride a tube on your *hundredth*

lesson because it's just very shallow in a tube. You know, a lot of people close their eyes! So you never really see it, because you're too scared to open your eyes up.

Word of Mouth pressed her for a definition: a *tube* is where waves are rolling over very fast, she explained, and the water is very shallow beneath and the surfer rides inside the rolling wave—or, in her words, 'You *back-stall* sometimes to hold yourself inside there. And then, all of a sudden, you just do— wait for it and then you pump yourself out of it. And it's a fantastic feeling.' though one she admits that gets tougher to enjoy as she gets older: 'We're so stiff we can't get back up! And people think we're catching these fantastic tubes, but they don't realise that our bones are too stiff to get back up after we've been surfing for an hour and a half and we're so cold!'

Susan is a survivor. In the pounding Pacific waves, you have to be, knowing what to do when the sharks are about, when the rips catch you unawares. After *Word of Mouth* recorded at Maroubra, Susan suffered a series of family tragedies that clearly shocked her deeply, knocked her back. But her spirit, along with her verve for the vocabulary of the waves, remains undimmed.

> You get—we get—a love for the ocean; we get a respect for the ocean. There's a meditation in the *gutters* (channels at the front of the beach) before you go out the back in the ocean. And you'll have this feeling of a heart-to-heart relationship through nature— through surfing—with people who surf as well. That's an emotional click that you do have through surfing. I have surfed in Biarritz and I have surfed in Ireland and I've been lucky enough to surf in Bali and Hawaii, and we've had a little surf in Fiji, and I've done a lot of areas around Australia. So you just take this feeling with you to other shores.

A Little Birdie Told Us

Martians who managed to unlock the mysteries of chess, arm-wrestling, and the Teletubbies confess that there's one human activity that utterly perplexes them: golf. They say that they can't figure out whether the players are playing with or against each other, why some wear strange socks and others don't, why the flat grassy bits are surrounded with sandpits, and why the men who carry the sticks in the big bag don't get a chance to use them.

But that's only the start of Martians' problems with the game. Non-golfing mortals can usually figure out some semblance of a game going on—who can get the ball to the hole with the least number of strokes—but many of them are felled by the game's jargon. It used to be possible for non-golfers to regard *birdies*, *bogies*, and *eagles* as avoidable as cloud-names, but with the sport available on cable and satellite channels all the year round and with all four days of the British Open played out hole by hole on BBC television, this strange language finds a way into all our brains. The Golfish language has a vast lexicon and we'll be able to do no more here than a *worm-burner*—the ball that skims the surface at high speed.

The name of the game is a borrowing—something you might guess, as you'd be hard pushed to find many other English *olf* words. Rolf, as in Harris, hasn't quite become a noun or a verb, though a particularly rough massaging technique named after its founder, Ida Rolf, is called *rolfing*. *Yolf* and *bolf* are recently invented games with golf in mind, and the *wolf* usually refuses to rhyme with *golf*. One of the old ways in which you could tell if someone was educated privately was if he or she pronounced the word as *goff*. This hid its possible Dutch origins in a game called *colf* noted as early as 1296. It was a wild hit-and-run sort of a game, where players aimed for doors rather than holes and pursued their wayward shots through graveyards, kitchen windows, and bakers' shops.

It was the Scots who introduced holes into the matter, inspired by people bashing pebbles from sand dune to sand dune and seeing who could get one to go down a rabbit hole. The Flemings meanwhile were playing *chole*, which was really golf on ice. A quick trip to a 1340 stained-glass window in Gloucester Cathedral will furnish you with a picture of Bob Hope (or is it Henry Cooper?) perfecting his swing.

In the fifteenth century, King James II of Scotland banned golf. This was to stop the populace wasting their time when they should have been down at the butts stringing their bows. Mary Queen of Scots was a keen golfer: her presence in the game also disproves the old acronym: 'Gentlemen Only Ladies Forbidden'. The first English golf course opened in 1604, the Royal Black Heath, and it's still there. The first true golf club—association, that is, not the stick—was founded in 1744 in Scotland. It was this 'Honourable Company of Edinburgh Golfers' who laid down the first rules of the game.

What has happened since is rather like Summer Pudding. In place of the layers of bread and soft fruit pressed down on top of each other, golf has its layers of custom, practice, rules, and nicknaming. One key to understanding what's going on is *par*. This is equivalent to saying something like this: if you're Arsenal and you're playing against Manchester United, you might be expected to score one goal. If you're Arsenal playing Halifax, you might be expected to score six. *Par* is the number of strokes a top professional player might be expected to take to get from one hole to the next. As the distances and difficulties vary between holes so the *par* changes too. It's called *par* because you, as a player, aim to be par with the expected score. So it is, with a little help from Latin (*par* meaning 'equal'), golf gives us the idiom *par for the course*.

Once this idea of par was established (in the 1880s, actually) you could unleash on an unsuspecting world a raft of nicknames for the scores that are under or over par. This is the part that makes trying to understand golf commentaries extremely difficult. Take the *bogey*—or is it *bogie*, or even *bogy*? Apart from giving children an excuse to giggle every time they hear the commentator say it, why should a score of one more than par be called a bogey?

You may not have heard of either Major Charles Wellman or the old music hall song, 'Hush, hush, hush, here comes the bogeyman', but both feature in the explanation. It was said that Wellman was out playing the Great Yarmouth when he shouted out that the expected score for the course (not yet dubbed the *par*) was a 'regular bogeyman'. The secretary for the course then ran with the idea and suggested that there was some kind of demon golfer at the club, the bogey, who played every hole at this expected score. The scene now moves to Alveston in Hampshire, where it's suggested that this bogey couldn't be just any old bogey. Anyone that good at golf would have to be an officer and a gentleman. He was, therefore, Colonel Bogey. (In case your mind is racing ahead, Sir Alec Guinness in *The Bridge Over the River Kwai* is not relevant to this story.)

What happens next is that golfers come out to play against Colonel Bogey. So in your game against Colonel Bogey, you read on your card that the expected score for the next hole is, say, four shots. Bogey, of course, does just that. You, you duffer, do it in five. You have therefore *bogied*—or *bogeyed* (and are even bog-eyed, but that's not relevant). And so it is the one-more-than-par shot came to be called the *bogey*.

If you're the greatest golfer the world has ever seen, i.e. Tiger Woods, many of your scores are *under par*. Strangely, the idiom means the opposite of the golf term. Rather than feeling queasy, when a golfer is *under par*, he or she is doing exceptionally well. So here is your guide to *under par* nicknames: One under is a *birdie*. Two under is an *eagle*. Three under is either a *double eagle* or an *albatross*. Four under is a *condor* or a *triple eagle*. A *hole in one* is sinking the ball in the hole with one's first stroke.

Why a *birdie*? Either because you played so well, the ball flew like a bird or because, in old American slang, a *bird* was a gifted person. Why an *eagle*? Because it's a big bird. Why a *double eagle*? Because golfers can't count. Why an *albatross*? Because it's a very big bird. Why a *condor*? Because it's a very, very big bird. Is a *condor* possible? Yes, if the par is five and you hole in one. Why not call it a *hole in one*? Because you like nicknames. Why a *triple eagle*? No comment. Why isn't there a nickname for a shot that is two over par? There is. It's a *buzzard*. Other nicknames for scores include, *snowman*, used if you score eight for a hole, because … er … a snowman is supposed to look like an 8.

There is something poetic about all this—we *are* talking metaphors here. Rhyme also has its part to play. In 1991, golfer John Daly was asked how he won a big tournament and he said, 'I just grip it and rip it.' That is, he gripped the club and took a rip at the ball. Meanwhile Loren Roberts was regarded as one of the greatest putters of the ball—quick explanation: the holes are situated in a flat, perfectly mown and rolled patch called *the green* because it's green. This is where the golfer taps or *putts* the ball along the ground to get it into the hole. Great putter Loren Roberts was known as the 'boss of the moss'.

Similes creep in too. If a ball lands softly on the green, it's said to land *like a butterfly with sore feet,* and if it falls on the green with hardly a bounce, it lands *like a dropped cat.*

More metaphoric and definitely more crude, a stroke can be described as *an elephant's ass.* This is one that has too much elevation, i.e. it's 'high and stinky'. On the other hand, a ball might seem to slide over the hole and won't go in. That's because the hole is covered with a *cellophane bridge.*

Apart from the idioms around the word *par,* golf hasn't offered too much to the language of everyday use. One exception is the phrase *the rub of the green.* In golf, it means any accident, not caused by a player or caddie, that moves or stops a ball in play. This is when your ball is deflected by agencies beyond your control, like a cat, a UFO, or rapidly sprouting rhubarb. Essentially it means a bit of bad luck. The idiom in common use sounds ambiguous, if not the opposite of the original meaning. When the manager of Blackburn Football Club, Graham Souness, said in February 2002, 'I just hope we enjoy the rub of the green in the premiership now,' he implied that whatever this rub of the green is, it was worth having.

We can guess that Tiger Woods will donate some part of his game to golf language—if he hasn't already. Some people have mistakenly thought that he is the first world-famous American golfer with a degree of African descent. In fact, when golfers all over the world place their ball on a small pointed stick topped with a cup, they are relying on the invention of the African-American golfer, dentist, and son of slaves George F. Grant. Patented in 1899, this object, sad to say, is not called a *Grant* or a *George* but a *tee.* Perhaps a *Tiger* or a *Woods* will feature soon.

Paying Court

'After you, madam ...' 'Ah, the age of chivalry is not dead!' The idea of respect, of courtesy, and of a certain deference and decency in day-to-day dealings, particularly as displayed by any self-respecting gentleman towards a lady, is still alive, though perhaps under threat of extinction as the equality and egotism of the Me generation increasingly hold centre stage.

Time was when *chivalrous* behaviour—like men standing when a woman enters a room, or the automatic surrender by men of a seat on bus or train to an unseated woman—was commonplace. Expected, even. It was *polite* to behave in this way; it was the done thing. Deference, consideration, courtesy are all abstract qualities that have been having a hard time of late. Compare the rise of the many *rages* (road, air, even supermarket) that lie at the other end of the spectrum and it is not surprising that chivalry is not what is once was. Edmund Burke it was who first declared, 'The age of chivalry is gone', and that was two hundred-odd years ago.

Burke's statement was, perhaps, literally true, since the origins of chivalry lie not directly within world of deferential behaviour by men to women, but in the much more vigorous arena of the medieval joust. Because *chivalry* is all to do with horses and the knights who rode them. Helen Castor, historian at Sidney Sussex College, Cambridge, explains that 'horsiness is a very important part of *chivalry*. What you're really talking about is fighting men who fight on horseback; that means they're aristocratic because it is the rank and file who have to get down in the mud on foot.' Helen Castor traces the word's roots to medieval French, where the common or garden *cheval*, a horse, has its rider, the *chevalier*, which is the normal term for a knight who fights on horseback.

Our knight—let us think of him as, say, Sir Michael de Rosen—not only displays horsemanship or *chevalerie* but also the qualities of being a knight, and that in turn gives us *chivalry*. This, confusingly, was a term which often in the Middle Ages was also used just to mean a body of knights on horseback. Not for nothing do the *cavalry* go into battle astride horses. Thus the French *chevalerie* has spawned two modern English terms, not entirely unrelated conceptually, though a good distance apart in usage—*chivalry* and *cavalry*.

Geoffrey Chaucer's Knight is an exponent of the chivalric virtues: 'A knyghte ther was... he loued chiualrie, Trouthe and honour fredom and curteisie...' These abstract qualities such as *courtesy* and *honour* are inextricably bound up with the aristocratic calling of knights such as Sir Michael de Rosen. And there is another etymological curiosity here too. Because Chaucer's *curteisie*—French *courtoisie*, essentially meaning 'behaviour appropriate to a Prince's court'—is directly related to the *curtsey* that is made to indicate deference. Helen Castor observes: 'the general sense of *courtesy* is very important in the chivalric ethos and means "courtly behaviour" in its widest sense. That might mean behaving appropriately towards ladies; it might mean not blowing your nose on the tablecloth—it generally meant conducting oneself appropriately for someone of noble birth and noble morals.'

Snobbish though it may seem in the twenty-first-century world, the key component of medieval chivalry, then, is the idea of high birth. This is the world of the *chevalier*—the knight—whose birth gave him a code of conduct to observe.

Historian Helen Castor picked her way through some of the other abstract notions that lay at the code's core. 'Many have to do with *giving* and with *generosity*. Again one of the interesting things is how many of them are associated with noble birth—with this assumption that it's people of the upper classes who will behave in this way. So for instance, *generosity* itself—generous—originally means "well-born".'

In fact the modern meaning, 'magnanimous', dates from as recently as the seventeenth century, and its former sense is obvious when you start unpicking the etymology of the word. *Generosus*, the Latin root, means 'noble' and it is in turn the adjective derived from *genus*, a 'kind' or 'race'. 'So originally,' says Helen Castor, 'if you refer to someone as *generous* you might well mean that they were a gentleman of good standing. Similarly *largesse*, which of course survives again in contemporary usage meaning the distribution of gifts by someone in a high position, but *largesse* was one of the key attributes of chivalry.'

Conversely, the low-born, the humble, the ordinary—the *poor*—are the antithesis of the virtues of the perfect knight. 'So if we think about words such as *poor* or *mean* or *low* or *common*, they all mean not well-bred, but they can also mean "not good", "inferior", "of inferior quality"—whether in practical or indeed in moral terms.'

Geoffrey Chaucer's Knight, to whom we have already referred, is also described as 'noble and gentil'. These qualities of nobility and what the French called *gentilesse* (not 'gentleness' but rather the quality of being *gentil* or 'of good birth') are undoubtedly displayed by our chivalric knight Sir Michael, being well-born as he is. Says Helen Castor:

If you are a *chivalric* knight *noblesse* and *gentilesse* are parts of what you're aspiring to. Because one of the most interesting things about chivalry is how the words that are used to describe the qualities of the perfect knight have a double meaning. They both mean 'well-born', 'well-bred', 'aristocratic', and then they also mean all these great moral qualities that you would have, because the underlying assumption of all of this is that if you are well-born, you will have all these great moral qualities and people who have all these great moral qualities—of course— will be well-born'.

A perfect gentleman, in fact. Which is where we came in. 'After you, Sir Michael'—'No, after *you* my lady…'

Chapter 6
Wording Your Eats

A SUCCULENT SELECTION OF LANGUAGE that's good enough to eat is on offer at the *Word of Mouth* Café—from the dubious delights of fashionable menu-speak to the mouth-watering prose of the doyenne of culinary writing, Elizabeth David. All natural ingredients on our menu, as we explore the fascination of all things *organic*—pure, wholesome and chemical-free—a celebration of the down-to-earth goodness of simple food terminology.

And as far as summer cooking is concerned, there is little more basic than that patio-perfect phenomenon, the barbecue. But why *barbecue*? Does it really have anything to do with French 'beards-with-tails'—whatever they are? And if your idea of an ideal Australian *barbie* is washed down with a few *tinnies* (cans of beer), time to follow it up with an investigation of the rich brew of terminology that flows from the kettles and the vats of our national tipple—from *ale* to *beer*.

To round off your meal, sir, madam, may we suggest something from the dessert counter at your local supermarket? Will it be the Hot Crunch Banoffee Cheese Cake or the Toffee Apple Torment? For today we have Naming of Tarts.

" "

Words of Mouth

Give us this day our daily bread—but don't forget to specify whether it's split tin or farmhouse, wholemeal or rye, ciabatta or cholla, pitta, baguette or flute... *Word of Mouth* has tackled the rich lexicon of filling our bellies from a number of different angles over the past ten years. For this anthology we thought we should look at some of the ways we use words to describe our nosh.

Television food guru Loyd Grossman deciphers some of the wilder linguistic imaginings of fashionable menuspeak while Lindsey Bareham, the distinguished writer on food, joined Michael Rosen at the *Word of Mouth* dinner table to discuss the words *she* employs to describe the sensations on the palate that the food presents. 'And it's difficult', she says, 'to make something sound tempting or appetizing without sounding pretentious.'

The language our food writers and restaurant reviewers deploy tends to follow the trends of fashion just as much as the food itself. As chef Keith Floyd writes in his book on French cuisine, 'The introduction of *nouvelle cuisine* swept chefs and diners alike off their feet in waves of gastronomic euphoria—for a while it looked as though the slow-simmering heavy winter stews and the succulent roasts were to become a thing of the past.' And as the food shrank and plates got larger and always, it seemed, octagonal, so the language metamorphosed into deep pretension. Even when old-fashioned robust victuals were available, it was not unknown for the words used to describe them on the menu to be—shall we say—*un tout petit peu prétentieux, non?*

'The other day,' reports Loyd Grossman, 'I saw something called *ragoût de boeuf anglaise en croûte*. And then in brackets it said, *"(steak and kidney pudding)"*. Restaurants will really try anything to sell a dish.'

Forty years ago, in 1960, perhaps the greatest word-spinner about food, Elizabeth David, used few adjectives to conjure the flavours of the food she was describing. Rather she painted pictures and evoked dining scenes that suggest Renoir luncheon tables under sun-dappled umbrellas: 'soups delicately coloured like summer dresses,' she writes in her classic *French Provincial Cooking*, 'coral, ivory or pale green ...'

Meals for Elizabeth David are a narrative, an adventure, and florid descriptions flavoured with too many mouth-watering adjectives are out. They would simply hold up the plot. Here, for example, she is sitting down to dinner in Alsace: 'an onion tart, flat as a plate but still somehow oozing with cream, preceded a subtly flavoured sausage served hot with a mild and creamy horseradish as the only accompaniment.' No frills, no exotic adjectives. Plain language, chosen carefully to be powerfully suggestive.

French Provincial Cooking is as much, of course, a piece of culinary travel-writing as it is recipe book, though the actual recipes and how to achieve them are absolutely central to the volume. In principle, on the other hand, the language of the menu is supposed purely to describe and evoke rather than offer a chef's working method—texture, not textbook. Yet these days, to read some of the elaborate descriptions that greet you on opening the great leather volume presented by the sleek white-aproned young man at your table is almost to rediscover the recipe book. Try this, from a fashionable central London eatery, for a method-in-all-but-name: *Brick-flattened baby chicken, grilled over an open fire, with sliced potatoes, baked with cream and garlic in a red-wine reduction.* You could almost cook it from that yourself.

'From the chef's point of view and certainly in top-class restaurants,' comments a leading British restaurateur, Brian Turner, 'and we consider we're in that league, the menu's got to give the diner that little bit of poetic feeling that you've created something artistically. And I love it when you go to a table and someone says, "Oh this is so awful", and you say—shock horror—"Don't tell me you can't find anything?" and the diner replies: "Oh no, I love *everything*."' I'm not so sure that *brick-flattened* does it for me in that way, though.

Twenty years after Elizabeth David was writing, food writers seemed to have forgotten that simplicity was the key: 'in the 1980s there used to be a great trend', explains Lindsey Bareham, 'for using the expression *scented with* when we were eating very pretentious French food. All these words borrowed from forests and music were plucked out—*leaves* of this and *symphonies* of that.' Now, she says, food writing has more or less regained its leaner look—'We've turned completely against that, I'm pleased to say.'

Mmm. Maybe not entirely. The trouble is, when your job is to describe how something tastes, how it smells, and how it will frankly feel in the mouth, the temptation to pull out the full toolbox of adjectives, adverbs, and metaphor is overwhelming—whether you are composing a menu or describing it in a newspaper column. Why call something *sliced potato pie*, protests Lindsey Bareham, when *pommes dauphinoise, sliced and baked in the oven with cream,* 'sounds so much more appetising?'

One of the problems food writers and menu composers have to contend with is that mainstream English food is often not so much *haute cuisine* as plain peasant cooking. Indeed, the very language used to describe it so often emphasizes the fact: *good wholesome plain English cooking* is to be found in pubs and cafés across Britain. (The fact that the *cooking* may in many cases involve slitting open a plastic bag and placing a deep-frozen lump of goo in a microwave and then twirling a bit of sauce along the edge of the plate to make it 'look nice' has nothing to do with it!)

There is nothing, however, intrinsically unsophisticated about simple food. After all, Elizabeth David sings the praises of excellent simple fare well prepared. Where we go wrong, it seems to me, is when the language of the menu and the decor and style of the restaurant pretend that it is something else. I remember about twenty years ago visiting the restaurant of a large county hotel in the heart of England where the design keynote was something called *Country Kitchen*. The waiters wore smocks, the tables were dressed overall in rough gingham and the menus were weighty slabs of six-ply, branded—yes branded—with the dishes in burnt-on lettering. Needless to say, the food was about as tasty as the wooden menus. It was 'concept dining' at its worst.

The precise linguistic excesses of these barn-door menus have long faded in my memory, but Loyd Grossman knows from bitter experience the sort of wording I mean:

> There are always a few sexy modifiers that can be thrown in, so instead of saying *roast beef and Yorkshire pudding* you can say *roast Aberdeen Angus*. And then something like *and Richmond Yorkshire pudding*. English cooking thrives on place names. This largely reflects the fact that, historically, English cooking has been very long on the quality of produce and rather short on the flashiness of technique. What makes an English diner excited is to know that, yes, their duck once indeed quacked its

way round the Vale of Aylesbury. So by throwing in a few judicious place names you can make even fairly standard English cooking sound awfully attractive.

But the game is up. We know the trick. Richmond is *not* famous for its Yorkshire pudding and the duck that may have made Aylesbury's name is almost certainly *not* the one you are eating. This sort of menuspeak stands revealed for what it is—a con. It is that famous political commodity applied to food—let us hereby christen it *Menu-spin*.

Word of Mouth decided to put Menu-spin to the ultimate test. Where better to try out the excesses of colourful description—without infringing the trade description act—than a works canteen? So we strong-armed Loyd Grossman along to the eighth floor of Broadcasting House in London to the staff restaurant, otherwise known to all as the BBC Canteen. An unnamed dish was brought steaming to his formica-topped table, laid with standard-issue stainless steel cutlery and paper napkin.

The mystery food, Loyd soon determined, was a savoury main course of leeks served in a cheese sauce. 'Not unappetizing,' was his verdict 'but it ain't pretty!' So how would he squeeze this simplest of simple dishes for every ounce of linguistic possibility? A *gratin*, he began, of leeks—*Staffordshire* leeks... or perhaps *Welsh*. Thus, he suggested the 'menu-spun' dish might adorn a table without fear of contradiction as a *gratin Owen Glendower*.

But there was more: 'Another trendy way of describing something like this is to use a total misnomer, so a lot of layered things like this are called a *gateau*. So you could call it a *gateau of leeks and potatoes*.' In fact, Menu-spin can create all sorts of levels of food-gobbledygook depending on how posh the establishment is: 'If it's in a downmarket restaurant I'd call it simply *leek and potato pie in white sauce*. If it were a mid-market, middle-brow restaurant, I'd say *gratin Owen Glendower*. But if it were a frightfully upmarket restaurant, then it would be *a gateau of potatoes and leeks with a Chewton cheddar glaze*.' Foodies beware!

To clear the palate, compare the way Elizabeth David conjures up a genuinely provincial feast of a starter (complete with 'judicious place names') composed from simple produce and the simplest of language:

> Served to us at a hotel at Les Saintes-Marie-de-la-Mer, it consisted of a very large round dish, quite flat, completely covered with overlapping circles of thinly sliced *saucisson d'Arles*; in the centre was a cluster of shining little black olives. Nothing much, indeed, but ... so potent that we felt we were seeing and tasting Arles sausage and black olives for the very first time.

Organic Panic

As spring steals across the early twenty-first-century British countryside, vast yellow patches of oil-seed rape join up the dotted lines of what remains of ancient hedgerows. Not quite yet the *Silent Spring* described by writer and early eco-whistleblower Rachel Carson, but still a less teeming countryside than half a century ago, more organized. Neatly turned furrows, all meticulously aligned, begin to sprout with tidy cross-hatchings of barley or oats, pricked out mechanistically across footpath and field edge, as if some casual industrial artist had unthinkingly overshot the border of his sketch. But tucked in amongst the rolling prairies, where hedges have long been grubbed up and industrial farming, phosphates, nitrates, and yield-per-hectare are the new lexicon of the land, there lie the *organic* farms serving the fashionable trade in supposedly healthier food. *Organic* ...

What is it with *organic*, this word that so effectively catches the Zeitgeist of now? This little adjective sits up there, right at the front of the shelf full of good-for-you lifestyle words, along with all those wholier-than-thou terms: *wholefood, wholegrain, wholemeal* and *holistic*.

It is a story that goes back centuries, but the recent semi-official usage dates from thirty or more years ago. *Organic* started its existence as a lifestyle definer at the end of the 1960s, according to Sir Julian Rose, who is a leading member of the Soil Association and himself an *organic farmer*. It was a time when those agriculturalists who opposed the use of chemical agents were looking for an adjective that would most effectively describe the product they were advocating and producing—'grown naturally, without pesticides, herbicides and fertilisers. We had to find a name for it, because we had to market it.'

At the time there were a number of linguistic contenders bidding for that official recognition. So *sustainable* was high on the list, but had to wait a good thirty years before it developed a sufficiently comfortable, convenient utility. Then there was *ecological*, already beginning to flower as a major international denoter of catastophe. The *Torrey Canyon* oil-spill crisis and the *Exxon Valdez* disaster were two major challenges in the 1960s and 1970s to the ecological balance of nature. Yet *ecological* was perhaps already too wide, too all-embracing to be really useful as a brand. And *eco-* (a prefix which seemed to breed compound terms across the Channel as freely as did *euro*-) never quite cut the mustard north of the White Cliffs.

Then again, in these linguistic survival-of-the-fittest contests, there always seems to be at least one term that never really caught on at all. Decades later it appears quaint and somehow stunted at birth, lacking the legs to clamber aboard a passing fashion and so achieve real currency. In the *organic* race, this seems to have been *pure food*. How often is *pure food* used as a set term today? Food is described as *pure*—HP sauce was classically described on its time-honoured label as 'absolutely pure'—but *pure food*? No. Perhaps it is precisely because we like to think of all food, whatever it contains, like HP sauce, as 'absolutely pure'.

And finally, there was *natural*. Fine word, saying all the right things, but perhaps, like *ecological*, just too wide. And so, it was *organic*. And *organic* was born as the official designator of this chemicals-free product the farmer so wanted to promote. Today, Sir Julian Rose explains, to be permitted to call food *organic* and to stick an 'organic' label on their food, farmers must demonstrate to the organizations that supervise the trade, such as the Soil Association and the government-spearheaded UK Register of Organic Food Standards, that for two years their land has been completely clean of chemicals.

So much for the technical use. Today, *organic* has become one of those useful catch-all fashion words that suggest pseudoscience. Journalists love them and regularly reach for them to give products, restaurants, social-action movements that good-for-you earthy feel. Yet *organic* already had a farming association going back to just after the Second World War, when it was used to denote naturally produced fertilizer—in effect, dung—as opposed to the chemical variety. Soon, the adjective attached itself—as adjectives have a habit of doing—to a useful noun, and *organic farming* and *organic gardening* were regularly being spoken of. By the end of the century, *organic* had been filed under 'wholesome' and 'beneficial', and it is today regularly used even in connection with the debate about genetic modification—a subject with which it has very little if anything to do.

But how did the word *organic*, related as it obviously is to *organ*—both the one to be found in your local church and in your local human body—come to have anything whatsoever to do with manure in the first place? All guesses seem to lead into scatalogical territory, so for an expert etymological view we consulted John Wells, Professor of Phonetics at University College London.

And it turns out to be a curious and fascinating trail. Professor Wells explains that *organic* is derived originally from the ancient Greek term *organon*, meaning 'a tool'—something that works. In fact, the word *work* and the stem of the Greek word *org* are also directly related. And still, in Modern Greek, *organicos* is an adjective with a 'doing' connotation, meaning 'instrumental' or 'having to do with a tool'.

From ancient Greek, the *organic* word takes the well-trodden etymological path to Latin, where it slips easily into something comfortably Roman-sounding—*organicus*—now meaning 'mechanical'. And this is where the king of instruments slips in by the back door, as it were, because Latin sees *organicus* taking on a vital extra shade of meaning: 'pertaining to a musical instrument'.

But it is not until the Renaissance that we see the anatomical connection. 'Organs are organized, I think that's really the point,' observes John Wells. 'Once we came to understand human anatomy and that things like the heart or the lungs are in some sense "mechanical instruments", that provides the link that we need.'

Eighteenth-century scientists took a much more direct view of *organic* and applied it to anything they deemed to have organs, ie any living being—and that could include both animals and (strangely, to our ears) plants. Chemists then hijacked the word, adding yet another refinement, contrasting the chemistry of compounds derived from carbons, which have hydrocarbons in them—like plants and animals (*organic chemistry*)—and those that do not (*inorganic*).

From this distinction, it is but a tiny hop to the dung vs. chemical fertilizer use of *organic* that we found back in the 1940s. Which is pretty much where we set out. As John Wells adds, somewhat resignedly as he sees this useful and resonant term expropriated by turn-of-the-twentieth-century food warriors, 'Today it's just all part of what people worry about in foods.'

" "

Summer Sizzle

A warm evening, the shadows lengthening, the sound of a desperate pair of bellows wheezing air onto the recalcitrant grey charcoal imprisoned under the griddle. A trayful of bloodily uncooked steaks and resolutely pink and mottled sausages await the gift of fire. But when?

The barbecue ritual is now as firmly ensconced a feature of the British summer as umbrellas at Lord's or the dashing of British tennis hopes at Wimbledon. For years, though, the barbecue was a feature of more clement climes, an American essential, the Antipodean sine qua non, the ultimate expression of food alfresco.

But why *barbecue*? *Word of Mouth* turned to one of Australia's top English specialists, Dr Pam Peters of Macquarie University in Sydney, to dish up the low-down on the Aussie summer sizzler. Interestingly, she told us, the word *barbecue* is West Indian in origin, filtered through the early Spanish settlers.

The indigenous Arawaks of the Caribbean called a structure formed from sticks on which they slept or used for smoking or drying fish, *barbacoa*. In the turbulent history of the string of islands that scroll across the Caribbean Sea, the word was probably taken up by Spanish colonists, of whom it is said, on arrival in the islands: 'They fell on their knees and then on the natives.'

During the seventeenth century, the word was mediated via Spanish on to the mainland of North America. There it tended to get applied to lavish outdoor feasts, though one description from 1815 equates it with an 'elegant dinner'. More typical of nineteenth-century American examples was the Brooklyn Barbecue seventy years later, where 8,000 kegs of beer were consumed.

It was during the heyday of the American barbecue that it suffered its linguistic truncation, just as the scale of the do itself took on the more modest proportions commensurate with the suburban backyard or deck. In keeping with the American passion for what we might call the alphabetization of ordinary words for graphic and advertising purposes (think of all those products called *E-Z* anything ...), *barbecues* became *BAR-B-Qs* and even *BBQs*.

And this was where, according to Pam Peters, the false 'French' connection stemmed from. *Barbeque* looks vaguely Gallic (compare that genuine French culinary item, the *pastèque* or watermelon), but, as Dr Peters observes, of course 'the spelling with *-que* would come out as two syllables (*bar-bek*)—and no true French person would own the word!' A *Word of Mouth* listener subsequently contacted the programme to point out that one suggested French-based etymology was via the phrase *barbe à queue*—'beard to tail' – which, though absurd, would get over the syllable problem.

In fact, Pam Peters, who has done cutting-edge research in her *Langscape* survey on the wide variety of ways in which similar words are spelled in the world's English-speaking countries, reports that the spelling with *que* at the end is an anomaly in both British and American usage. On both sides of the Atlantic, the *-cues* outnumber the *-ques* twenty to one.

But when did Australians turn the *barbecue* into the *barbie*? Affectionate abbreviations are a striking and individual feature of Australian English: musicians are *musos*, politicians *pollies*, and even the venerable Salvation Army becomes the *Salvos*. So *barbie* is merely another example of regular Australian linguistic practice. Australian *barbies* are a mid-twentieth-century phenomenon, and pigging out outdoors, helped along with lashings of alcohol, is illustrated by the expression *barbecorgy*, which was noted in Australia during the Second World War.

But fifty years on, reports Pam Peters, 'the backyard barbecue is changing from the rather blokey meat-and-beer-laden spree of its origins to a more diverse cuisine, inclusive of fish, chicken, and even vegetarian kebabs, and lubricated by chardonnay and pinot noir as well as the inevitable *tinnies* or *stubbies* of beer.'

To describe the failing would-be barbecue lighter we began with, Australian English suggests a splendid metaphor which has taken its place alongside a wealth of like expressions, as reported by *Word of Mouth* listeners. 'Someone who is *three sausages short of a barbie*', observes Dr Peters from Sydney, 'has not merely failed the test of hospitality, but exposed the limits of their intelligence—in Australian lingo. Not that they can be said to have *kangaroos in the top paddock*, but they are in the terms of the urban Australian *probably not acceptable as brain surgeons...*'

Cakes and Ale

The very word has 'old' stamped all over it—*Traditional Ales* boasts the sign outside the scruffy suburban pub. *Cask-conditioned ales* trumpets the advertising slogan promoting the product of a modern glass-and-steel urban brewery. *Ale* says antique: *Real Ale*, the badge of the serious beer drinker, the CAMRA aficionado. Today, beer marketeers, wise to the image conjured by those three little letters, help confer a spurious antiquity on their product by calling it *ale*. Yet it is only Americans in my experience who actually ask for 'ale' by name and are naturally surprised when people look at them quizzically, like the subject of some latter-day H. M. Bateman cartoon: 'the New Yorker who asked for "a quart of your best ale, landlord" in the public bar of the Rat and Parrot.'

The thing about the word *ale* is that—like *stout*—it is one of those words that exist, that we see on signboards everywhere but (almost) never utter aloud (unless in the company of *real*). Beer, lager, bitter, or *best* do the trick at the bar, when you are not asking for a particular brew by name. But *ale*, never.

First off, a definition: so-called 'real' ale is ale that has not been pasteurized or filtered so that it continues to live and develop in the cask, and, according to the writer on beer Michael Jackson, 'when the Campaign for Real Ale started, the brewers hated the name because they said that *all* their ale was "real".' This is what brewers mean by *cask-conditioned ale*.

Ale is of course a very old piece of English indeed. It was one of the earliest English drinks and comes from the Old English word *alu*. No French imports here, as brewing pre-dates the Normans. As *Word of Mouth* heard when we began an investigation of the antique history of brewing and drinking language at a small local brewery in Shoreditch in London.

Steve Christopher of Pitfield Organic Brewery—as twenty-first-century a man as you would wish to meet—was quite unselfconscious about drawing on the medieval lexicon of brewing in describing the process he supervises: 'We start with a grist of the malt,' he explained, 'and we add this to a mash-tun to form a mash. We sparge the remaining grains. We take the liquor from the mash-tun and put it in a kettle... so we might boil this wort...', and so on. A linguistic brew almost as heady as the product of Steve's mash-tun itself, and almost all Old English, rather than post-Conquest French in origin.

Grist, incidentally, is the product of *grinding*, a word as well as a process to which it is directly related at source in Old Teutonic dialect. Its use in brewing to describe crushed malt is relatively recent—less than two hundred years ago, according to the dictionary. But the milling process in which grist was used *or* produced —it curiously came to mean both ends of the process—goes back to the earliest quern-stones. (*Quern*—another Old English term, a fact that is indeed, *all grist to the mill* of this enquiry...)

But back to Steve and his mash-tun (both *mash* and *tun* come from Old English roots too, as does the *wort*, or pre-fermented ale, that he talked about. Only the solitary verb to *sparge* (sprinkle) has a Latin root which arrived via French (*espargier*). Like the ale that the brewery produces, the language is overwhelmingly indigenous. Ale, a sweetish liquor—not beer—was the ubiquitous drink of medieval England. Beer, with its hops which gave it its bitter taste, arrived later, from the Netherlands in the sixteenth century.

Beer writer Michael Jackson says there are in European culture 'three big words' for fermented grain liquor: first, there is a group of terms related to *cereal*, from *Ceres*, the Goddess of grain—most prominently the Spanish word *cerveza*, but also found in the antique French term *cervoise*. (The famous French cartoon character Astérix, when travelling through Roman Britain, famously and to his disgust is served warm beer or, in the French original, *la cervoise tiède*). Second there is the *beer* family—*bière* in French, *bier* in German and Dutch, *birra* in Italian and so on. And third, of course, there is our northerly *ale*.

In Domesday Book days, ale was a useful way of staying healthy, 'drunk day and night by everyone who could afford it—men, women and children—as the safe alternative to the risky business of drinking water', according to Helen Castor, historian at Sidney Sussex College, Cambridge.

In thirteenth- and fourteenth-century England, ale was drunk (though not *quaffed*—that onomatopoeic term did not turn up till 200 years later) in *alehouses* or *taverns*. But notice the French roots of this alternative word (*taverne*, deriving directly from Latin). A *tavern* was a sure sign that French wine was also on offer.

But if *vintners* were wine makers, *brewers* were the producers of good old ale (a medieval trade that—as with tanners, dyers, and a thousand other professions—ended up as a traditional British family name (remember that standard work of linguistic reference, Brewer's *Dictionary of Phrase and Fable?*). As, indeed, did the *brewster*, who was the aleman's female counterpart, just as a *spinster* was the *spinner*'s. But that particular language trail is taking us a long way from our ale.

Yeast, one of the essential ingredients of ale production, was, says Michael Jackson, known to medieval brewers as *Goddis good* ('berme, otherwise clepid goddis good' lists a brewers' manual of 1468) 'because I suppose they felt God was being very good turning this grain into beer!'

Equally good, though no doubt not particularly godly, was the medieval drinking session. And 800 years ago, the term *ale* was indeed widely used to mean just that—a sort of boozy party—a gathering at which ale was served. Here too there is a fascinating little linguistic byway, because it leads us to the compound form *scotale*. Given a drop of ale too much, you might be forgiven for thinking that *scotale* was just another name for whisky. But this medieval phenomenon has no Caledonian connections. These *scots* were what the lord of the manor charged for communal entertainment, the *scotale* was the name for his knees-up where every guest had to pay his or her fair share towards the ale consumed, and if you managed to wriggle out of paying up, you were inevitably described as getting away *scot-free*.

Weddings were at that period great places for ale consumption, and the celebratory ale-drinking in honour of the happy couple was, inevitably perhaps, called *bride-ale* (or *bryd-eale*). Thus today's *bridal* suites, *bridal* gowns, and *bridal* bouquets all started their journey down the long linguistic road of English in a celebratory pot of ale. Somehow I feel today's real ale brews, with names like *Sexy Satsuma, Dishwater, Cunning Cucumber*, or *Piddle in the Wind*, are not quite the appropriate libation with which to toast the happy couple.

Finally, spare a thought for the medieval representative of *Which?* magazine, whose job it was to check the quality of the local brew. He was the *ale-conner*. He knew his onions where ale was concerned, since he had *conned* ('studied') it well. Historian Helen Castor explains that the ale-conner's expertise was deployed on the palate—he simply tasted it—and on the seat of his trousers.

> He wore special leather breeches and sat down in a pool of ale and stayed there for half an hour while he downed another tankard to test its flavour. At the end of that time he tried to stand up. If the ale contained a lot of sugar—and was therefore of poor quality—his trousers would stick to the bench. But if all the sugar had turned to alcohol, his breeches wouldn't stick and the ale was declared to be good!

With the spirits of such great literary boozers as Sir John Falstaff and Sir Toby Belch in the offing, a certain John Shakespeare was appointed in 1557 to be ale-conner in the little Warwickshire town of Stratford-upon-Avon. And his son ... well, the rest is history. Amazing where a little drop of ale can get you.

The Naming of Tarts

Marketing. The very word is today ambiguous. Here, for the most part, we think of *marketing* as being associated with products and advertising. Companies set *marketing* budgets to promote their new lines, and in this advertising-rich world of global capitalism, where we are no longer, for instance, seen as *passengers, patients,* or—heaven knows, maybe even one day *students*—but *customers,* we need to be promoted to. *Marketed* at. But then again, I recall one of those 'divided-by-a-common-language' moments a few years ago when I was confronted by an American matriarch who assured me that she loved to *market* at such-and-such store. And she certainly was not in the business of pushing product. She meant, quite simply, 'shopping'.

Perhaps it has something to do with the changing trading culture across the Atlantic, where *shops* have become *stores* and most downtown department stores are in decline compared with the vast, thriving, out-of-town *malls*. Food shopping is done almost exclusively—as it is in Britain now—in supermarkets. But while British buyers still go *shopping* at the supermarket, Americans are happy to do their *marketing*.

But whether we are being marketed *to* or are in the business of doing the marketing ourselves as customers, the products that we have at our disposal on the shelves of the supermarket are today products in another sense too—products of the most detailed, sophisticated, and intense scrutiny that money can buy. From package design to typeface to the name of the product itself, all are crawled over, held up to the light, and subjected to the most intimate analysis. So when you hear that a humble bathroom cleaner is to change its name, there is a marketing story behind it. When a major public company decides to rebrand itself with a fresh title, there is assuredly a tale of marketplace penetration underlying the change. And when the humble shopper sidles up to the frozen food counter of the local supermarket, he or she is certainly being subtly marketed at by the names of the delights on offer.

Word of Mouth, captivated by the mouth-watering linguistic trifle presented to our eyes and tastebuds by the marketeers of frozen desserts, indulged in a little fanciful speculation about what lay behind the names. What associations did *Razzleberry Bliss* and *Toffee Apple Torment* set up in the shopper? *Bliss* and *torment* are not normally parts of the culinary lexicon. And what in the world do *2 Individual Raspberry Revenge* (apart from throwing up a succulent grammatical puzzle in the new collective plural *revenge*) do to you? *Revenge* for what? Against whom? Is this the raspberry's Finest Hour?

Of course, exotic pudding names are nothing new. Generations have been delighted—perhaps—by the very individual flavour and texture of *Angel Delight*, and who was it back in the 1950s who first thought of calling an ice lolly with vanilla ice cream covered with strawberry-flavoured water ice a *Mivvi*? As Michael Rosen discovered at his local supermarket, today's freezer cabinet is full of more exotic dreams —faraway places and foreign cuisines inspiring the concoction of puds that sound as though they might have been dreamed up at one of Europe's grandest restaurants. But which were probably manufactured on a trading estate in the outskirts of Leeds. *Hot Crunch Banoffee Cheese Cake* ('short-crust pastry with a filling of creamy banana-flavour baked cheesecake and banana purée with a crunchy streussel topping and a sachet of toffee sauce') or *Large Black Forest Gateau* ('moist chocolate sponge layered and topped with cream and cherry fruit filling decorated with chocolate-flavoured curls'), not to mention the *pineapple and peach strudel* or the *lemon torte*.

It is now common knowledge that supermarkets have experimented with wafting around pheromones that suggest the smell of baking bread to encourage shoppers into the stores because marketeers have found that we respond positively to certain smells. Inspired by such fantastic marketing realities, *Word of Mouth* invited the poet Nigel Forde to indulge in a little marketing *fantasy*. He drew his inspiration from Henry Reed's memorable wartime evocation of weapons training, 'The Naming of Parts', and came up with the dessert-counter manager's address to the team:

> Today, we have naming of tarts. Yesterday
> We had detergents. And tomorrow morning
> We shall have how to steer a trolley, But today,
> Today we have naming of tarts. Sad old men
> Peer with glistening eyes into the humming freezers.
>   And today we have naming of tarts.
>
> To start with, you must not say *cake, trifle,* or *flan*
> If you can pronounce *gateau, strudel, compote.*
> This, you see, is the *torte*, well-named after the Latin
> For a terrible wrong. Ingredients are not named, only
>   numbered.
> The sad men hold in their memories a mother rolling out pastry
>   Which in our case we have not got.
>
> Here is the Heritage Section, where permitted adjectives
> Are used like a sauce to mask or manipulate:
> *Rich, deep, thick, fresh, countrystyle,* are favourites,
> Or *traditional*, usually paired, paradoxically, with *New!*
> The puddings lie on the stomach and on the teeth. The old men
>   sigh.
>   They call it lying in your teeth.
>
> Here you will find the Specious Genitive: Mr. Kipling's this,
> Mrs. Hudson's that. Their non-existence lends true authority.
> You can do it quite easy if you have few brain cells. Tomorrow We
> expect Harold Bishop's kiwi-fruit blancmange,
> Grant Mitchell's Devil's food cake
>   Which, in their favour, we have not got.

They call it marketing the glutamate; it is perfectly easy
If you have a thesaurus, a small I.Q.
And a single-minded drive to increase your bank balance
Which in our case we have not got.
Sadness in all the aisles, and the bewildered old men going
       backwards and forwards,
    For today we have naming of tarts.

Chapter 7
Between Ourselves

YOU KNOW THAT MOMENT when you want to tell someone something but you don't want anyone to know— what do you do? Indulge in a little Franglais (*pas devant les enfants*), adopt a home-made code like Aggy-paggy or backslang, or do you—good Wykehamist that you are—indulge in a few high-class Notions? Because this chapter is all about private codes of one sort or another. What, you may ask, is the true meaning of half the words people wear emblazoned across their chests and their backs? Tee-shirt-speak has its own history of statement and response, of unspoken context and deliberate mystification— only those who really *know* get it, geddit?

In the jazz cellars of the 1930s, *dirty* was good and if you were any good, you were a real *gasser*. Likewise, art— whether performance or plastic—has a coded language all its own, and our excursion into the heady world of art criticism with its secret subtext of good and bad takes in the vacuous and the vapid in a celebration of what some reviewers call, less than courteously, 'artbollocks'.

To round off this canter round codespeak, enter Julian and Sandy, classic figures of radio comedy, with a flourish from the celebrated lexicon of homosexuality, Polari. All *omies* and *polones* welcome.

" "

Sshh! Don't Let On!

Have you ever found yourself inventing code words to talk about adult things that you don't want the children to understand? Or maybe it was the other way round and your mum and dad were 'the enemy' from whom secrets must be concealed. Well, you are not alone. By no means. Secret languages are thriving in homes across the land.

A few years ago a BBC programme asked members of the public to write in with examples of their own private languages. The result was a torrent, a cascade of codespeak, some of them fully worked-through languages complete with grammar, syntax, and original pronunciations. But without somehow the resonance of the great constructed tongues of history. The nineteenth-century Polish oculist Dr Ludwik Zamenhof's linguistic baby took the mellifluous name *Esperanto* ('one who hopes'—originally Zamenhof's pseudonym), while that other attempt at a manufactured world language (in 1879, at least seven years before *Esperanto*) was dubbed *Volapük*—less mellifluous, but still resonant with meaning ('world-speak', no less).

In contrast, these languages that arrived at the BBC by the sackful bore names like *Lalpen* (because the inventor liked a particular breakfast cereal) and *Slime*. Slime, I recall, arrived in a roll of paper a good thirty feet long.

But these private codes are by no means the preserve solely of the eccentric. I distinctly remember the joy of discovering the key to what my mother used to refer to as Acksly Angbay, or Backslang and for days afterwards driving everyone insane by using it incessantly. When *Word of Mouth* surveyed Radio 4 listeners, they offered a variety of private languages, often depending on the insertion of syllables. *Wouldaraga Lucaragayraga likearaga anaraga icearaga-creamaraga?* was the question posed by one correspondent suggesting a delicious frozen comestible for daughter Lucy. Meanwhile another parent intimated that their son's bedtime was surely approaching in *eggy-peggy*: *Egis egit negot agebegout tiga megis begoy wegent togu begad?* (is it not about time the boy went to bed?) I guess it is something that parents and children must have done for generations. The hybrid form, involving both backslang and eggy-peggy (for example *amscray* for *scram*), is usually called Pig Latin.

Backslang has its professional applications that take it well beyond the domestic arena and *pas devant les enfants*. In Liverpool, the Jewish community has traditionally used a form of backslang known as 'Wej Patter', inverting words and syllables, mixing rhyming slang and imported Yiddish terms into standard English in order to preserve trade secrets, while a prize dog-breeder from Cumbria once confided to me that he and his wife would adopt a private form of the Romany language when ear-wigging competitors were about. Other forms of concealing language derive, they say, from Victorian slang, such that the English *yob*—backslang for 'boy'—rears his aggressive and unpleasant head as early as 1859.

Backslang is not confined to these islands either. Across the Channel in France, they call it *Verlan*, but it works on much the same back-to-front principle and is used to the same concealing ends, among young people. Thus *musique* (music) becomes *siquemu* in French Backslang.

But perhaps the most exclusive and richest (in every sense) of these private languages stems from southern England. Hot on the trail, *Word of Mouth* went to Winchester College in Hampshire to investigate the extravagant lexicon of the so-called 'Winchester Notions'. The Notions are one of the most institutionalized and formalized secret lingos in the country, the most prominent example of a widespread tradition amongst Victorian public schools, and the only one to have a formal title. Amazingly, the Notions contain, it is claimed, fragments of Anglo-Saxon and Latin that reflect the 700-year history of the school. A recent dictionary of the 'language' ran to 300 pages, but these days Wykehamists lament its decline from its heyday at the turn of century, when students took delight in creating new words to emphasize their apartness.

Today, opines a recent paper, 'using Notions is contradictory to students' desire for conformity... Through a process of linguistic natural selection, only the terms that are essential or beneficial will survive.' So current denizens of the great public school still refer to their free periods as *Bookie* but in future years, it is suggested, the Winchester *brock* will succumb to the standard *bully* and the arcane *Mathma* will revert to good old plain *Maths*.

Backslang, though far less exotic and regularized than Winchester's quaint but dying elite-speak, turns up everywhere. *Aggy-Paggy* is how many people refer to it, but variants abound: *Aggo-Paggo*, *Eggo* language, *Egg and Bacon* language, *Pig Latin*, *Dog Latin*, *Aggotalk*, *Rug* language, or simply *Cut* were other names supplied by *Word of Mouth* listeners. Most of the versions the programme heard about involved inserting extra syllables into words, as in the examples above, or—as in the version I grew up with—additionally removing the first sound in a word and tacking it on to the end with *-ay* attached.

To celebrate this apparently national domestic linguistic

pastime, Michael Rosen composed a verse entitled 'Not in Front of the Children':

> The name of the club is 'Parents'.
> Children—you can't join.
> Around the tea-table, my brother and I think
> we're fully paid-up members,
> entitled to hear of every event—
> the miscarriage, the eviction and the new Ford car,
> but we learned that our membership cards
> did not cover every single moment.
> Year after year, just before Christmas,
> the house would go mysteriously French
> until my brother reached secondary school
> and learned to unpick *les cadeaux pour les enfants*.
> And later, in the dark, he whispered hotly:
> "Don't you see? A *bicyclette* is a bike!"

Puts Words on Your Chest

When the definitive fashion history of the twentieth century comes to be written, what, I wonder, will be the place occupied by the humble tee-shirt? This essential item of casual wear has become a universal and unisex garment of choice when the weather gets warm. And the tee-shirt too has in recent years replaced the definitively unsexy and unfashionable men's vest as what's worn under the shirt.

But if the garment has become the ubiquitous fashion equivalent of hamburger and coke, what about its role as a walking, talking billboard? Wearing words on your chest and your back seems at first thought an odd thing to do. After all, sandwich-board advertising was frankly always a curiosity on Britain's streets. But men and women seem perfectly happy, day and night, to walk the pavements advertising everything from international brands of beer to the local Chinese takeaway, not to mention the long-past-their-sell-by-date dates of a dingy European tour by some long-forgotten band from the 1970s. The fact is that *wearing* words has become as acceptable and as unremarkable a linguistic feature of our contemporary lives as the souvenir mug or the commemorative tea towel. Even *Word of Mouth* has in its time had a tee-shirt!

But try your own survey and read the passing throng on your local high street and you soon find that tee-shirt texts fall into many distinct categories. As we have seen, there are the strictly commercial variety—a portable billboard that puts your product under people's noses in every location imaginable. But think about it. That is wonderful if you are advertising, for example, the Maroubra Bay Café in downtown Sydney, but it is not going to pop a lot in the tills when the same tee-shirt is parading down, say, Prince's Street in Edinburgh. Nor, one might think, is the advertising value assured of a legend that commends a chic and stylish beauty product perhaps when worn by some less than prize-winning specimen rather too many days since the last visit to the laundrette. You get my drift.

But the legends that are really interesting both for wearers and watchers alike, that add gaiety to life and enrichment to the urban landscape, are those that have more to them than brands, bands, or boasts. These are the literary, witty, or downright rude tee-shirt texts.

Michael Rosen believes the modern tee-shirt wearer to be a latter-day secular sampler-sewer, like those Victorians who so intricately wove—frankly—sanctimonious statements into rectangular scraps of cloth, such as 'Let Self-Sacrifice Be Its Own Reward'. Martin Raymond, a fashion analyst at the London College of Fashion, goes further. He says that the sporters of tee-shirts are today's equivalent of the Pamphleteers. 'That's what good tee-shirt writing is about—pamphleteering. And the best ones happen instantly where you get an event happening and someone prints the tee-shirt after it.' In the struggle for the new South Africa, for instance, tee-shirts precisely took on this polemical, often subversive role. 'In Search of a New Experience?' read the chest of an election-rally specimen. Turning round, the wearer revealed the punchline at the back: 'Vote!'

And that's one of the great joys of the tee-shirt. It permits that exciting advertising fundamental, the 'reveal'. One text teases, the other pleases. Now you see it, now you don't. To get the full effect, you have to be a people-watcher on a street full of passers-by, so the two-part process happens before your eyes as front, then back is revealed in succession. The best legends are these two-parters: 'Lead Me Not into Temptation—I Can Find it Myself' or 'Be Different—Act Normal'.

The other way the shirt-borne text can pack a powerful punch in its message is by sheer volume and ubiquity. Artist Andy Warhol's 210-Coca-Cola-bottle image or multiple Marilyn Monroe silk-screen makes a striking visual statement by virtue of repetition. In a similar manner, reporter Elizabeth Ohene of the BBC's World Service remembers, the 1997 general elections in the African state of Liberia were characterized by the mass impact of a tee-shirt slogan: 30,000 supporters of the presidential candidate Charles Taylor all turned up at a rally wearing identical tee-shirts printed with the legend YOU ARE OUR MAN. The effect was overwhelming.

The course from the linguistically nude tee-shirt to verbal political activism is in some ways a potted social history of the second half of the twentieth century. Martin Raymond reckons that the verbal invasion of the chest started with designer wear:

> Originally you had logos on jeans and on jumpers for example — tee-shirts were traditionally the white, single-pocket tee. I think what happened from the 1960s onwards was that people realised what they had was a personal billboard or showing-space whereby they could put information on the tee-shirt. And certainly from the 1960s through to about 1985 the majority of slogans on tee-shirts were political or making statements about things in the greater culture. And I think certainly, the better and funnier ones traditionally related to politics.

This was the era of student protest, of Vietnam, Watergate, and the CND. So just as the tee-shirt was being adopted by the youth of the West as a convenient easy-to-wear, easy-to-wash garment for all seasons and a form of uniform *anti*-uniform, so the causes they embraced could be emblazoned and worn literally as a badge literally across their heart. Martin Raymond remembers there have been great tee-shirt moments, such as the time when Catherine Hamnett met Margaret Thatcher and had emblazoned across her chest '58% Don't Want Pershing' (in protest against the presence of American missiles). And during the miners' strike we had 'Dig Deep for the Miners'.

Puns, familiar texts subverted, rallying cries—these are the staples of classic tee-shirt-speak. But just as in the past five years or so the Internet grapevine has bred a rapid-fire 'cap-that!' post-modern linguistic culture in which one witty statement is outwitted, developed and subverted almost day by day, so twenty years ago the medium was the tee-shirt. Martin Raymond remembers with affection the evolution of shirt legends featuring that epitome of 1980s chic, Holly Johnson's band *Frankie Goes to Hollywood* (whose hit 'Relax' created a bit of a stir with its suggestive lyrics). He recalls how they started with 'Frankie Says Arm the Unemployed', then they evolved to 'Frankie Says Do Something Political', to 'Frankie Says Relax'—and then finally into that ultimate postmodern statement 'Who Gives A **** What Frankie Says'.

But the great days of tee-shirt dialogue appear to be over. 'My Son Went to London and All I Got was This Lousy Tee-Shirt', with its slightly mournful, self-parodying text, is somewhere near the high-water mark in this postmodern post-Millennium age. These days, as I've indicated, texting and the Net can say more... and faster with all the same levels of wit, subversion, and style, but at the speed of electronic communication.

So as the legends subside back towards band names, tour venues and the name of your local pub or the dates of last year's summer fête, let us remember the great days before texting when tee-shirt words were witty and self-knowing, when, as Martin Raymond says, 'those jumps and word-plays meant you had to bring something to the tee-shirt to take something else away from it. Like "Time Wounds All Heels" or "Children Should be Herded and Not Seen". They work on many levels because you've got an engagement with the tee-shirt and they show that the wearer has understood it.' The cliché "Been there, done that, got the T-Shirt" is recorded from the early 1990s.

Jazzin' it Up

A phonograph turntable, horn akimbo, rotates wildly, seventy-eight or more times per minute. From the fluted sound-funnel pour the scratchy notes of a dance tune called 'Uncle Josh in Society'. The year is 1909 and dancers swaying to the rhythms of the ragtime melody are surely unaware that linguistic history is being made. Because deep among the lyrics of 'Uncle Josh' (not the snappiest title the popular music world has ever come up with) is buried a line that marks the first ever recorded occurrence (in every sense) of one of the English language's most significant words. The line, for what it is worth, runs: 'One lady asked me if I danced the jazz'. And what was *the jazz*? At this moment, it was not the idiom that was arguably the twentieth century's greatest musical invention, but a form of ragtime. The transfer of the meaning from the name of the dance to the music itself, the syncopated, improvised rhythms that accompanied it, would not be seen in print for another four years.

But what a rich well of language jazz ushered in! Demotic, extravagant, imaginative, drawing its vigour like the music from the African-American traditions of the Deep South, of Louisiana, with its musical cadences and Creole dialects. Most jazz words are slang, and often invoke sexual imagery. The word *jazz* itself remains deeply mysterious. Many ingenious explanations have been offered for its origin, including a corruption of the nickname of a travelling Mississippi singer called *Jasbo* (Jasper) Brown. Rutgers University in New Jersey devoted a whole seminar recently to attempting to determine the origin of the word, to no definitive avail. What is certain is that by 1913, *jazz* was being used to describe the music itself, though the *Ragtime Review* of 1916 was still unfamiliar enough with the term as to spell it with one z, *jaz* ('the jaz bands that are so popular at the present time').

As the craze spread north towards the end of and after the First World War, so did the term acquire its modern undisputed meaning. The New York *Sun* writes in 1917: 'jazz is based on the savage musician's wonderful gift for progressive retarding and acceleration guided by his sense of "swing". Louis Armstrong was one of the stars whose rich playing with language alongside the rhythms and melody helped develop the craze for jazz-talk. According to Dan Morgenstern, Director of the Institute of Jazz Studies at Rutgers University, 'during the Swing Era, there was a very rich load of language and Armstrong used to do a little patter on his recordings'. He quotes the dialogue between Satchmo and the vibraphonist Lionel Hampton at the opening of the number called 'You're Driving Me Crazy'. 'They talk about *muggin' lightly* and use words like *gate*, *Pops*, and *viper*, which is a famous term for "pot-smoker" that was popularized amongst others by Louis Armstrong.'

And even in the cold light of formal print, you can still savour the richness and colour of jazz-talking in the song's patter interlude:

> [MUSIC STOPS]—*Hey, hey! What's the matter wid you, cat? Don't you all know you all a drivin' me crazy!*
> —*Oh, oh, Pops. We ... we just muggin' lightly.*
> —*Oh, oh. You got me talkin' all that chop-suey language! Listen you cats. You all crazy!*

One of the interesting features about jazz talk is its subversive, inverted nature. Just as with the popular rap talking and 'black London' talk that is about as close a definition of 'cool' language as can be found right now, the surface meaning of jazz terms is usually the reverse of what is meant. So *square* and *straight* are pejorative, *dirty* and *low-down* are terms of approbation and then, as now, to refer to something or someone as *bad* was a term of high praise: *Man, he's really a bad cat!*

'Some people theorize', comments Professor Morgenstern, 'that that was deliberate, so that people who came from a group that was looked down upon would turn around and say "OK, if you call us *dirty*, well that's great! *Dirty* is good!"'

When jazz-talking leapt the Atlantic on a wave of popularity for the new idiom, it became inextricably mixed up with that other great demotic linguistic tradition, Cockney rhyming slang. This appears to have produced some fascinating hybrids, so *bread and honey* representing *money* comes to be the universally accepted jazz term—*bread*.

Another jazz term that today has gained a currency way beyond its original confines and well beyond the musical arena is *gig*. An abbreviation, it seems, of *engagement*, it now means any performance date (though formal etymology is notoriously hard to establish in this essentially *spoken* idiom). The late Benny Green, the eminent jazz writer and broadcaster who drew on a vast fund of knowledge as a performer—on sax—remembered being confused when as a child at school learning to read he was presented with a picture on the wall of a farmer's small carriage, with the word *gig* beneath. 'I thought, "Why is my father going about pushing one of these things?" Because he said, "I'm going on a *gig* tonight". And it was years before I discovered that there were two kinds of *gig.*' *Gigs* were short-term engagements as opposed to *perms* or permanent or long-term bookings. Trumpeter and band-leader Alan Elsdon remembers the magazine *Melody Maker* advertising for 'trumpet-player wanted: gigs or perm'. If you were no good, Alan remembers, jazzers would say you were 'a bit strong'—shades of that subversive inversion, again. On the other hand, if you had genuine strength as a performer you would be known as a *gasser. he's a real gasser!*

So has the golden age of jazz-talk passed on with the likes of Armstrong and Charlie Parker? Are new terms still being coined? Dan Morgenstern is well placed in his Institute of Jazz Studies to comment, and he says there is plenty of new language joining the mainstream. And he quotes a phrase most likely drawn originally from the smoky halls where billiards are played, *in the pocket.* 'It means everything has gelled and it's really swinging. Back in the 1930s, the phrase would have been *it used to be in there*, meaning, "That's where it all belongs". Today they say *it's in the pocket*!'

" "

The Ire of the Beholder

Years and years ago, there was a BBC programme called *The Critics.* It was an opportunity, as you may have guessed, for a bunch of reviewers to say nice—or nasty—things about books, films, plays and art exhibitions.

And boy did it get some stick!

As a reviewer of the review, tongue firmly inserted cheek-wise, might have put it: *despite its noble title, simple in its aspiration, freighted with a full charge of meaning encompassed within those two simple words, yet possessed of a level of possibility sufficient to satisfy the most demanding of imagination-junkies,* The Critics *only serves to fuel the vitriol-laden pens of metropolitan art-critical pranksters.* Not least amongst those who turned their pens against the show were Peter Sellers and Joyce Grenfell, who loved to poke fun at the endlessly vacuous musings of the interpreters of what were frequently abstractions on the wireless.

The Critics was not the first such excursion into the wilder linguistic exploration of art. According to Simon Wilson, who is the so-called 'Media Co-ordinator' and former 'Curator of Interpretation' at Tate (note, not *The Tate* or even *Tate Modern*; just naked, unadorned ... and somehow satisfyingly simple *Tate*—sorry, one gets carried away), 'at least since the Italian Renaissance, language has been inextricably bound up with Art or Art has been inextricably bound up with language'. But the laughter and parodies that *The Critics* engendered were certainly the best-known modern assault on the language of art-fashion. Nearly fifty years on, the critics are still all hard at it. And having a field day.

Back in the 1950s, the artists who were being dissected and hung out on the linguistic stretcher of abstraction were such approachable artists as Francis Bacon, John Osborne, or Benjamin Britten. Today—in the field of the plastic arts alone—the names of Tracey Emin, Carl André, Damien Hirst, and, heaven preserve us, Martin Creed are the ones to conjure with.

This invokes language heaven. Because what can the art-critical establishment do when confronted with an unmade bed, a segmented beast, a row of firebricks or, in 2001's Turner Prize £20,000-winner's submission, a white room with a lamp switching on and off, but dip their hands deep into the goody-bag of polysyllabic pointlessness and have them some fun?

Creed does things called *Work 203: Everything is going to be alright* and *Work 232: the whole world + the work = the whole world*. Then there's the masterpiece that carried off the Turner, *Work 227: the lights going on and off.* (In fact, you just begin to wonder whether the titles are not also part of the linguistic hoodwink.)

And true to form, the spirit of those hoot-worthy wireless critics of the 1950s lives on. The judges, wrote the *Independent* with a perfectly straight face, 'admired [Creed's] audacity in presenting a single work in the exhibition and noted its strength, rigour, wit and sensitivity to the site'. This was a white room, remember, with a flashing light in it.

'No object is so banal or so uninteresting', the art critic Brian Ashbee explained on *Word of Mouth*, 'that you cannot find something to say about it. For example, if the object is devoid of any interest you can say—well, maybe that's the point: 'this video is very likeable mainly I think because of its *desperate aimlessness*'. Or again: 'It is their very *mediocrity*, their *monotony* and their *emptiness* that attracts us.' If a work is incoherent and apparently meaningless, then you identify that as the reason for its production: 'The work invites a *construction process* undertaken by the viewer as much as that of the artist.'

I feel the shade of Joyce Grenfell walk.

Not that she—or Peter Sellers for that matter—would have used the expression with which Ashbee labels such exercises in linguistic emptiness: *Artbollocks—Drivel for the New Millennium* was the title of a series of articles in the magazine *Art Review* during the year 2000 which poured scorn afresh on the pretentious terms of contemporary art criticism. Language, Ashbee contends, has become absolutely essential to undestanding what art is about because it's no longer an art of *perception*, it's an art of *concept*. Thus it is almost impossible to say anything of interest about much contemporary art, 'so the critic is thrown back on his own resources for something to say.'

At the heart of the contemporary critic's lexicon are memory, sensation, the body, the spiritual, the medium, perception, and culture, says Ashbee. 'Which of these concepts you choose is entirely a matter of fashion or personal taste.'

So he quotes: 'Tait's paintings have a kind of blankness that reflects both a fascination with an image and yet denies it.' And—of a sound piece—'Although the sounds heard would not be those that normally expect or require particular attention, they do however articulate the "middle distance", a sense of place and time, a shared experience and evocations of proximity and distance.'

Ah yes, it's so easy! On *Word of Mouth*, Michael Rosen challenged Brian Ashbee to a little bit of *live* artbollocks by gently removing his spectacles and declaring them to be, Marcel Duchamp-fashion, a ready-made, a *trouvaille* that would forever be... Art.

The key verbs to deploy, says Ashbee, are *subvert* and *deconstruct*. 'Most of these activities or objects require legitimation by the art world so that they may be read as Art.' So for M. Rosen's newly exhibited ready-made *Sight* (a pair of spectacles, remember): 'Rosen's work wryly deconstructs popular notions of vision.' Another, equally valid vacuity from the Ashbee stable would be 'Rosen's work mockingly subverts stereotypes of sight, or Rosen's work cunningly disrupts archetypes of vision.' Or 'Rosen's work innocently parodies popular notions of representation.' 'It's a very useful little formula', he declares, 'because you can apply it to any piece of art, however inept, however lacking in interest.'

Well, as if Ashbee's little *jeu d'esprit* about Rosen's optical equipment were not enough, listener Ted Millichap penned a full-length review of the groundbreaking *Sight* in coruscating, no-holds-barred artbollocks ...

> In his one man-one exhibit show *Sight*, Michael Rosen brilliantly and wittily works through the history of art. At first hearing, the exhibition seemed simply to be a man placing a pair of spectacles on a table, but the clue was in the 'seemingly' passing reference to Ernst Gombrich.
>
> Consider the following—the exhibition is called *Sight*, but was 'displayed' on Radio 4, so that the observer had to exercise interior vision in order to *see* the show. No spectacles would be needed for such a show, since we all see with 20/20 vision in our mind's eye. A perfect example of postmodern irony, coupled with minimalism.
>
> However, our deconstruction of *Sight* does not stop at the twentieth century. Whilst we had to accept an impression of the spectacles—although on a hard desk surface, no impression would have been made—we were forced to consider that the spectacles would give Rosen the sharp sight, bold outlines and perfect colour sight of the Pre-Raphaelites.
>
> Of course, the art critic being interviewed in *Sight* could only give an outline of a critique of the exhibition, finally arriving back at the starting point of art, in the cave represented by a BBC studio. I can recommend that all readers should hear *Sight* at the earliest opportunity.

Nuff said?

" "

How Nice to Vada Your Eek

They were outrageous, they were hilarious, and they were distinctly odd. Yet the British nation loved them and came back for more week after week. Julian and Sandy were the creations of two men—or rather *four* men, two performers and two writers—who created a pair of characters who danced, or more accurately *minced*, across the humorous airwaves of the country throughout the 1960s. The rattle of a BBC sound effects door and 'Hello, I'm Julian and this is my friend, Sandy' became a catch-phrase that heralded the funniest creation of the radio decade. Nothing else came near. It was the high point in *Round the Horne*, the show into which Hugh Paddick as Julian and Kenneth Williams as Sandy erupted every week. And their arrival was expectantly awaited, each delaying tactic in the script raising the hilarity-temperature another degree, until the set-up became obvious, their arrival could be delayed no longer, and those flaunting creations could at last utter their now immortal cue-line. The applause was instantaneous and overwhelming.

With the coruscating characters that scriptwriters Barry Took and Marty Feldman created came their eccentric language. Some of the words we could discern—*how nice to... your dolly old... again!* The meaning was clear... *ish*. It was a greeting all right, but what were those strange bits of vocabulary in between? *Vada* and *eek*—'how nice to *vada* your dolly old *eek*'. Riffle through the dictionary as we might, there was no trace of *vada* (or was it *varder* or *vader*?) or *eek*. And yet these flamboyant men, with their camp manners and suggestive innuendo, seemed to know well enough what they were talking about. So, half understanding it by inference, we accepted it, albeit baffled.

And it *was* strange. Full of terms like *omi* (pronounced '*oh*-me') and *polone* ('puh*loan*'). What was quite clear to anyone with an ounce of imagination was that the eponymous Mr Horne was playing straight man (in both senses of the term) to two over-the-top gay guys (except forty years ago we didn't call them *gay*) whose strange conversation was littered with a private lexicon which only they seemed to understand. What were these *lallies* they kept referring to? What was the *latty* they lived in? And why was everything they seemed to approve of dubbed *bona*?

JULES: Morning. I'm Julian and this is my friend Sandy.

SANDY: Hello, hello, nice to see you again—nice to vada your dolly old eek ... Yes we're from the *Daily Polari*—yes.

JULES: Can we 'ave five minutes of your time?

HORNE: Well, it depends what you want to do with them.

SANDY: Ooohhh! Well our Editor said 'why don't you troll off up to Mr 'Orne's latty ...

HORNE : ... that's flat or house—translator's note ...

SANDY: That's right ... and 'ave a polari with 'im, you see. Polari.

JULES: Yes, we like to 'ave something 'ot and personal, see ...

The astonishing thing about Julian and Sandy was that they were two quite obviously homosexual characters strutting their stuff through a piece of mainstream comedy on the still very strait-laced BBC at a time when homosexuality was still illegal and gay sex punishable with a gaol term. The key to why they got away with it lies, I think, not simply in the fact that it was always—and still is today—outrageously funny, though that must have been the principal reason, but also because they expressed themselves in this curious language. The point was that it seemed in some ways vaguely familiar—*omi*, it became obvious, was a word for 'man', and anyone who had studied basic French knew that *homme* was the term in that language. So maybe there was a link there. And *bona*—again the French word for 'good' could help out there; it clearly was a term of approbation. But as for the rest, well, it was a mystery.

And in these mysterious indefinable terms, of course, lay the crux of the innuendo, and the biggest laughs. *Lallies* could mean anything, if you had a mind that worked that way, and though it *sounded* as though it meant 'legs', did it *really* have some ruder significance?

Most listeners will have heard the words, laughed at the jokes and gone away none the wiser. But for homosexuals in the audience, Julian and Sandy were, quite literally, speaking their language. The lexicon that was getting the big laughs actually *meant* something—and something special and secret—to gay men whose lives were blighted by the threat of exposure, prosecution and ruin because of their sexual preferences. They could laugh at the innuendo as enthusiastically as the straight audience—or more so—yet the words were their *code* too, their (albeit fragile) protection against the threat from the rest of society.

It is hard in these times, when multi-million-selling young pop stars can reveal themselves to be gay and 'comfortable with their sexuality' with barely a ruffled hair, to imagine how important it was before the law was changed for gays to shelter behind a protective wall of language. Because that was the serious purpose that underpins the strange language that made us laugh so uproariously when it was used by Julian and Sandy.

In fact, it has a formal name, *Polari*, and has a heritage which stretches back several centuries. Ian Lucas is a writer who devoted a chapter of his book about gay theatre, *Impertinent Decorum*, to an analysis and history of Polari. He has traced the roots of the lexicon in other closed communities where also, not surprisingly, it was important to be able to converse without being understood by the outsider.

'I think you have to look at Polari as "strands" of language rather than as a language in itself,' comments Lucas, 'and most of the major strands go back to things like the thieves' cant which was brought over in the fifteenth and sixteenth centuries, which was used to create a subculture—a coded language for people to use.' Codespeak rarely gets written down, so it is little surprise that word historians date the appearance of the term *polari* or *parlyaree* in print only to the late 1800s.

Now, every profession has its own technical terminology and its working lexicon of slang, from rubbish collectors to car mechanics, stone masons to computer programmers. They are fascinating and often poetic in their resonances and all represent a level of precision that the general word-store of daily life cannot provide, nor needs. That's why they exist. Likewise, most people do not on a daily basis need to distinguish between a *morpheme* and a *phoneme*, or identify *th-fronting* when they come across it, though they are perfectly common features of language which all of us know and hear all the time. On the other hand they are the professional code of the linguist with which to read more finely the world in which he or she operates. Polari and its antecedents have some of those functions too. But above all these old private lingos operate as a smokescreen.

Many communities that have over the years suffered persecution have resorted to this kind of linguistic protection and to a certain extent share with Polari some aspects of its history and vocabulary. The gypsy language—sometimes called 'tinkers' cant'—is an integral part of the travelling community's history (and as Roma has a long and distinguished history that stretches across the whole of Europe). Yet like Polari and thieves' cant it also provides a bulwark against the power of those who see travellers as a social incubus, a pest and a nuisance, and who seek their removal. In the unlikely surroundings of a shoe-shop near Carlisle, the owner, a breeder of champion dogs, had the great pleasure of explaining to me how he mystified other breeders about his rivals at the big national shows by passing critical comments to his wife in Romany. And many of the same words, or similar-sounding ones, crop up in the talk of other travelling communities like circus and fair folk.

Polari, while fulfilling the same protective functions, grew, as we have seen, out of the criminal underworld, which lent its *cant* to the private code of another closed group, the acting fraternity. Writer Ian Lucas picks up the story: 'Parliare was the theatrical language of the seventeenth, eighteenth, nineteenth centuries used by actors, showmen, the circus. And by the 1950s, 1960s, you've got that very much within the gay community, with emerging homosexual identities, gay identities.'

To each his own. So while itinerant Cumbrian horse dealers developed a fine line in code for describing the qualities or demerits of the animals that came to market, homosexual code, reports Ian Lucas, inevitably centred round sex: 'the thing which people most want to talk about, but don't want people to listen in to. So you get people talking about *trade*, what people look like: their *lallies*—their "legs"; *TBH*—"to be had", somebody who's "to be had". *Omi* is "man", obviously coming from the French *homme*; *polone* is "woman", "female"; *omi-polone* is "feminine man".' How you actually spell these words is open to confusion and disagreement. 'You have to know what you're doing,' says one Polari specialist, 'because a specific word might mean two or three different things. So one *zhooshes* one's *riah*—combs one's hair—before *zhooshing* some *dubes*—that's swallowing some Speed, before going out *zhooshing*—shoplifting.'

As Polari is essentially a spoken code, there has never really been any need to formalize the orthography. So you can find *omi* cropping up as *omee, omie,* and *omy,* while *polone* can be *paloni, palone, pallone,* or *paloney*.

One sourcebook offers the Italian *pollone*—a chicken—as the etymology for this common Polari word, and there is no doubt that the language drew on many sources, European languages amongst them (filtered, as we have seen, through many other social groups) in accumulating its vocabulary. Another popular contributor to encoded language is backslang (see page 180), which has given Polari such terms as *riah* ('hair', spelled backwards and pronounced '*rye*-uh') and its rather fanciful extension, *ogle riahs,* meaning 'eyelashes', where *ogle* is another standard Polari term for 'eye', claimed to derive from the Italian *occhio*. (Fascinatingly, though, the mainstream English term *to ogle*—'to cast amorous, coquettish, or lecherous glances'—comes into the story, too, along the way, arriving according to the dictionary—via cant—from Low Dutch, meaning 'to look at'.)

With the word *gay* itself now firmly part of the mainstream, the whole ecology of what word can and *cannot* be used without offence to describe homosexuals has become skewed. In the mouth of a homophobe, *queer* is seen as offensive, yet when used by homosexuals themselves, it is an honourable term. Writer Ian Lucas listed some of the words gay men and women use to describe each other.

Well, Polari has any number of terms, affectionate terms. *Molly* is one, *nellie* is another one. But I think that straight society uses any language against gay men. So for gay men—when I refer to myself as a *nellie queen*—I'm identifying myself as 'camp as Christmas' and that's fine. But if somebody else calls me *nellie*, or if somebody else calls me *queer* from across the street, then that's an attack on me. And it's not *what* the word is that's being used; it goes back again to *how* it's being used and in what context.

Leafing through the various extant word-lists of Polari, it is hard not to be struck by the preponderance of sexually specific terminology, so *bod* (body), *butch* (masculine), *camp* (effeminate), *carts* (penis), *carsey* (lavatory), *chicken* (young boy), *cottage* (public lavatory), *dish* (buttocks), *naff* (bad), and so on. Many of these words, in part thanks to the glittering presence of Julian and his friend Sandy, have slid quietly out of the shadowy world of coded words associated with illicit practices into the mainstream. So to talk of a *camp* comedian has for many years now been perfectly comprehensible, and *naff* has completely lost any of its purported original sexual connotation ('not available for f***ing'*)*.

But if *Round the Horne* did much to familiarize the general public with this hitherto restricted terminology, it was the decriminalization of homosexuality that ultimately has rendered it to a large degree unnecessary: 'I don't know anyone who speaks the whole Polari, because they can be upfront and open about whatever they want to say' was one comment we heard. 'I first hit the scene at the beginning of the '60s and there were hangovers from the '40s and '50s,' comments Peter Burton, author of a book about homosexuality entitled *Parallel Lives* who remembers Polari in its heyday,

And it was '*vada* this' and '*vada* that', '*bona, girl*'—*girl* was always at the end of a sentence as a sort of full-stop. It was really just a vocabulary. It was really talking about whether someone was good-looking or not, whether they were absolutely appalling. 'Vada the bona feely-omi ajax' which translated would be: 'Look at the attractive young, slightly feminine man next to you', *ajax* meaning *adjacent* (and pronounced 'uh*jacks*') and *feely*, 'young'. Or if it was someone naff, it would be 'Vada the naff bitch ajax'."

Today, Peter Burton both hears it and uses it little: 'I mean if I use it now, it's me being slightly old-fashioned, and I don't think there are many young queens who are particularly interested in it though there are those who are interested in it now from a more academic point of view as part of our history.'

Word of Mouth joined a group of young gay men in Brighton, camp capital of the south coast, as they were putting on their finery for a night on the town. Little or no trace of old-style Polari remained amongst the repartee of this highly unscientific sample, though there were plenty of words that were not part of mainstream vocabulary, or if they are, that these guys used with a very specific homosexual meaning. To get an idea of the flavour of the scene, imagine a dimly lit flat near Brighton's seafront. It's nine o'clock on a Saturday evening and the CD is playing the requisite Kylie Minogue number in the background. In keeping with the classic *Round the Horne* routine, there is a ring at the bell, and the door opens to reveal a young guy, known to all as Christina ... 'Hi girl. You all right? Did Andrew tell you the other night about what happened? This man was really really *butch*, he really was *bulldog*. And he goes into the kitchen and puts the light on and ... You were wearing make-up?—Well *purlease* it was Wednesday night, please. Oh fantastic! And he was like "You're a *femme*". Oh shocking! 'Don't want ladies in my life ...'

And so on and so forth. The occasional *butch* ('masculine') and *femme* ('feminine') are poor substitutes for the glory that was Julian and Sandy. Peter Burton remembers:

> I did rather think the whole thing had gone till I went to Manchester for the Gay Mardi Gras weekend and we spent the whole time waiting for the parade in a pub which seemed to be entirely populated by people who were speaking Polari. There were lots of *trannies* ('transvestites', 'transsexuals') and there were lots of people who'd starred in 'Soldiers-in-Skirts'-type shows who suddenly ran along Princes Street saying '*Vada* the *carts* on the *leatherqueens* on the float coming up Princes Street'. Never thought I'd see it.

I guess Peter Burton thought he would never *hear* it again, either: 'Polari was something that was of its time and served its purpose and is amusingly nostalgic now, but no more.'

Chapter 8
The Name Game

WHAT'S IN A NAME? Well, a lot of dosh, for one. If you get it right. Naming products and businesses is itself big business. Over the next few pages we investigate a few specialist corners of the name game. Coffee, for example, where the whoosh of steam-propelled frothy milk has brought with it a rich, dark crop of new terminology, from the *skinny latte* to the *flavoured moo*.

Since the mid-1990s, coffee emporia have sprung up nationwide, from the Duchy to the Principality, from Caledonia to Hibernia. As far as coffee is concerned, a *latte* is a *latte* is a *latte*. That's marketing. But what about us? What do we like to call *ourselves*? *British*, *Scottish*, *Welsh*, *English*? Or do we define ourselves more closely? *Cornishwoman, Yorkshireman, Bristolian*...?

Bristol is, of course, famous for lending its name to aircraft —Bristol fighters served the RAF with distinction. And it works; it remains a name with a resonance to go with its reputation. But what makes a good aircraft name? Would you go for the *Tadpole* and the *Titwit*, the *Cannibal* and the *Caterpillar*?

We ring down the curtain on this chapter of names with a brief burst from the bell-loft. Among the Stedman Triples and the Bob Majors, the arcane and ancient nomenclature of one of Britain's great gifts to the world—change-ringing—is deployed, like a skein of chimes across the valley on a summer's evening.

Naming Names

In every era something new but intangible creeps through the fraternity of namers. New cafés, bands, poems, cars, businesses, and the like all need names, but new naming processes come in on waves of modishness. Giving French names to cafés, restaurants, bars, and takeaways has a long history and looks like having a long future. Why a high-speed, stainless-steel-floored food outlet should be called *Pret à Manger* rather than *Ready to Eat* can't be discerned from its parsnip crisps and pasta salads. A chain of places called *Bar Med* and *Café Med* has nothing to do with the Mediterranean, though most of the eateries called *Café Rouge* are at least red.

One trend appeared in the 1990s that had no links to all this Rive Gauche, Toulouse Lautrec stuff, though the Pompidou Centre might have had something to do with it. It was the arrival of functionalism married to minimalism. While architects produced buildings with 300-foot ventilation flues exposed, the rise of Zen in the West had people throwing out their padded sofas.

So how can language follow this? With the throning of the monosyllable. Many decades earlier, Rudyard Kipling was a notable precursor, calling his stirring poem simply 'If'. Little did he know that two English bands of the 1980s would go similarly monosyllabic: Suede and Blur. Note: not 'The Blur' or 'The Blurs' or even 'Suede and the Suedettes'. Just one clean-cut, time-saving, clinical, one-syllable noun.

But it wasn't only nouns that were summoned. Surely verbs are even more functional. They reek of doing-ness. Why else do you call an airline *Go*? Notice it's nothing lengthy and cumbersome like *Travel*. It must marry functionalism with minimalism, otherwise they could have called it *Go and Come Back*. Similarly, there's an estate agent in London called *Move* and a café called *Eat*—not *Move House and Lose a Packet on the Fee* or *Eat Sandwiches and Sandwiches and Sandwiches*.

Grammatically, you'd feel inclined to call these imperatives— the voice that orders you to do something: jump! Smile please! Get on an aeroplane and Go! Order your removal van and Move! Come in and Eat! There's a supplement addressed to graduates that comes with the Guardian newspaper called *Rise*. It's easy, but not accurate, to imagine the hand of the state behind this, commanding the rabble rolling out of universities to gird their loins and Rise!

Another way of looking at these verbs is to imagine something more charitable: a you-can-Go, you-can-Move, you-can-Eat, you-can-Rise, but there simply isn't enough time in a day, on a letterhead or hoarding, to write a massive three words. This means they ought to be called Charitable Imperatives.

Sometimes the grammar can be even more ambiguous. This isn't difficult. In English there's no noun that can't be verbed. That's why we can sit in a home-brew hostelry called *Mash* and not know whether we've been commanded to mash beer or admire the mashed potato. Here, the functionalist–minimalist axis is aided by the lettering: a matching clean-cut sans-serif font. Another way in which words can do two things at the same time is with something we could invent called an adverbial noun. An exhibition on Shackleton's expedition to the South Pole was cleanly dubbed 'South'. At one level, this is obviously 'The South' slimmed down to Kylie Minogue proportions. But in the back of your mind, you can't help but think of 'going south' and 'sailing south', which is fairly adverbial in sense.

All this offers up enormous possibilities for namers. *Consignia*, the new name for the Post Office and the Royal Mail, has been greeted with hoots of derision all round. They should have gone with the Zeitgeist and called it simply *Post*. Don't we talk colloquially of 'the Post', anyway? Churches often describe the need to reach new audiences, so on offer here, free of charge is the name *Pray*. The national newspapers, usually heralds and creators of fashion, should break with all those *The*s and *Daily*s and adopt *Read* or *New*—no time for the usual plural *News*.

Within the BBC, we can reveal that scarcely anyone refers to the channels by their full names but simply say 'Four' or 'Knowledge' as in 'An afternoon show on Four', 'A repeat on Knowledge'. In the spirit of Greg Dyke's desire to 'cut the crap', surely the Corporation should drop all that wasteful talk of Radio this and BBC that. What we need is economy of effort. Think how much money the NHS could save if it called itself *Cure* (not *The Cure*—that's been done both by nineteenth-century spa towns and a 1980s band). In line with the new ideas about devolving power to the locality, each hospital could call itself what it wanted. We might see tired old names like *St Bartholomew's*, usually shortened to *Barts*, being further shortened to *Bart*; the Reading General Hospital could become *Bed* and a general surgical ward could be something friendly like *Cut*.

Eventually all talk could be pared down. You could sit round at home, at meal-time say, and have conversations like this:

'Work?'
'Bad.'
'Spud?'
'Yup.'

'Cat?'
'Ill.'
'Vet?'
'Jab.'
'Salt?'
'Nope.'
'Rain.'
'Right'
'Leave.'
'Who?'
'Me.'
'Now?'
'Yup.'

Anyone familiar with teenage boys talking to each other on the phone will know that they've already reached this level of communication.

" "

Coffee-Breaking the Mould

One of the most commercially appealing and fashionably invasive aspects of this soft-footed American linguistic landing on British high streets is in what we buy to put in our cups and mugs. Once, John Major saw it as politically correct to be seen and photographed consuming tea and fry-up at Little Chefs and Happy Eaters up and down the land. Now, Islington Man wouldn't be seen dead in a 'greasy spoon'. The description says it all.

So, for Cool Britannia, a cooler image. And the rise of the American-style coffee house, fuelled by the popularity and perceived sophistication of such American television imports as *Frasier* and *Friends*, has brought a whole new lexicon to our lips. Witness the appearance of the *javahead* or coffee enthusiast.

'A new country like America tends to grasp any new phenomenon and turn it into a form of social coding in order to denote class differences,' reports the British-based but thoroughly American psychologist Dr Aric Sigman. 'So coffees are given a hierarchy and the lower orders would deal with instant coffee, while those more in the know—the Great Literate—would want to familiarize themselves with all the various European-sounding blends in particular. Coffee snobbery has become the daytime version of wine snobbery.'

And it seems this snobbery and its accompanying language is not merely American-sourced, but can be localized even further. Seattle, capital of the American North-West, is not only the home town of the giant and prodigiously successful Starbucks chain of coffee houses, but also the locale of *Frasier*'s 'Café Nervosa'. 'Seattle' has in fact become a sort of brand, a word for slick, cool sophistication, cropping up in the name of British-based chain (now owned by Starbucks), the *Seattle Coffee Co.*

Ally Svenson was the company's American co-founder: 'When I first came to Britain and started getting coffees, I had no choice: there would be one size only and one type of coffee and that was it.' Now she says, the *barista* (Italian for *barman* or *barmaid*, but in today's coffee-bar-speak a fully fledged loan word meaning '*coffee*-bar server') will offer a *short* coffee drink, a *tall*, or a *grande*. All terms are, incidentally, always pronounced (even by thorough-going British) *à l'américaine*, as in 'grawn-day').

As for composition, the basic *classic latte* ('lah-tay'), consisting of espresso coffee with steamed milk, the familiar *cappuccino* and *mocha* ('moh-kah'), or black espresso, may be given a whole range of different treatments to suit the drinker's taste (*customized*) depending on how many doses or 'shots' of espresso you want, and how you like your milk.

Linguistically, this is exotic territory; so you can specify a *wet* or *dry* coffee (less or more foam), a *harmless* (decaffeinated coffee with skimmed milk), or—spotted in Manhattan—a *flavored moo* (made with flavoured milk). This is where Americans get to deploy their graphic love of imagery and no-nonsense monosyllabic punchiness, so *no-fun* means 'decaffeinated' while *rocket-fuel* is the opposite, and probably double or even triple strength and almost without need of explanation is *skinny* coffee, brewed with skimmed milk.

Oh, and if you want to drink your flavored moo or your wet skinny latte grande off the premises, be sure to specify *with wings*.

" "

True Brit

In his classic study of the British and Britain, *How to be an Alien*, expatriate Hungarian George Mikes told the story, back in 1958, of a woman whom he had met in London and who had, to his surprise, asked to marry him. No, replies Mikes, his mother could never agree to his marrying a *foreigner.* 'She looked at me a little surprised and irritated, and retorted: "I, a foreigner? What a silly thing to say. I am English. You are the foreigner. And your mother too."' Mikes opines:

> I saw that this theory was as irrefutable as it was simple. I was startled and upset ... It was a shame and bad taste to be an alien, and it is no use pretending otherwise. There is no way out of it. A criminal may improve and become a decent member of society. A foreigner cannot improve. Once a foreigner, always a foreigner. There is no way out for him. He may become British; he can never become *English*.

There is an ineluctable truth about this timeless piece of Mikes wit. We always seem to be confused and confus*ing* about what we are and what we call ourselves. And about what exactly it means.

This was never more clearly brought into focus than after the disaster that afflicted the United States on 11 September 2001. The idea that British men might have been fighting for the terrorist forces of Al Qaeda in Afghanistan, driven by their adherence to the form of Muslim fundamentalism advocated by Osama bin Laden, struck a jarring note. How could British citizens fight with a declared enemy? Was this treason? Were they Muslims first and British only by nationality, as many of the more outspoken claimed? Wherein lay the central locus of their identity? The ugly semantic and patriotic debate that raged reminded many of the equally unsavoury observations some years ago of the then cabinet minister Norman Tebbit, who suggested that Britons who supported a cricket team other than the English national side were somehow inferior and not worthy to call themselves British. Claim and counterclaim ensued, together, inevitably, with allegations of racism. Yet the idea of the so-called 'cricket test' of nationality and patriotism stuck as one extreme and crude measure of judging 'Britishness'.

When a BBC programme claimed to take as its subject 'the history of our language', many Welsh listeners complained that English—the subject of the programmes—was not *their* language, and that the assumption was English supremacist. In recent years, too, the creation of the Scottish Parliament and Welsh Assembly has directed attention once again to our national differences rather than to our similarities. Little surprise, therefore, that what we call ourselves—the way we refer to ourselves and the way others like to think of us—has become a critical linguistic as well as social issue. We may laugh, mockingly and with a confidence born of nearly fifty years of evolution, at George Mikes's anecdote, yet the subtly different resonances of *English, British*, and *foreign* are as real today as they were when this wonderfully ironic Hungarian first arrived on English—or was it British?—soil.

'There's no wonder we have a bit of an identity crisis in this country,' observes Professor April McMahon of Sheffield University, where she heads the School of English. 'For a start it isn't always clear what "this country" is. I remember in primary school learning that "French people live in France and speak French and Spanish people live in Spain and speak Spanish, but Scottish people live in *Britain* and speak *English*". So it's no wonder that there are some difficulties.' And that is not to mention the quandary faced by the citizens of Guernsey, Jersey, and the Isle of Man, which as Crown Dependencies are not part of the United Kingdom at all. As Jeremy Paxman writes in the preface to his recent volume, *The English*: 'Being English used to be so easy. They were one of the most easily identified peoples on earth, recognized by their language, their manners, their clothes and the fact that they drank tea by the bucketload. It is all so much more complicated now.'

An informal survey of some schoolchildren in the north-east and north-west of England as to what label they would pin on themselves revealed in every case an allegiance first and foremost to their village or town of origin. So the Cumbrian kids were *Wigtonians* (Wigton is a small manufacturing town, ten miles or so from Carlisle), and their counterparts from the former pit village of Ashington north of Newcastle were *Ashers*. *Cumbrians* was certainly acceptable as an alternative tag for the Wigton sixth-formers, while some variant of *Northumbrians* or *Geordies* passed muster in the north-east. But *English* was well down the list and *British* and *Europeans* pretty well unplaced.

Of course, the labels that we use to define ourselves are always to an extent the product of our local context. Bretons are proudly nationalistic, and would probably identify themselves in that way before saying they were *French*. Likewise the Corsicans, and the Cornish for that matter.

The problem in Britain is—as April McMahon identified in her anecdote—that we have two national names for our country—a historic one, Britain, which in some way defines our national heritage as the peoples of a group of islands, and a political one, the United Kingdom (of Great Britain and Northern Ireland). We also have a language which serves most of this country—and indeed a number of other bits of the globe—but is known by the epithet describing only one part of it, ie 'English'.

Despite the clear assertion in the *British* passport that 'Her *Britannic* Majesty's Secretary of State requests and requires in the name of Her Majesty all those whom it may concern to allow the bearer to pass freely without let or hindrance and to afford the bearer such assistance and protection as may be necessary', travel makes us all think twice about the way we speak about our national identity. Snapshot of a Boeing 747 in the last hour of its flight from London to—say—JFK in New York. Amongst the passengers, furrowed brows, earnest consultation of the flight attendants and quite a number of screwed-up first attempts to fill in the US immigration forms that have just been doled out round the cabins. The passengers know all too well how fierce the officials on the ground can be—no crossings-out or amendments—they have been warned. Everything to be filled in ship-shape and Bristol fashion (now that's what I call being a tad provincial!). So when it comes to the box identifying your country of residence, what do you put? *Britain? Great Britain? United Kingdom? UK?* Gotta be right, or the tough questions will hold up the line, like the man said. Yeah, you got it. *UK*. Right, next one: 'Nationality', what do you put there? *Ukonian?* Come again. Sounds like something out of a 1950s SF film with pointy heads. No, this time it is *British*. See what I mean?

And then when finally you manage to negotiate Immigration with your identity unimpaired, this sort of confusion leads to all sorts of labelling confusions when it is not Brits doing the defining. So Americans have an irritating habit of calling anyone from Britain 'English', without appreciating the deep hurt they are doing when the person to whom they are referring is, for example, a son or daughter of Wales. And then who are those *Britishers* that occasionally seem to pop up in discussions Stateside? Never known one myself.

'I never used to think about the question of my identity, maybe because I grew up myself in a service family,' comments journalist and author of *The Abolition of Britain*, Peter Hitchens, 'and the Services are one of the parts of the country which are most *British* rather than English, Welsh, Scottish or Irish. I'd always thought of myself as *British* and it took some time to realize that anybody might think of me as being *English* or that I might have to think of myself as being *English*. And it's only been when I've been living abroad that it's become an issue for me.'

But then, Peter Hitchens would perhaps not baulk at being called *English*, either, but I should just like to be a fly on the wall when an uninformed or simply unthinking Californian sidles up to Billy Connolly with the opening gambit, 'You're English, right?' Just like that US immigration form, you gotta get it right. Professor April McMahon comments: '*Britain* for instance and *British* were originally the terms for the native Celtic-speaking tribes here, and that was opposed to the Romans, and then it was opposed to the Anglo-Saxons. But then when the broader union came into being subsequently, the terms *Britain* and *British* were recycled.'

Again from an etymological point of view, the *Welsh* are simply 'foreigners' as far as the English are concerned, the modern word deriving from Old English *Welisc, Wælisc*, which arrives via a Germanic word meaning 'foreign (Celtic or Roman)', in turn derived from the Latin name for a Celtic people, the *Volcae*. And while we are about it, the dictionary lists a couple of other names that have long dwindled into the distance, thankfully, *Welsher* and *Welshy*. I don't somehow think anyone would be keen to put that particular name on their immigration form. 'I think the difficulty in regulating or regularizing any of these terms,' says April McMahon, 'is that they become very much emotionally coloured and we become very proprietorial about them. The difficulty is that they reflect a truth which is that we do belong to more than one group.'

Max Jarrett is an African journalist who was born in Liberia, and he confirms the rather blurred linguistic profile that our nationality seems to show to the world.

My original concept of what someone from these islands was called was formed in Liberia, where we were taught that it's *Great Britain* and *the British Isles* that anyone 'up there' belongs to—including the Irish! They're British because they're from that part of the world. It wasn't till years later when I met someone from a former British colony—from Kenya—and they kept referring to *UK... UK... UK*. I was wondering 'What's this *UK* he's talking about?' And they said, 'Oh it's the *United Kingdom*'. I said 'the *United Kingdom* of what?' And they said, 'the United Kingdom of Great Britain'. Then I realised that it meant *Great Britain*. So *UK* really didn't mean anything very much when I was young in Liberia.'

Max speaks fluent and perfectly accented English, as we know it in the UK. His language is what linguists today refer to—in shorthand—as 'BrEng'—British English. This is to distinguish the English language as spoken within the United Kingdom from the varieties that thrive in North America ('AmEng') and Australia ('AustEng'). Because, while once Americans and Australians would have been quite content to say that they spoke simply *English*, the language that we speak is such a badge of the place we come from that there is an increasing trend for inhabitants of the United States to say they speak *American* and even for Australians to talk about their language as *Australian*. And though this sounds to a British ear a little unusual—after all, despite all the well-known and overquoted lexical differences like *sidewalk*, *vest*, and *cobber*, the fundamentals of the language remain the same—maybe it is not quite so eccentric after all. As April McMahon demonstrates:

Take one term that we think we know what it means, which is *English*. Actually the term 'English' for the language has been around for a long time—as long as people have written in the vernacular language—so from about the seventh century AD. But the term *England* for the country is quite a lot younger than that. It only comes into use about the year 1000, and before that England is called *Angelkuin*, which is 'race of the Angles'. And of course the Angles were only one of the tribes who came to Britain in the first place. Why should we use the term for Angles and not the term for Saxons?

So maybe we should actually be calling our language *Sassenach* (a usually derogatory epithet from the Gaelic *Sassunach*—'Saxonish'—which derives originally from the Latin *Saxones*)?

And if all this fuss about language and identity strikes you as being a little over-fussy, spare a thought for the Dutch, where at a recent royal wedding much of the ceremony was conducted in English. The power of the English language internationally to provide a common medium of expression for business, information exchange, and a multiplicity of other functions is today unparalleled by any other language. Not surprising, therefore, that in countries where the British influence was colonial, and where the colonial inheritance is today viewed with—shall we say—a certain ambivalence, the *English* language should carry a political charge all its own. (Interestingly, in South Africa the English language is often looked upon favourably by the former disenfranchised African majority as representing the lingua franca of the freedom struggle, of which the enemy tongue of oppression remained, despite South Africa's status as a former British colony, Afrikaans.)

In recent years, with such events as *the Brits* making biggish headlines, and titles such as *Brits Abroad* gaining a certain currency, the abbreviation *Brit* for *British* has begun to gain acceptability. Short enough not to be an uncomfortable mouthful and slangy enough to feel at least not entirely official, *Brit* has more or less classless appeal. Not *Briton*, though. No self-respecting Brit would accept the use of that strange formulation. After all, it was in the middle of a particularly gooey mud-pile in the film *Monty Python and the Holy Grail* that Terry Jones poured linguistic ridicule on it in the form of Graham Chapman's King Arthur. Arthur was protesting, you recall, that he should be afforded some respect because he was 'King of the *Britons*'— 'King of the *who?*' splutters back the peasant with a speech impediment, 'Who are the *Bwitons?*' No, *Briton* (or indeed *Bwiton*) simply won't do. Peter Hitchens comments: 'It's a newspaper headline word because it usefully sums up something in a very few letters which will fit a headline and otherwise it's not used in speech. It's like other exalted expressions such as *Albion* that nobody would now actually use in normal speech.'

The only safe way, if you are uncomfortable with *Brits* (too trendy? too slangy? too young?) is to stick to your national designation. After all, they are always going to get it wrong half of the time, anyway. Especially in sport. Wearing her best Scottish accent, Professor April McMahon says:

> It's not always obvious what we mean by *the national team*. In the Commonwealth Games, for instance, there's a Scottish team, but in the Sydney Olympics there was *Team GB* and that's for the whole of Great Britain. And ask any Scot and they'll tell you, for instance, that any losing Scottish athlete is always *Scottish*, but a winning one miraculously becomes British, or even *English*, indeed, which is beyond the pale of course.

To return to where we began, and the wry, puzzled observations of Hungarian George Mikes. Writing just after the Second World War in his first and best study of the weird and wonderful British he observed on arriving here, Mikes concluded:

I know a naturalized Britisher who, talking to a young man, repeatedly used the phrase 'We Englishmen'. The young man looked at him, took his pipe out of his mouth and remarked softly: 'Sorry, Sir, I'm a Welshman', turned his back on him and walked away. The same gentleman was listening to a conversation. It was mentioned that the Japanese had claimed to have shot down 22 planes. 'What—ours?' he asked indignantly. His English hostess answered icily: 'No—*ours*.'

How to Name a Plane

Planespotters, like their confrères, trainspotters, are usually put in the category 'harmless funsters'. That is, until a group of them were locked up in a Greek jail. It brought to mind the possibility that all the people you see jotting down car numbers, collecting bus numbers, and spotting motorbike names might all be spies.

To be fair, planespotters are treading a path full of potential danger. This may not be immediately apparent, if you're standing, say, at London's Heathrow airport whiling away the time watching a planespotter watching a jumbo. Move the same spotter to a military airbase—or even to the perimeter fence of Boeing's complex in Seattle—and the harmless fun takes on a different appearance.

But let's keep things simple: human beings invented flying machines. They did this as (1) a way of killing each other and (2) a way of moving more quickly round the earth's surface. Different human beings invented different flying machines. Human beings gave all of them names and nicknames. Some of these are so famous, they are part of history: *Spitfire, Lancaster, jump jet* and *stealth bomber*. Some are not so famous: *Gasbag, Cow, Bullfinch,* and *Pisspot*.

Unlike most fields of linguistics with its phalanxes of competing experts, the naming of military planes is a subject mastered by one person and one person only. For reasons only known to psychoanalysts, you will know that this person has to be male. He is one Gordon Wansborough-White—someone who has collected together all the names and naming systems of aircraft and their engines flown by the British armed forces between 1878 and 1994.

On meeting him, in the presence of old aircraft, you become immediately aware of a jovial reverence—the planes are sacred but the naming of them was a bit of a wheeze. This might be a disguise. To compile his encyclopedia Wansborough-White had to grapple with the fact that aircraft have often had more than one name, some of the records have been destroyed, some of the records are wrong, some aircraft had no name, while many others, like human beings themselves, existed with two parallel, competing names: the official and the nickname.

Let's begin at the beginning. The very first British military aircraft was an 1878 balloon. Pause for a moment and put yourself in the shoes of the manufacturers of this prototype of air warfare. You have to name it, so will you reach for the gods, Greek, Roman, Norse, or otherwise? Will you think of the winds blowing your balloon over enemy lines? Or will you have a sense of your place in history as a first? Yes, it was the lattermost. It was named, by an unknown namer, the *Pioneer*. Other great balloons quickly followed, and it wasn't long before governments stepped in and took up the role they've had ever since, as naming supervisors. Unlike France with its Académie Française, the British have never created a national language overseer, an institute to determine whether we should say *napkin* or *serviette*, *diaper* or *nappy*. Perhaps, then, governmental control of the naming of military aircraft is a rare, if rather specific, similarity to French-style intervention in language matters.

Here is an example of the tone a government official took up over wayward naming:

> ...on the question of naming Bristol Bomber... you will shortly receive a circular letter informing you of a general scheme for naming machines, and the steps you will require to take.
>
> In the meantime, it would be wise if you did not go on with the idea of naming your machines by star names, as this will not fit in with the scheme now awaiting approval.
>
> I am, Gentlemen
> Your obedient Servant
> Tunswick (?)
> Captain RFC
>
> Air Board Technical Department
> Embankment WC2
> 17 January 1918

For those who yearn for an Académie Anglaise, this might be the kind of letter that any of us might receive if, say, we had been heard splitting an infinitive or hanging a participle. A letter would arrive on your doormat with an official insignia and you would open it to find, 'It would be wise if you did not go on with the idea of using the plural form of the verb following singular collective nouns, etc. etc.'

We digress.

The kinds of scheme that the good captain at the Air Board was referring to was an amazing classification system, so complex and fantastic that there's only space here to give a flavour. If, say, you had produced a single-seater one-engine aircraft for use on land or from ships' decks (and therefore not a seaplane) you would have to give your plane the name of a reptile—but not a snake—or a land bird—but not a bird of prey. If, on the other hand, you had produced a seaplane with more than one engine with a gross weight up to 11,000 lb, then you would have to give your craft the name of an English or Welsh seaboard town. And so it was that the manufacturers—firms like Bristol, Fairey, Sopwith, Supermarine, and the like—were asked to fall in line.

In case you should think that this matter was lacking in poetry, a further letter from Wing Commander Alec Ogilvie of 14 February 1918 reminds us that alliteration was desirable if not always possible: 'the name selected should fall in the class of "Insects", "Reptiles", or "Terrestrial Birds" and should commence with the letters "BR", "CO" or "KO" to indicate that the design emanates from yourselves.' The 'yourselves' in question were the 'Messrs' of the British and Colonial Aeroplane Co. Ltd.

From now on, these artificial birds could take off with such memorable names as the *Blackburn Blackbird*, the *Sopwith Snail*, and the *Westland Weasel*. However, don't imagine that this naming process was left to the manufacturers themselves. It wasn't long before the regs became even tighter, with the demand that all RAF aircraft should be forced to take the names that the air ministry demanded. The naming system would now follow more closely the function of the aircraft. So fighters would have 'F' names, spotter planes would have 'S' names, trainer planes would have 'T' names, and so on. The relevant civil servants got stuck in with suggestions of their own. It must have been exciting times in the ministry offices when the chaps burst out with such names for fighters as the *Faggot* and the *Fairy*; for bombers, the *Baboon* and the *Bustard*; for spotters, the *Sardine* and the *Skunk*; for training planes, the *Tadpole* and the *Titwit*, and for troop carriers, the *Cannibal* and the *Caterpillar*.

All this seems to have proved too arbitrary. As linguistic forerunners to the French semiologist Roland Barthes, the men from the ministry figured out that names do not merely denote things, they also connote. With war beckoning, and the need to keep the minds of fighting men inspired, a more subtle scheme was introduced. Here's a sample:

Fighters: general words indicating speed, activity of aggressiveness

Bombers: place names—an inland town of the British Empire or associated with British history

Gliders: historic military leaders

Meanwhile, the Fleet Air Arm (planes under control of the Royal Navy) had its names placed under control of the Admiralty. The high-ups there soon dived in with *Benbow, Drake, Hawkins, Trafalgar, Royal Oak, Victory, Revenge*, and the like. They clearly had a naval point to make.

With Britain standing alone and destruction possible, apparently there was still time for a ministry meeting to modify the naming systems yet again. Fighter planes could now have the prefix *Fire*, dive-bombers could have the names of seabirds, torpedo bombers would carry the names of oceans, seas, and estuaries. With the RAF using some US planes, the Americans had to be informed, and were given some suggestions: for dive-bomber *Skua*, for bomber *Blenheim*, and so on. It seems that this ran into difficulties, and with the war raging in every continent of the world, Sir Charles Portal, Commander-in-Chief, Bomber Command in the Second World War, wrote to Churchill pointing out the great difficulty they were having in finding a unity of naming systems with the Americans. 'Thus a P-40 can either be a *Tomahawk* or a *Kittyhawk*... whilst both the A-28 and the A-29 were called by us the *Hudson*.'

In the postwar period, further modifications were introduced. You will remember that the sun was setting on the British Empire, so bombers were now to be named after places in the British Commonwealth. Helicopters had to be named too, and it was deemed that the best source for their names was trees. The sycamore was the inspiration here, with its rotating seeds.

Gordon Wansborough-White, the aforementioned king of aircraft names, has not merely been a passive nomenclature noter. It is to him that history owes a debt for coming up with the name for the military application of the civil aircraft, the de Havilland *Comet*. Not happy with the cumbersome *Maritime Comet*, the ministry compiled a shortlist: the *Plymouth, Osprey, Cormorant, Slessor, Trenchard, Bideford, Calshot, Albatross*, and *Blake*. Most of these were dismissed with such arguments as: the *Osprey* (not maritime—er, but it is!), *Cormorant* (it dives into the sea), *Albatross* (unlucky to shoot at—what's wrong with that? asked G W-B), *Drake* (bound to end up with the nickname *Duck*).

In stepped our Gordon. He was having dinner with Lord Shackleton at the Royal Aeronautical Society and suggested the name *Nimrod*, the 'mighty hunter' of the Bible, also a king, to be found in Genesis. And that's what it became. How many planespotters, trainspotters, any-kind-of-spotters are there who must wish that one day they could name one of the objects of their spotting? The privilege only falls to the very few.

Perhaps the final note should be left to the daughter of Sir Robert Maclean, the Chairman of Vickers. She, according to her father, was something of a spitfire. If you think you can guess what's coming, you're right, though with reservations. The lady's nickname is one version of how the RAF's most famous plane got its name. It seems as if Reginald Mitchell, the designer of what was officially the Vickers F7/30 thought it was a 'bloody silly name'. This plane was modified into the F37/34 with a new engine, and there was every chance at one point that the plane that won the Battle of Britain would have been called the *Shrew*. Well, at least it rhymes with *the few*. Some say that it was the General Manager, Sir James Bird, who suggested *Spitfire*. Mitchell was heard to say that it could be called *Spit Blood* for all he cared. Mrs Anne Penrose, the spitfire herself, Maclean's daughter, claims that as time was running short at the board meeting, it was she who suggested the name. And if she really was a spitfire, perhaps we had better believe her.

❝ ❞

Appeal of Bells

Claud Corderoy straightened up, his face red with effort and creased with long days spent labouring in the sun. 'Nothing quite like country towers,' he sighs, 'the sound of bells from country towers.' A quarter of a mile away across the summer evening fields, a peal had started up from the little Berkshire village church. In the loft, the ringing team were beginning their weekly practice. The tumble of notes wavered on the breeze, carried in floating modulations, now faint, now strong, rather as the tinny old Bow Bells peal used to sound on the BBC Light Programme fifty years ago.

The sound of what is known as 'change-ringing' (the process of going through all the possible changes of sequence in ringing a peal or set of bells) seems these days to epitomize a certain British timelessness. John Betjeman, like the former Berkshire farm labourer Claud Corderoy, knew this well and returned to it ceaselessly in his poems, and even called his poetic autobiography *Summoned by Bells*. In 'Church of England Thoughts Occasioned by Hearing the Bells of Magdalen Tower', Betjeman captured the essence of that sound:

> A multiplicity of bells,
> A changing cadence, rich and deep
> Swung from those pinnacles on high
> To fill the trees and flood the sky
> And rock the sailing clouds to sleep.

And William Cowper wrote lovingly of the landscape around the river Ouse dominated by a

>   square tow'r
> Tall spire, from which the sound of chearful bells
> Just undulates upon the list'ning ear ...

Just as the sound of change-ringing has framed our romantic notion of rural Britain, the language of bells has also left its mark on the lexicon. *Ringing the changes* is perhaps the most obvious example, where the sense of 'going through all the possible variations of any process' is a direct metaphorical transfer from the original campanalogical meaning. 'Ringing the changes is making a noise, actually.' Speaking in the bell loft of St Mary le Bow church in London—the church whose prewar peal was used in that famous BBC recording—is Mark Regan, the church warden and steeple keeper. 'It's telling the people outside the church that there is something going on, because bells were used as a sort of signal in medieval times.'

But the change came quite literally 400 years ago, when it was realized that pleasing cadences of notes could be established by applying strictly observed rules of sequence in a peal of tuned bells. And here it is worth perhaps making a short etymological diversion. The word *peal* orginally referred to the actual *ringing* of a bell—shortened from *appeal* and derived from the Old French word *apel*, meaning 'a call' (in this case, to worship.) By the eighteenth century, the word *peal* had become transferred to the set of *tuned* bells hung in the tower of a church and used for *change-ringing*. The earlier term for a set of bells, dating from the 1550s, was a *ring* (how many towns and villages in Britain boast a *Ring o' Bells* pub next to the parish church?).

With the discovery that, by applying mathematical formulae, a peal could be constructed which never repeated itself, sounding the bells from the church tower ceased simply to be a call to devotions. 'Ringing became a competitive sport as it evolved in the seventeenth century and when people rang the bells they just rang sequences or *changes* of bells; that expression does probably come from the seventeenth century where all our early language comes from. It's language which we still use.'

'The art of change-ringing is peculiar to the English,' wrote Dorothy L. Sayers in *The Nine Tailors*, a detective fiction largely built round change-ringing, and, like most English peculiarities, unintelligible to the rest of the world. To the musical Belgian, for example, it appears that the proper thing to do with a carefully tuned ring of bells is to play a tune upon it. By the English campanologist ... the proper use of the bells is to work out mathematical permutations and combinations.

A *change* in a rung peal occurs when, thanks to the ringer applying a different touch to the bell-rope, the bell swings to less than its full deflection. As a result, the swing back is shortened and the next stroke of the clapper against the rim of the bell occurs sooner, so breaking the rhythm of chiming. 'In this way two bells can change places in the tone row (or *change*),' explains an authoritative guide to the art of ringing, resulting in a sort of dancing in and out of the different notes of the various bells, treble, tenor, and so on.

It is an arcane sport, and a handful of basic rules define the process, including, for instance, that each bell should sound exactly once in *change*, that a bell may move only one position at a time and that no *change* is repeated within the full sequence or *method*. And as so often with such arcana, it has its own vocabulary. I remember being fascinated by notes on scruffy pieces of paper pinned up in the porches of country churches that announced, for example, that the peal for a forthcoming Sunday would consist of *Stedman or Grandsire Triples* or *Plain Bob Triples*.

Too laborious and obscure to be worth examining in complete detail here, these different *methods* are amongst the most traditional forms of ring. A *plain bob* is a simple (or plain) form of change-ringing which *hunts*, or weaves, a simple course through the other bells. (And why *bob*? Well, some dictionaries suggest that the term is connected with the notion of *bob* meaning 'a sudden movement up and down'—like the *red, red robin* that came *bob, bob, bobbin' along*—though it may also be related to the late sixteenth-century meaning of 'a blow with the fist'. The evidence, as they say, is not conclusive.)

The essential difference amongst all these rings is one of complexity and thus of length. *Plain Bob Minimus* is the simplest, and means Plain Bob rung on four bells. This only allows for twenty-four changes (because, as we have already seen, repetition is forbidden) and takes less than one minute to ring. Add a bell (a total now of five) and the ring becomes *Plain Bob Doubles*, yielding 120 separate permutations. As the number of bells in the peal increases, so of course do the mathematical permutations, to the point that a full peal can last three hours or more and consist of 5,000 or more changes. What stamina—both for the bells and ringers (not to mention the poor parishioners and the drinkers in the Ring o' Bells)!

In the bell loft of St Mary le Bow, in London, there is a reconstruction of the original eighteenth-century sign-board (lost when the church was gutted during the Blitz in 1941) which recorded such a mammoth peal: 'The Company rang on Tuesday January the Twelfth 1730 in three hours and forty minutes a complete Peal of five thousand and forty Plain Bob Triples.' Mark Regan explains: 'The board records the first known piece of long bell-ringing—that's the first known record, and in fact one of the men there, William Laughton, belonged to a group of ringers called the "Rambling Ringers" who used to travel round the country ringing and drinking and eating at the same time.'

The art of making bells chime perfectly in tune and with a sweet noise is practised not so very far away from St Mary le Bow, in Whitechapel, in a teeming street now full of exotic market stalls and as ethnically diverse a population as you are likely to see in Britain in this third millennium. The Whitechapel Bell

Foundry is an ancient and venerable institution, one of two great British bell-makers—the other is Taylor's of Loughborough—and which was responsible for casting some of Britain's (and indeed the world's) most celebrated bells. At least half, or so they say, of the churches whose peals are commemorated in the time-honoured nursery rhyme 'Oranges and Lemons' (say the bells of St Clements)' were originally manufactured at Whitechapel. The celebrated 'Liberty Bell', on permanent display in Philadelphia in Pennsylvania, which played a central role in the achievement of American independence, is a Whitechapel bell, as is 'Big Ben'. Manufactured in 1858, this was the largest bell ever cast at Whitechapel, weighing 13½ tons.

At Whitechapel, where all those rather more run-of-the-mill bells whose destiny is to ring out the changes across the British countryside are made, they have their own very specific local lexicon to describe bells and the parts thereof. 'It's very easy to talk in a language that outsiders won't understand,' says Alan Hughes, an executive with a finely tuned ear for bell-like tone, 'and we can even confuse each other, because there are two bell founders in this country and we both have our own language. Some of that language is even unique to the company.' Now, dialect and local terminology is one thing, and we are familiar with the fact that what linguists refer to as 'regional variation' is one of the richest and most characteristic features of British English. But to find such variation within one industry—and a very small one at that—is astonishing.

So is there, then, a sort of bell-founding *dialect*? Alan assures us it is true: 'When we talk about the top of the bell where inscriptions are placed we call that the *inscription band*, the other foundry call it the *mulley groove*'. When we talk about the harmonic tones of a bell, we will talk about the *extra*; they will talk about the *fundamental*. But it's the same harmonic. We will talk about the *fifth*, they will talk about the *quint*; we will talk about the *third* they will talk about the *tierce*. We do agree on the *hum note*. We both call the 'hum note' the *hum note*!

Look up the supply list of the foundry, and you will find a range of bells that run from a little C-major bell with a diameter at its *lip* (as the mouth of the bell is called) of nine and five-eighths inches right up to a C-major monster with a lip measurement of sixty inches. (Incidentally, the other extremity—the top section—of a bell is known as the 'crown'.)

But beyond the precise note to which the bell is tuned, the essence of that sound with which we began, the gentle wafting torrent of changes rung in country towers, that is the territory of the ear and a quality savoured by the trained faculties of the foundry master. 'There are two elements to the bell—there is *tone* and there is *tune* and people confuse the two words,' says Alan Hughes. 'Tune is the pitch of the bell. It is the actual note of the bell, it is a measurable thing. Tone is the quality of sound, therefore it is subjective. And we are left with subjective-sounding words to describe it. So we will talk about bells sounding *thin* or *rich*, or *tight* or *panny* or *fruity*, rather like describing wine actually.'

And Alan Hughes claims authorship for *fruity* in the vocabulary of the bell:

> It's a word that I've tended to bring in because I think that there are some bells which are genuinely *fruity*. You get this very round, full, velvety quality. It's smooth, there are no sharp edges to it, it's not rough, it's not raucous. It doesn't grate in any sense. It's warm, it's like a blanket on a cold day, it's lovely, it wraps you in warmth and smoothness at the same time. I know of no better way of expressing that in a single word than to say *fruity*.

And if the language of wine appreciation has taken over at the bell-foundry, the computer has moved into the ancient art of change-ringing. All those mathematical permutations are now calculated on laptops and PCs, and the names by which they are known have escaped the millennial lustre of Plain Bob Triples and Grandsire Majors. Now the *methods* go by names like *Abba Bob, Biryani Bob, Flatiron Bob,* and even *Rhododendron Bob,* 'and a recent group of ringing methods like Grandsire or Plain Bob have been called after stars in the Orion constellation: *Orion, Rigel, Betelgeuse, Andromeda, Aldabaran,*' says Mark Regan of St Mary le Bow. 'Now, as ringing has got I suppose a bit more sophisticated and we like to have a bit of fun, we also ring some silly names. And because I quite fancy Michelle Pfeiffer, we rang a peal of *Michelle Pfeiffer Delight Major* for her fortieth birthday. My wife wants to ring a peal of *Sean Connery Delight Major* to sort of balance the books a bit.'

In the little Berkshire village where Claud Corderoy laboured long into his seventies, the last notes of the change-ringing practice are dying away. Solitary notes escape the tower, falling away across the roar of a passing 125 on its way to Paddington. Despite the train, despite the computers and despite the quirky names, bellringing remains essentially timeless. As an ancient set of rhymed 'rules for bellringers', pinned up in a country church bell-loft, concluded over seventy years ago:

> And when the bells are down and ceased
> It should be said or sung
> And God Preserve the Church and King
> And guide us safely Home.

Chapter 9
Country Natters

A**ND WITH THE SOUND** of those bells still in our ears, the rolling road wanders, like the rolling English drunkard, up hill and down dale through some of the linguistic thickets of the British countryside. Here are the words that bloom in the spring, the lexicon of love and the rising sap of passion. Here, too, flourish the *floribundas* and *flowering currants* of hothouse and herbaceous border. How *did* Erica find her way off the heath and into the garden? And spare a moment to listen to the *plunk, plunk* of axe on bark as the roots of the ancient terminology of the woodsman's craft are laid bare.

Meanwhile, high above, soars a hawk, poised to *stoop* before being returned to her *jesses*. We follow the trail of writers T. H. White and Barry Hines, whose stories of wild falcons tamed inspired generations of readers with a fascination for the ancient and bloody sport of falconry, yet one which has given the English language some of its loveliest words.

"We'll weather the weather, whatever the weather, whether we like it or not!" runs the old rhyme, and there are still few subjects on which the British are better able to wax lyrical than the ways of the weather. But do you know what a *willy-willy* is, and how you would recognize it? We end our country wander as the leaves are turning and the nights are drawing in with some thoughts on the fall of the leaf—and an ode to autumn.

" "

Writes of Spring

As the new year frosts are melted by warming days and the sun's narrow angle widens to a higher more theatrical spotlight, the countryside yields up its stark and brown colours and almost imperceptibly fringes off into green.

The great Victorian poet Gerard Manley Hopkins famously wrote:

> Nothing is so beautiful as spring—
> When weeds, in wheels, shoot long and lovely and lush ...

Or, as the musical *Seven Brides for Seven Brothers* more demotically and certainly more tunefully has it:

> Oh the farmyard is busy/in a regular tizzy/and the obvious reason is because of the season./Ma Nature's lyrical/with her yearly miracle: Spring, Spring, Spring ...

To celebrate the start of the growing year, *Word of Mouth* invited countrywoman Pam Ayres to reflect on the vernal vocab. 'I suppose I think of the ploughed fields with a lovely mist of green as it all starts to shoot up. And I think of the hawthorn, which is such a lovely shade of green at this time of the year.' In fact, that sense of burgeoning newness and freshness lies at the heart of the list of spring words—verbs like *fertilize* and *fructify* and adjectives like *fecund* and *fruitful*. It is a spirit that Pam Ayres celebrates with a deft pun in one of her poems:

I am a bunny rabbit, sitting in me hutch,
I like to sit up this end,
I don't care for that end much.
I'm glad tomorrow's Thursday
'Cos with a bit of luck
As far as I remember
That's the day they pass the buck.

Broody is how hens, rather than rabbits, are said to turn when the mating call goes out, and it prompts a memory of the farmyards of Pam's youth: 'When I think of the word *broody*, I think of lovely big Rhode Island Red chickens.' She recalls the spectacular sight of a hen with a great crowd of chicks round her, 'but it was always irritating if one of them went broody!' And Pam points out that *broody* is often used—somewhat jocularly—to describe a young woman in a certain condition: 'you'd look at each other at school and say, "Oh yes, she's getting broody."'

Pam Ayres has a sort of daisychain of words with springtime connections, and top of the list comes *burgeoning*: it suggests a nice urgency and upthrust, she reckons. Then comes *succour*, in the sense of nurturing and supporting. '*Fruitful* is another simple word I like very much; it's quite feminine: a *fruitful* woman. I can just see her in a flowery frock enormously pregnant.' In fact, *pregnant* is far too formal a term for the village fruitfulness Pam Ayres remembers from her childhood: 'People usually said "she was *expecting*", or *in the family way*, or *radiant*—she's looking *radiant*.'

Radiant women, *broody* women, young men's fancy on the prowl—the pulse of a country spring was enough to make a young girl's blood race: Pam remembers going to the local dance, the Wantage 'hop', 'where you'd give each other the *glad eye*'.

But there is one strange spring-word that forever has a particular resonance for her. It was uttered during a flower-arranging demonstration that she was attending, given by a young man—'a rather affected young man, I have to say'. Having constructed a magnificent spread of fresh blooms, to the accompaniment of a continuous suggestive patter ('it was very *juicy* the way he described it all'), the young man added, with a nudge and maybe half a wink, 'Be sure, ladies, that your stems are *turgid*.'

'*Turgid*—it always makes me smile,' adds Pam Ayres, 'and it always stuck in my mind. I can't think why!'

A Rose by Any Other Name

'Daisies pied and violets blue', wrote Shakespeare, 'paint the meadow with delight', and it is an eternal truth that the beauty of flowers, whether wild or cultivated, has done almost as much to inspire the poetical imagination as love itself. And a garden full of blooms is a garden packed with an abundance of lexical luxuriation: *aconites* and *adder's fern, Adam's needle* and *amaryllis, edelweiss* and *elderberry, narcissus* and *none-so-pretty*... right the way through to *zinnias* and *zebra grass*. The overwhelming richness of plant names is as heady as a sealed-up room stacked with orchids.

There are old names with a strongly international flavour like *ilex* and *lobelia*; there are Latinized names that define the plants according to the taxonomic system devised by the Swedish scientist Carl von Linné (almost always known by the Latinized form of his name Linnaeus, 1707–78) like *Eranthis hyemalis*. There are those names that bless the discoverer or propagator with immortality—*fuchsia* (after Leonhardt Fuchs) and *buddleia* (from the Revd Adam Buddle), and then there are the old English names that sing of an era of flower-dappled meadows and folk remedies. Open any compendium of flora and simply list the names, and the riches of poetic associations pour off the page. Little surprise that this nation's greatest poets have so often used floral metaphor and analogy.

This, at random from one classic botanical encyclopedia:

> Bear's breech, pheasant's eye, prickly thrift, alligator apple, chokeberry, milkweed, sneezewort, fairy moss, blessed thistle, bloodberry, devil's apple, dropwort, farewell-to-spring, treasure-flower, hedge hyssop, dutchman's breeches, lad's love, lady's mantle, toadflax, codlins and cream, good king henry, pearl everlasting...

'The standing objection to botany', wrote the Revd Gilbert White in his celebrated study of the fauna and flora of the peaceful little Hampshire parish of Selborne, published in the otherwise revolutionary year of 1789, 'has been that it is a pursuit that amuses the fancy and exercises the memory, without improving the mind or advancing any real knowledge: and, where the science is carried no further than a mere systematic classification, the charge is but too true.' Thus we should be wary of merely luxuriating in the linguistic pleasures of such resonant folk names as those quoted above. As Gilbert White says: 'The botanist that is desirous of wiping off this aspersion should be by no means content with a list of *names*; he should study plants philosophically, should investigate the laws of vegetation, should examine the powers and virtues of efficacious herbs, should promote their cultivation.' In other words, dividing up the plant world by name, the science of botanical taxonomy, is not enough, he says. 'Not that system is by any means to be thrown aside; without system the field of Nature would be a pathless wilderness: but system should be subservient to, not the main object of, pursuit.'

However, our subject here is not botany but language; and the considerable diversity of ways in which plants are defined—with many different names for the same species, acquired across diverse cultures, some names pseudo-scientific, others renamed following later reclassification—offers a fascinating study in its own right and unlocks doors onto a number of worlds and histories.

How far back can one trace what we call our flora? Gardening writer Robin Lane-Fox claims one of the oldest names goes back to the thirteenth century BC, halfway through the second millennium, and thus three and a half thousand years old. It is that harbinger of spring that carpets public parks, arriving with the daffodils and hyacinths to daub the still long, wet grass of winter with brush-strokes of yellow and purple. It is the humble *crocus*.

The name *crocus* comes down to us via Greek—*krokos*—probably originally from the Hebrew term for the flower, *karkom*, which is in turn related to the Arabic for saffron, *kurkum*, itself the product of the autumn-flowering crocus (botanical name *Crocus sativus*). But the real origins of *crocus*, according to Robin Lane-Fox, are to be found much earlier, along a linguistic historical route that lay through Mesopotamia and came ultimately from India. 'Wall-paintings found on the Greek island of Thera and dating from between 1600 and 1400 BC show the crocus, and the name originates further to the east well before then.'

The naming of plants, however, has been in very many cases far more recent and far more mundane. There are literally hundreds of species that simply bear the names of the man or woman who identified the genus or the variety. Surf the compendious classifications of plants listed on the Internet by gardeners inordinately proud of the multitude of varieties to be found in their back patch, and you can find whole genealogies of such names: *hudsonia* and *kochia, howea, kohleria, huntleya, kleinia,* and the well-known Scottish cousins *jamesia, stewartia,* and *gordonia.*

Some, like *fuchsia* or *buddleia,* are familiar enough and their patrons well known. But rather like the long-forgotten nobility memorialized on ornate tombs in country churches, many of these often resonantly named flowers have become quite detached from the person who identified them. This is the stuff of the imagination. Could one perhaps construct a murder mystery in which the man who lent his name to the lemon-yellow buttercup *F. M. Burton* that disappears after four years' growth was somehow mixed up with the perennial forget-me-not *Brunnera macrophylla* 'Betty Bowring'? Betty Bowring... Who she? And what relation is *Dianthus* 'Mrs Sinkins' to *Dianthus* 'Gran's Favourite'?

Often in the plant-naming business it is not so much a separate species that bears the name of its discoverer as what is known as 'the *cultivar* name'. Names of new varieties have to be approved by an official naming committee who will validate them. So Robin Lane-Fox cites the example of the variety of sisyrinchium called 'Mrs Spivey'. 'This was a form that arose in somebody's garden and was named after their friend Mrs Spivey because it was distinctive. But it wasn't a new species so it was granted a new *cultivar* name.'

It is the sad fate of the gentleman who gave his name to that hardy rock plant with myriad purple flowers that we know as *aubretia* that, in the English-speaking world at least, his fame is forever compromised. Claude Aubriet was an eighteenth-century

French painter famous for his pictures of flowers and animals who died in 1742 and whose name is commemorated in the Latinized classification of the Purple Rock Cress, or *Aubrieta deltoidea*. But as linguists frequently observe, his position as a hero of horticulture has been nibbled away by the inability of English-speakers to get their tongues round French. So *aubretia* has the slightly dubious distinction of being one of the very few words in the language whose mispronunciation has become not only accepted, but regularized: *aubrieta* [oːbʀiːˈetə] has become *aubretia* [obˈriːʃə]. As the keen gardener and distinguished writer Dr Germaine Greer lamented one year while examining a particularly splendid display at the Chelsea Flower Show: 'If you actually pronounce it correctly, OR-BREE-AY-TA, gardeners will giggle because you're being pedantic and foolish—so poor old Aubriet has lost his plant!"

'Gardeners abuse language frightfully,' adds Dr Greer, 'and the word they abuse the most is *blue*'. She says that, for the horticulturalist, colour is a fairly approximate matter when it comes to description: '*Blue* in gardener's-speak means anything from 'puce' to 'purple', and as for *scarlet*, they keep calling plants 'scarlet' that are in fact the colour of liver!'

Latin or pseudo-Latin dominates the naming of plants. We saw how names like *Howe, Gordon,* and *Stewart,* not to mention the good Revd Buddle's, became 'Latin' by the addition of an ending in *-ia* or *-ea* or simply *-a*. The relation of Latin to the English language has always been one of superiority. In the Middle Ages, while demotic speakers were quite happy to converse in Old English and then in Middle English, the scholarly language in which books were written, and indeed in which scholars could even converse aloud, was Latin. Additionally, French was the language of the medieval court, and so it was not uncommon for an educated man or woman to be trilingual. But gradually, the demotic English became the only language in which to express even ideas, helped along in no small measure by the Reformation and the translation of the Bible into English. Science remained, however, the last bastion of Latin usage amongst the educated classes, and it was not until the time of Sir Isaac Newton that science began to abandon Latin, his early work (like his *Philosophiae naturalis principia mathematica* of 1687) being written in the classical language, for example, and his later *Opticks* (1704) in English.

But science persisted in looking upon Latin as both a universally understood way of describing its mechanisms and a worthy linguistic source when inventing new names for newly discovered compounds, properties and species. Botany is no exception. Linnaeus devised his genus and specie ('binomial') system of classifying all living organisms, including plant types, in a way that could be unambiguous and internationally comprehensible. But, as Robin Lane-Fox points out, the so-called 'Latin' of plant names is really what he calls 'dog-Latin', 'with a bit of Latin pun or Latin description thrown in. New Latin has been added, fights have taken place to rename things after Latin that existed before somebody thought their name existed: these names are going round and round.'

To end with, two examples of how this plant-naming merry-go-round operates. In recent years, there was an official move to change the name of the popular flower the *chrysanthemum* to the more 'accurate' *dendranthemum*. 'This was the most unpopular move made in Britain for about a hundred years,' Lane-Fox says, 'and the pundits—who are always investigating naming—had to give way to popular fury, even though, technically, they were right because it was a *dendranthemum*; it is an earlier name.'

On the other hand, a name change that has taken place successfully and without causing much stir occurred in the hothouse world of rose-growing, where *Rosa* 'Duchess of York' has lost its royal tag, to become simply *Rosa* 'Sunseeker'. 'I wouldn't like to hazard the reason,' concludes Lane-Fox, 'but it is slightly appropriate.'

" "

Woodcraft Folk

It was the great Italian Renaissance writer Dante Alighieri who wrote so movingly of the *selva oscura*—the 'dark wood' —of language. And there's no doubt that the image of the great dark forests of Europe into which medieval souls strayed with a stout heart played powerfully on the imagination of past generations whether in a literal or, as in Dante's case, a figurative one. Today, with our tidy plantations courtesy of the Forestry Commission, you have to try pretty hard to conjure up the terror that the medieval traveller felt, lost amid a dark and forbidding forest, prey to whatever outcasts and beasts lurked in the shadows of endless columns of tree trunks stretching far out across half of western Europe. Gone, then—at least in most of Britain—is the reality that Paolo Uccello painted so luminously in his medieval depictions of hunters in the forest.

And yet, tame they may be and riven with the sound of buzz-saws and distant motorway traffic, woods still abound across much of our land. And just as the creak, crack and crash of a falling tree has the power to catch the imagination as one of these great pieces of living history keels to the forest floor, so it comes as a powerful imaginative jolt to realize that down in the woods, the language and craft of felling is alive and well ... and some of it as old as the ancient trees themselves.

For Marcel Croiffet, a young forester at Bramshill in Hampshire, to talk even now, in the twenty-first century, of a tree that presents a real danger when it comes to be felled as *a widowmaker* is quite normal. Yet it has a poetry and a mythic quality that could come straight out of the pages of that great chronicler of Victorian rural life, the novelist Thomas Hardy.

Neither is it unusual, according to Marcel, for a forester to go into the woods looking for *wolf trees*. While perhaps evoking amongst the more imaginative a picture of those ancient dark European forests we referred to earlier, wolf trees are for the forester simply those that have a difficult or unpleasing shape in timber terms: perhaps very heavily branched or with multiple stems, making felling difficult.

These, though, are the wild trees, the grow-out-of-shape trees, the bad boys of the forest, and are dubbed *wolf trees* as a result. 'You might also hear them called *stag-headed* trees, which means that they have branches literally like a stag's horns,' adds Marcel Croiffet, with half a glance backwards to the forester's traditional proximity to the animal kingdom. 'The forester's vocabulary is rough and tough and close to nature.'

When he comes to fell a tree (and there is only that one word for the process, to *fell*), the forester cuts a wedge-shaped notch with his chainsaw, on one side of the trunk; this is the *gob*, a cut, perhaps unsurprisingly shaped like a crude mouth or 'gob' that will cause the tree to fall in the particular direction the forester wants: 'The tree always falls in the direction of the *gob*.' To lever the tree over he uses his *breaking bar*, and once the timber is on the ground, the woodsman will need to remove the branches. This process is known as *snedding*, a word that doesn't hide the rough angularity of its Old English origins (*snǣdan*) meaning 'to prune or divest of branches', in recorded use well over 400 years ago.

If the tree needs to have its branches removed while still standing, the process is then known as *brashing*, another centuries-old word that may well come from French, and the resultant litter on the forest floor is known, perhaps unsurprisingly, as *brash*. In Scotland, though, the word is *hag*. This has nothing to do with Macbeth's three old crones (a different origin) but sweeps in directly from the Old Norse, where a *hogg* was 'a cutting-blow, or strike'. Thus the Scots word *hag* came to mean 'a cutting, hewing or felling', and two centuries ago the term is recorded in the sense of 'a lot of felled wood'. Maybe Macbeth's blasted heath was covered in brushwood after all.

After all this colourful talk of *snedding* and *brashing*, of *wolf trees* and *widowmakers*, it comes as a bit of a twentieth-century let-down to learn from Marcel Croiffet that these days the pile of felled wood is just as likely not to be *brash* or *hag*, but something more redolent of the cash-and-carry, pick 'n' mix generation: *lop and top* is what most modern forestry manuals call the wood that falls to earth. And while a *sprag* is still the descriptive old word foresters use for a useful protruding branch at one end of a trunk (perhaps related to the *sprag* of wood that propped up a mine-workings—a pit prop), the modern hydraulic grapples that foresters attach to the felled trees have a distinctly unmedieval feel to them. They call them *clambunsculars*.

Sounds as though the 'dark wood of language' just got up to date.

" "

Flights of Fancy

Fifty years ago, the writer T. H. White, author of the Arthurian epic *The Sword in the Stone*, published a graphic account of the very real trials of his initiation into the ancient art of falconry. It was called *The Goshawk*, and it remains one of the most compelling modern insights into the strange chivalric world—and linguistic tradition—of man and wild beast:

> ... terrified, but still nobly and madly defiant, the eyas goshawk had arrived at my small cottage in his accursed basket ... a wild and adolescent creature ... He was born to fly, sloping sideways, free among the verdure of a Teutonic upland, to murder with fierce feet and to consume with that curved Persian beak, who now hopped up and down in the clothes basket with a kind of imperious precocity, the impatience of a spoiled but noble heir apparent to the Holy Roman Empire ...

Having received his goshawk in its basket direct from Germany, White sets to work training it to fly from his wrist and return—an arduous and long process. On the wrist the hawk is attached by leather thongs secured round its legs; more or less the first technical word White introduces us to is the name for these straps, known as *jesses*. The *Oxford English Dictionary* offers the full technical definition: 'A short strap of leather, silk, or other material, fastened round each of the legs of a hawk, usually bearing on its free end a small ring or *varvel* to which the swivel of the leash is attached.'

The modern word derives from Middle English *ges*, in turn a borrowing from Old French (*gez, getz*) which meant a 'cast' or 'throw'. Reaching back through the etymological mists, you find the bedrock of Latin *iactus* (thrown) famously memorialized in the original classical version of the phrase 'The die is cast'—*alea iacta est*.

The medieval French roots of *jess* are unsurprising, as Nick Kester, Secretary of the British Falconry Association, explained on *Word of Mouth*. Much of the terminology connected with falconry is Norman French in origin, because the sport was popular with the French court. And it is another French word that lies behind the name for the place where hawks were placed for moulting during the summer, a *mews*, because, according to Nick Kester, it is not usual to fly birds of prey at quarry all year round. The *mews* were originally the cages in which falcons were placed while undergoing their change of plumage, or moult, and as early as 1386 Geoffrey Chaucer, author of the *Canterbury Tales*, writes in the Squire's Tale how 'by her bed's head she made a Mew'. In turn, the name for the bird's temporary home during the moult came from the old French word for 'to moult', or 'undergo a change'—*muer*. *Mutatis mutandis* perhaps?

It makes you look at that desirable mews cottage in quite a different light, doesn't it? Perhaps not so surprising to learn, though, that what a sixteenth-century chronicler described as 'the kynges stable at Charynge Crosse, otherwise called the Mowse'—the Royal Mews in London—was built on the site of the cages in which the court formerly kept its hawks.

The art of falconry, however, dates from long before Henry or even the Normans set foot on English soil. As T. H. White points out, it is perhaps the oldest sport persisting in the world, an ancient Babylonian bas-relief showing a figure with a fist bearing a hawk that dates from over 3,000 years ago. 'Hawks were the nobility of the air, ruled by the eagle; they were the only creatures for which man had troubled to legislate,' writes White, observing that the medieval *Boke of St Albans* had laid down the accepted hierarchy of permitted birds. Thus eagles befitted monarchs and emperors, an earl could fly peregrines, goshawks were the province of ordinary yeomen, while a kestrel was worthy only of 'a knave'. (Strange coincidence that it is precisely this ancient hierarchy that resonates through the title of Barry Hines's modern classic novel that later became the film *Kes*, 'A Kestrel for a Knave').

Despite the observation by one fanatical falconer, the British character actor James Robertson Justice, that 'though it takes a comparatively short time to train a falcon, it takes about seven years to train a falconer', White's daily record of training his goshawk shows it to be a painful, day-by-day process.

The *austringer* (how alien these hawking terms seem to a twenty-first-century ear, ringing with echoes of nobilities lost in the passing of custom) is the formal name given to a keeper of goshawks, borrowed and Anglicized from an Old French word *ostruchier* meaning just that, an *ostour* being Old French for 'goshawk'). He (or she) must perform feats of considerable endurance, going regularly without any sleep whatsoever: 'The austringer', writes White,

> since he rode to battle in the train of William, had been accustomed to perform this feat for three nights every time he acquired a passage hawk. Man against bird, with God for an umpire they had sat each other out for three thousand years. The watching of hawks, the triumph over them ... the weary joy with which the succeeding capitulations of the enemy were noted one after the other, it was these things which ... I must try to remember.

Some of the vocabulary associated with falconry remains, like *austringer*, firmly locked into this tight little world. So a falconer will describe a bird who is ready to fly as *in yerk*. The word, says Nick Kester, is an 'untranslatable' term, maybe of Turkish origin, he wonders, though the *OED* suggests it to be Middle English. Certainly, in its obscure meaning of 'desire', *yerk* has long been associated with what Elizabethans knew as *Venerie*—hunting: 'Ciucius did much delight to goe on hunting, & had a fine *yeark* to kill the Bore & other uenerie in the mountaines' is recorded in 1577.

Whatever its origin, there is no mistaking the exhilarating sensation of holding a bird that is 'in desire' (so to speak) to soar from the wrist: 'You can tell a goshawk *in yerk* instantly by its attitude. They are actually nothing more than avian killing machines and when they are *in yerk* they look fantastic, just desperate to kill something.'

When airborne, the hawk will stand high above the earth ready to kill, descending like a precise arrow-shot on its prey: this vertical dive at quarry is known as a *stoop*. 'She waits', recorded James Robertson Justice in a long-forgotten conversation in the BBC archives, 'five hundred feet above your head; and then, once the grouse are flushed, she turns over in this breath-taking *stoop*, knocks one down, stone dead, a puff of feathers on the wind.' Although the action of the plunging hawk is essentially to *swoop* on its prey, the two terms should not be confused and for the true falconer, such a dive is always a *stoop*. Yet Nick Kester assures us that they excuse Shakespeare when he gives the following exchange to Ross and Macduff in *Macbeth*. Note how, immediately, Shakespeare sets the hunting imagery running (*on the quarry of these murder'd deer*) as Ross reports that all Macduff's family have been slain:

> MACDUFF: Your castle is surprised; your wife and babes
> Savagely slaughter'd: to relate the manner,
> Were, on the quarry of these murder'd deer,
> To add the death of you.
>
> MACDUFF: My children too?
>
> ROSS: Wife, children, servants, all
> That could be found.
>
> MACDUFF: And I must be from thence!
> My wife kill'd too?
> [...]
> All my pretty ones?
> Did you say all? O hell-kite! All?
> What, all my pretty chickens and their dam
> At one fell *swoop*?

But Nick Kester would still have preferred *stoop*.

Let us return to the words of T. H. White in *The Goshawk*. His is the chronicle of a love affair with a bird, a relationship of harsh training and gruelling living over a period of years that manages thoroughly to dissolve the gulf between the early 1950s when he was writing and the high-water mark of falconry, the Tudor period. This book, with its glorious casual use of words caked with the patina of history, has a powerful sense of past, weaving the lexicon of falconry throughout, and gathers together in his postscript a rich scatter of diary thoughts about the world of the hawk:

> Falconry is as old as Babylon. It has never been a dead sport, and is ... extraordinarily tenacious. To have existed since Babylon, it must have had a regular fount of sap in it. Even in the Second World War, the art managed to find a foot-hold. It was discovered

that small birds were lethal to aircraft. So ... the business of the Squadron-Leaders of the Falconry Squadron to train hawks [was] to keep little birds off airfields. The science was officially recognised, and it kept alive. But no hawk can be a pet. There is no sentimentality. One is matching one's mind against another mind with deadly reason and interest. It is a tonic for the less forthright savagery of the human heart.

Under the Weather

When that I was and a little tiny boy,
With hey, ho, the wind and the rain;
A foolish thing was but a toy,
For the rain it raineth every day.
   (Shakespeare, *Twelfth Night*)

With a climate as variable and as altogether interesting as the British, it is hardly surprising that weather not only absorbs an inordinate amount of conversation time and space in the press and on radio and television, but also mightily preoccupies our writers and poets. The BBC Radio 4 Shipping Forecast, with its mantra of *sea areas Dogger, Fisher, German Bight* and the rest, has exercised a curious fascination over the public and over composers and poets for years. The great Irish poet Seamus Heaney has written lines inspired by the forecast, and even the rock band Blur composed a song based around it.

On *Word of Mouth* we have examined weather words more

than once over the ten years of the programme's existence. The poet Maura Dooley memorably detailed the poetic lexicon of cloudscapes and gentle rain—*a soft day* she singled out as a peculiarly expressive Irish metaphor for that sort of gentle, drizzly atmosphere where the rain is more *sensed* than actually felt.

Helen Young, the broadcasting 'synoptic meteorologist' (as we are assured one should officially refer to her), uses *mizzle* these days to express that half-mist, half-drizzle. Though it is by no means a formal scientific term, *mizzle* is sufficiently widely accepted as to be found in specialist meteorological and geographical dictionaries. It has a splendid linguistic pedigree, with its roots deep in dialect and a history stretching back to the fifteenth century; a Dutch dialect verb, *miezelen* and a term from Low German, *miseln* or *museln,* mean roughly the same thing.

Rain, not unexpectedly, occupies a major place in the British weather lexicon:

> The rain is raining all around,
> It falls on field and tree,
> It rains on the umbrellas here,
> And on the ships at sea.

wrote Robert Louis Stevenson in his wonderful *Child's Garden of Verses*, and there are more than sixty entries listed in the *Oxford Dictionary of Quotations* under 'rain'. It is ubiquitous, penetrating, one might say, like a good British *drizzle* (or maybe *Scotch mist*). *Drizzle*, unlike *mizzle*, has a precise definition ('light continuous rainfall', says the meteorological dictionary, 'the droplets of which are less than one hundred microns in diameter, i.e. like a fine spray'). 'All meteorological phrases, like *rain* have clearly defined definitions,' confirmed Helen Young; 'for example, a *shower* is rain from a certain type of cloud' ('often associated with a *cumulonimbus* cloud form' according to the official definition), 'and even within *rain* there's *moderate* rain, *heavy* rain, and *light* rain'.

As well as the *mizzle* and *drizzle* we have already talked about, *moisture, dampness, wetness, dankness, precipitation, shower, downpour, drencher, soaker, cloud-burst, foul weather, monsoon, torrents, spitting,* and *The Rains* make a real splash in Roget's *Thesaurus* under the innocent notion of 'rain'. For the record, the word *rain* is a good old drop of Old English (with an Old Teutonic root)—*reġn* or *rēn*.

> The rain it raineth on the just
> And also on the unjust fella:
> But chiefly on the just, because
> The unjust steals the just's umbrella.
>
> Baron Charles Bowen (1835-96)

As a weather forecaster and a scientist, Helen Young has to be careful to distinguish amongst all these different types of precipitation, yet she must also make her summaries clear and understandable to listeners and viewers for whom a *downpour* may be more expressive than the more technical *heavy shower*.

> There are lots of things I would love to be able to say, like *explosive cyclogenesis*, which I think is a fantastic phrase and which basically means it's going to be extremely wet and windy because we've got an area of low pressure developing really quickly. Another is *castellanus cloud*, which is medium-level cloud giving a few spots of rain and it can signify the start of some thunder activity—that type of phrase I would love to be able to say!

Castellanus or *castellatus* cloud, as you might deduce, is cloud which towers into castles in the sky 'with cumiliform protuberances in the form of turrets'.

And therein lies the linguistic allure of weather words: *castellanus... turrets: castles in the sky* quite literally it seems, though composed of nothing more substantial than a mass of water droplets.

> Great is the sun, and wide he goes
> Through empty heaven without repose;
> And in the blue and glowing days
> More thick than rain he showers his rays.

Robert Louis Stevenson's childhood world is full of delight in the weather. His summer sun is a smiling, serene 'golden face' that brings fruitfulness—'the gardener of the World', he calls him. From her strictly scientific standpoint, Helen Young nonetheless also takes huge pleasure from the linguistic riches the weather brings—the *haar*, a cold coastal sea fog that drifts onto the coast of Scotland and England in spring and early summer, is one she particularly treasures. Likewise its synonyms, the *sea-fret* and *sea-roke*, and the adjacent colloquial Yorkshire adjective *parky*, used to describe a 'nippingly cold' day, according to the dictionary.

Roke and *haar*, incidentally, both reflect the ancient Scandinavian influence on the north-east of England—as so do many dialectal terms in that corner of the United Kingdom, *roke* ('drizzling rain') being derived from Old Scandinavian *rauk*, and *haar* from an Old Norse word meaning 'hoar' or 'hoary'—*hárr*.

> O you that are so strong and cold,
> O blower, are you young or old?
> Are you a beast of field and tree,
> Or just a stronger child than me?
>   O wind, a-blowing all day long,
>   O wind, that sings so loud a song!

Winds have traditionally been the bringers of misfortune to man—a *lazy wind*, according to Helen Young, is one which is especially bitingly cold 'because it lazily goes *through* you, not *round* you'—and the crofters of the Western Isles speak in some awe of the *equinoctial gales* that sweep across the bleak landscape in autumn. Beyond our shores, they actually give their winds names, not as—famously—in the song where 'they call the wind *Maria*', but by names like *mistral*, the violent, cold, northerly wind blowing off the Alps and funnelling down the valley of the river Rhône, meaning 'master wind', and the *sirocco*, a hot desert wind of the Mediterranean. Australia, incidentally, has three strikingly named winds: the tornado-like *willy-willy*, also known as *cock-eyed bob*, from Western Australia, the cold *southerly buster* of New South Wales, and the hot dusty *brickfielder* that always precedes it.

The story of how the *brickfielder* got its name is a curious one. Apparently the wind is named after Brickfield Hill, a piece of high ground in what is now central Sydney where, until the mid-nineteenth century, there was a large brickworks. In Sydney at that time a sudden squally wind from the south, bringing relief at the end of a hot day, but sometimes characterized also by an accompanying storm of brickdust, became known as a *brickfielder*. By a curious inversion the name was subsequently used across other parts of New South Wales and Victoria for a *hot*, dusty wind. It was even commemorated in verse:

> My Jenny dear, that many a year
> So well hast done for me,
> Come in, here comes a brickfielder,
> Let's have a pot of tea!

But, for the real evocative poetry to be found in weather words, little surpasses the folk names for clouds. The scientific names can themselves be poetic—we referred earlier to towering *castellanus* cloud, and there is a rhythm and a sussuration to *stratocumulus* and *cirrostratus* that has its own magic—but, says Michael Rosen, the vividly descriptive *mackerel* sky, where the clouds resemble the mottling of a fish's back, or the high-level, ice-crystal clouds known evocatively as *mares' tails* contain a poetry all their own as they presage the wind and rain that are bound to follow. As the old saying goes:

> Mackerel sky and mares' tails
> Make tall ships carry low sails.

" "

Fall Tales

It is a curious and yet eternal fact about language that deep down in the business of communication, far removed from the surface traffic of irregular verbs and split infinitives and sentence structure, lie the unwritten rules. They are a sort of web, a substructure that in some very substantial ways controls the shape of our utterance, but which is hard to define. Poets mine it richly, sometimes bringing it right to the surface so that it becomes audible and even visible. We are talking here of rhythm, rhyme, beat, pace, patterning, assonance, alliteration and song. Advertisers, too, know it all to well (*On and on and on—Ariston, the appliance of science* both using assonance and even rhyme to sell, heaven knows, washing machines).

So consider, in this chapter full of country words, two terms that outwardly mean much the same, yet have found their ways into different parts of the English lexicon, and different corners of English-speaking civilization. They are two words with different weights and rhythms, with divergent resonances and secondary meanings; and in many respects it is that secondary web of usage that determines how we use them.

The two words denote what the *Oxford English Dictionary*, a little prosaically, describes as the 'third season of the year': *autumn* and *fall*. Two little words that say the same thing, yet are not quite synonymous, or at least do not possess what linguists call the same 'distribution'. That is to say: you cannot interchange them at will in all contexts. So we may happily describe the Queen as *in the autumn of her years*, yet it would clearly be quite wrong in this context to use *fall*.

In part, the division is a matter of usage, so *Autumn Sale* sounds 'correct' to a British ear, and Americans would not be surprised to see *Fall Reductions* posted in a downtown US store window.

And that is, of course, how we rather crudely define the two words—on the *sidewalk* vs. *pavement* principle. (And here, a little diversion, because, as usual, scratch a truism and a lot of the truth ebbs away. So Americans do happily say *pavement*—it is merely that they mean the road-surface, or the carriageway. And as for *sidewalk*, it is neither perverse nor unique but belongs to a whole family of US *-walk* words denoting pathways of various types— *crosswalk* for 'pedestrian-crossing' and *boardwalk* for a slatted wooden pier are just two.)

So *fall* is the American for what the British call *autumn*. Certainly the *OED* does note that *fall* is 'chiefly US, now rare in English literary use'. Yet linguistic equivalences are never quite as simple as they seem—just try exchanging some of Dr Roget's synonyms and you soon realize how not-quite-synonymous they are. And as well as simple meaning, it is as much the rhythm and word-length that we mentioned at the beginning that has a part to play. No word operates solo. So *Fall Sale* might well sound inharmonious, yet *Fall Reductions* not so. Conversely, Keats did not—could not—have written his famous ode *To the Fall*. Certainly, at the time he was writing at the beginning of the nineteenth century, it would have been too ambiguous, as *the Fall* would almost certainly have been interpreted with a Christian connotation—*The Fall of Man*.

Likewise, *To Fall* would not have worked either. The expression does not function properly without the definite article. *To Autumn* is good English; *To the Autumn* works well too; yet, as we have seen, neither *To the Fall* nor *To Fall* would have been on John Keats's list of top titles.

Thus the distinctions between *fall* and *autumn* are much more than purely the American and British expressions of the same idea. Their meanings do not have the same distributions, and function in different ways. Nor do the two words display the same 'hidden' properties—their rhythms differ (monosyllable against disyllable) and their resonances are very dissimilar.

Autumn is only autumn, unless used as a metaphor. *Fall*, in the sense of 'the third season of the year', was originally not so much a metaphor as the stem of a longer description, *the fall of the leaf*. Then a process occurred much like the actual physical process of abscission, whereby the stem of the leaf becomes blocked, sap no longer circulates (producing luminous colours in the process), and the leaf dies and falls. So too, with the expression *fall of the leaf*, the trailing, cumbersome, flapping vane *of the leaf* finally died and dropped off. *Fall* now stands alone, meaning the season following summer.

Fall of the leaf is first recorded in 1545. *Autumn*, which started out on its journey north as the French word *autompne* (compare modern French *automne*) was a fourteenth-century import. Geoffrey Chaucer, author of *The Canterbury Tales* and many other masterpieces written in the language of his age (he died in 1400), which was known as Middle English, chose to make use of the new word: 'Autumn cometh again, heavy with apples' he writes in his poem *Boethius*. *Fall* goes on carrying its fall-of-the-leaf connotation quite comfortably through the Middle Ages, still cropping up in this sense as late on as Elizabethan times, when westcountryman Sir Walter Ralegh wrote of 'Fancie's spring, but sorrow's *fall*'.

Autumn, the upstart import, was unambiguous; soon it began to supplant the cumbersome *fall of the leaf* and the ambiguous *fall*. Except in America. It was carried there with the Pilgrim Fathers and took ready root on the new continent. Diana Trefry, Editorial Director for Collins English Dictionaries, suggests that *fall* may have been preferred owing to the new settlers' preoccupation with matters of the land, the growing and handling of timber. 'Trees were important to them,' she says and *fall* might well not have presented the sorts of ambiguity that it did in the old continent. Maybe too there was a regional factor that favoured a particular use amongst the communities most numerous amongst the first settlers.

In Britain, *fall* continued to find favour particularly with poets because of its ambiguity and resonances. So Dryden, writing in the late seventeenth century, uses it to mean 'autumn', but with satiric intent:

What great crowds of patients the town-doctor kills,
Or how, last *fall*, he raised the weekly bills ...

And Gerard Manley Hopkins, a hundred years later in his poem 'Spring and Fall', writes:

> Margaret, are you grieving
> Over Goldengrove unleaving?
> Leaves, like the things of man, you
> With your fresh thoughts care for, can you?

Chapter 10
The Word Has Landed

It's DEPARTURE LOUNGE TIME, but before we go, a quick trip round some of the ways the principal tongue of the British Isles is taking on flavours from other corners of the globe. Strapping our seatbelt tightly across our waist, returning our seats to the upright position, and stowing our tray-tables (in pursuit of the wording of airline safety announcements), we take a quick flight to Cardiff and the South Wales valleys to hear from so-called *Wenglish*-speakers the distinctive flavour of the English of Dylan Thomas and Neil Kinnock.

Then it's a 5,000-mile trip to upstate New York, where David Barnhart, a lexicographer with his finger on the latest language to emerge from the powerhouse of verbal invention, the USA, has been eavesdropping on what's hot language-wise round the water cooler.

Last stop for this volume is Sydney, and a brief history of Australian English, from *kangaroo* to *cobber*. Now that's something to talk about round the *barbie* this *arvo*, a full *tinnie* ice-cold from the *eskie* in your hand. Cheers!

" "

Seated One Day at the Mouse-Mat

Ah, a snoozy afternoon in the open-plan office! Heads down behind *dividers*, flat screens glowing in the half-light cast by the regulation *uplighters*, nimble fingers tip-tapping their way across smudged and smeary keys of once ivory keyboards. In the corner, a yucca—can we run to that?—reaches towards filtered daylight behind the venetian blinds. Headsets bob assent to near-silent conversations at the other end of a scratchy line from head office. The water cooler gurgles volcanically with each dispensed carton of fluid fuel. Watch it! Here comes Ms Manager, checking the staff. Or indulging, as we like to say these days (because we're ultra cool and have logged on to that Californian website where they list these things), in a bit of *MBWA*. *MBWA*? No idea? Hold on— explanation anon. But the word round the water cooler is that Ms M hasn't really got enough to keep her busy. The ritual walkabout fills up another little quarter-hour before the four o'clock meeting: what we call *MBWAWP*...

It's the scenario of every office worker in the country, give or take a yucca or two. And—sent up rotten on telly in the hit BBC sitcom of 2001 *The Office*—the rituals of contemporary desk dramas hit home with unerring accuracy. As the MBAs arrive with the spring and new business gospels spread, teleconferenced from Tallahassee, like an information-technological gold rush, so does the jargon of the new office environment. Oh yes, *MBWA*. That's one of the favourite techniques: *Management By Walking About*. And how many executive washroom users have *you* noticed putting it into practice recently, then? And *MBWAWP*? Well, that's just what people who haven't got their MBA yet do (*Management By Walking About Without Purpose*).

I used to think that all these bits of mashed-up business jargon only really existed in email-land, or on that website. But no. Overheard—well, she was *shouting* down her moby— just the other day in an airport departure lounge: 'Well, I have to tell you that I have *issues* with that. No. There are several issues that I want to *bring to the table*. Can you *source* that information ...' And so on and so forth. People were actually *conversing* like a textbook. In fact, when *Word of Mouth* ran one of our periodic items on the latest state of play in office talk, we were sent several versions— we should call them *iterations*, I think, out of courtesy—of a 'random bullshit generator' currently doing the rounds, in which a grid of hot, yet meaningless, terms could be read off in any direction and seem to make some sort of sense—or nonsense.

Sadly, they are never quite as funny as the real thing, as evidenced by this (true) extract from a BBC internal circular email about

> the creation of pan-BBC delivery teams, supported by a small outward-facing enabling centre. This central team will be the axis by which all activities are prioritized to maintain our strategic focus, to manage key partnership projects, and to have an effective support and communication service for the devolved teams ... Each will 'own' the vision ...

Blah blah blah. Just listen to those terms cascade! And then cascade them to your teams: delivery team ... outward-facing ... enabling ... central team (again) ... axis ... prioritized ... strategic focus ... partnership ... effective support ... devolved teams (again again) ... 'own' the vision ...

Frankly, these days, if you don't network with your team and prioritize your strategic focus, then you've *missed the clue train*. 'I think I heard this on the radio and I immediately wrote down a few notes.' The attentive listener is David Barnhart, an American lexicographer who has for many years been keeping a watchful ear and eye on the latest language to emerge on a multitude of different stages of activity in the United States. His findings he publishes every three months as a digest called *The Barnhart Dictionary Companion*, listing source and—as far as possible—the first date the term was used.

And then I went into a very large electronic databank and I found out that it is not just *clue train* but a whole slew of idiomatic expressions such as *get on the clue train, ride the clue train, take a ride on the clue train, buy a ticket for the clue train,* or *miss the clue train*. And *the clue train* is just 'being up to date' about attitudes, issues and conditions around us. But it's a clever, colourful expression.

It is impossible to keep abreast of the vast stock of fashionable buzzwords constantly flowing from the portals of US industry and from MBA courses the world over. Collect them up one day and the very next another tide will have washed up a further tangle of fashionable business flotsam along the linguistic highwater line. So you can be sure that, as soon as the canteen supervisor or the washroom supremo starts talking about *Chinese walls*, and *glass ceilings*, and *having issues* with something or other, the boardroom have long ceased finding them useful. It's rather like a linguistic version of label one-upmanship: those lower down the food chain are always playing catch-up with head office. (Did you spot the jargon there, incidentally?)

The rate of turnover seems easily accounted for. Seated for

hours at desks and in meetings, head hunched over computer screen, hand hardwired to the mouse, the modern office worker is permanently on-line, both literally and metaphorically. The language has simply to tumble onto the screen in an email from someone up the chain—the boss, the boss's boss, the Big Boss, or from that Californian website, and the would-be boss in the Hugo Boss suit has logged it, filed it and is ready to drop it into his next smartass conversation at the water cooler.

And the terms manifest their sources. Technology and computers unsurprisingly are favourites, with all the forms based on *cyber* being pretty well top of the tree. (*Cybernetics*, 'the theory or study of communication and control in living organisms or machines', was coined in 1948 by an American mathematician, Norbert Wiener, based on the Greek word *kubernetes* meaning 'steersman'. Dozens of compounds have flowed forth since, such that the prefix *cyber-* is now loosely attached to almost anything referring to computers; c*yberspace*—the root of all the current cybercoinings—was invented in 1982 by the science fiction writer William Gibson only to be quickly copied—*cyberpunk* followed in 1983, *cybernaut* in 1990, and *cybercafé* in 1994.)

So current hot terms from the desktop include *cyberslacker* (too much surfing, not enough real work), *cyberpiracy* (theft of intellectual property via the internet) and *cybersquat* (the unauthorized occupation of an internet domain). These last terms illustrate another favourite coining technique, where an existing word is yoked to another (or a prefix like *cyber-*) to form an attractive and buzzy compound. So colleagues—never oneself, natch—are accused of *multishirking*.

Another little detour, here, by way of explanation. Because the genesis of these terms is so rapid and competitive, they are inevitably endlessly self-referential. Great piles of jargon result, each coining attempting to cap the previous one, in a form of competitive linguistic duel. So *multishirking* is a witty modification of that bane of modern office practice, *multiskilling*, that arose when one person seated at a computer took over the functions of many traditional office staff. (So one *multiskilled* operative could draft, type, and send letters and memos, design presentations for the board meeting, do the sums, draft the tables, and make the coffee. No, just joking there. That's what the office junior does.)

If, on the other hand, you are failing to perform all these miracles simultaneously, you are said to be *multishirking*. David Barnhart sets the scene:

> What happens is that you're sitting there at your computer and you're bored to tears with your assignment—your children might be doing this to you too if they're working on their homework—and they decide that they need a little vacation from homework and they slip over and they play Minesweeper or Solitaire or Freecell or something of that nature—and they see you coming and they can get right back to their work with the push of a button.

It is all too familiar; that spreadsheet for the finance meeting tomorrow where the figures (or, in true financial jargon, the *numbers*) are not adding up but dance merrily across the screen as you desperately scroll up and down. It is just so easy, isn't it, to slip away to the Accessories menu and those silly games. But—joy—that spreadsheet is just one keystroke away (another favourite there, *keystroke*): 'It's been called the *Boss Key*,' says Barnhart. 'When the boss is coming you push the Boss Key and you're back to work before the boss comes and looks over your shoulder.' Those who indulge in this behaviour, he says, are called *multishirkers* and a verb even exists, to *multishirk*. As for MBWAWP

(*Management By Walking About Without Purpose*), 'that's the boss's form of multishirking!'

Another favourite way of cooking up new words for the world of work is to employ metaphors, frequently involving a pun and preferably drawn from fields of reference as far removed as possible from the techie, results-driven arena of the business plan. So David Barnhart's *Dictionary Companion* lists *working-wounded*, *the prison-industrial* complex, and *accordion scheduling*:

> That's a term that's been kicking around for a while. I have evidence for it at least as early as March 1999. It is the use of workers—such as part-time employees—whose work schedule can be adjusted (squeezed and expanded like an accordion) to meet changing labour requirements. And it's reminiscent of such innovations as *just-in-time publishing* or *just-in-time manufacturing*.

Finally, a couple of usages which capture in their imagery, I think, the essence of the modern office. And they are related. Picture the scene: the open-plan office: row upon row of staff sit, locked to their screens, headset clamped over the ears. (We could be anywhere, but the main office at the *Oxford English Dictionary* is quite like this too.) Near-silence reigns. In fact, you could hear a pin drop. And thus was born *pin-drop syndrome*, where such is the absence of whirring machinery or the clatter of traditional typewriters that any slight disturbance of the quiet causes people to look up, stare around, and stop work. This phenomenon received huge publicity when the BBC decided to pipe noises into one of its otherwise near-silent office areas in order to achieve higher levels of concentration. The press derided the Corporation for it, yet the existence of the term on David Barnhart's database proves that it is more widespread—and of more concern—than we may have been led to believe.

And if you are listening out for that metaphorical pin to drop, what happens when it does is known as *prairie-dogging*. The words betray their origins in middle America. The image transferring from the wide open grain-lands of the United States to the humdrum environs of the call centre, the insurance office, and, heaven help us, even these days the BBC, is the habit of dogs to act in unison. Just as dogs on the prairie all start up together at a sudden unexpected noise, so do the denizens of the open-plan office, disturbed by a sudden irruption of noise. Heads go up, backs straighten from screens, eyes swivel—that's *prairie-dogging*. Sort of makes the office sound fun, doesn't it?

Oh, well, time to water the yucca plant, I suppose.

In-Flight Entertainment

You know the moment: you've found your seat, you've stuffed your bag in the overhead rack. The magazine you were going to read you've left in your bag and you're wondering if you can get up again to dig it out. The little boy in the seat behind, your travel companion for the next seven hours, is pummelling the back of your seat with his feet. What's that in the pocket in front of you? Behind the copy of the latest well-thumbed copy of *Air Smiles*. Oh boring—it's the in-flight safety card, complete with those weird pictures of people 'adopting the brace position'. You start to read:

> If you are sitting in an exit row and you cannot understand this card or cannot see well enough to follow these instructions please tell a crew member.

This sentence is taken from the safety instructions issued by United Airlines on their transatlantic flights during the 1990s. Does it make sense? Surely if you 'cannot understand this card', then how can you understand it well enough to know that you could 'tell a crew member' that you 'cannot understand this card'? As for not seeing 'well enough to follow these instructions', then presumably you wouldn't be able to read that there's something you could do about not being able to read them.

There seems to be a principle here: the harder the service industries try to tell us how helpful they are, the harder it becomes to understand what they're on about. In the case of air travel, we can detect a certain nervousness in the language we meet.

This is how we're greeted as we're getting on board:

> Ladies and gentlemen, as you're taking your seats we must inform you that all hand baggage is to be safely stowed either under the seat in front of you or in the overhead bin prior to departure.

We're so used to hearing this sort of thing as part of the musak and airline self-promotion that it's easy to overlook how peculiar it is. Take: 'We must inform you that all hand baggage is to be safely stowed' etc. This is really saying: 'You must stow your baggage where we tell you', but the *must* is attached to the idea of us informing you, rather than to you being obliged to stow your bags. This is a way of making it sound less commanding, as if they're saying, 'We're the ones following orders here, not you.'

Fans of the passive mood will also notice the wording: 'baggage is to be stowed'. What a miraculous construction this is. The person who has to stow the baggage is invisible. Quite simply it will be done. No one here is telling you that you should do it. This too sounds as though it was written with the intention of making it sound less like a directive.

By the time you settle in your seat you should be feeling reassured that you're doing things as they should be done, but not because some domineering bossyboots has ordered you to.

And so back to those safety instructions. A particular kind of delicacy seems to fit the bill here. No one is going to remind you that in certain circumstances there is no chance of survival. Instead, we are informed of various bits of apparatus: a life jacket (with whistle), an oxygen mask that drops out of a panel above our heads, chutes that we will be able to slide down, and, of course, exits.

The airlines have very little leeway in how these instructions are written. The Civil Aviation Authority has very strict guidelines. Even so, you can't help but wonder why a child's life raft is described by some airlines as *a separate flotation aid for infants and children*. According to Patrick Hoffman, a professional writer of instructions, the overriding intention in the minds of the airline companies is: how can we temper any possibility of people freaking out? In other words, the term *separate flotation aid* is intended to sound more reassuring than a *life raft*. It may or may not be reassuring, but it's certainly harder to understand.

Hoffman has spotted another message between the lines of the instructions. In times of emergency on a plane, an announcement will be made to this effect: 'Ladies and gentlemen, please. The captain has informed us that due to [whatever], we will be making an emergency landing.' This tells us that the captain is in charge. He's the one responsible for the plane. This is a kind of delaying action, put in place of a direct statement like: 'We are experiencing extreme turbulence.' Hoffman sees that kind of language as the opposite of technical instructions, where there is a need to simplify and speed up the language. The job of technical language is to make remembering and digesting as quick as possible, whereas flight instructions seem intent, he thinks, on delaying the message to maintain what he calls our 'level of comfort'.

The emergency announcement continues: 'All cabin attendants are thoroughly trained in emergency procedures. With your calm cooperation and attention you will be able to assist us in preparing the cabin.' This tells us that the cabin crew are in charge of us, whilst implying that when things get nasty we'll all be equals. We assist them in doing what has to be done. So far so good, says Patrick Hoffman. More disconcerting, he thinks, is what comes next: 'Please remain calm and listen carefully. Look at the person sitting next to you; you may be able to help each other later.' 'I'm not sure how comforting that is,' Hoffman says with studied understatement.

The job of reassuring though, rests with the flight attendants. Helen Jameson from Easyjet told us that part of her job is to help the passengers (what is the collective noun for all the passengers—a *congregation*?) feel like a family, a community. Then, if there is an emergency, we will behave as a community and not like a bunch of warring, air-raging hooligans.

As they say, as we leave the plane: 'Please fly with us again.'

" "

Indeed to Goodness, Look You

It is the misfortune of certain national characteristics to become caricatures, cartooned versions of reality that, for all their occasional wit, do little more in the end than obscure the truth and give offence. Such is the fate of the image of the former mining valleys of South Wales. Perhaps because the intense activity that for centuries dominated these closely knit communities—the social solidarity, the male voice choirs, the political activism—bred in the minds of the outsider a sense of otherness, to which supposed attributes and caricatured characteristics adhere like iron filings to a magnet. The English have always looked down on the Welsh. When they referred to the mining towns of the Rhondda and Aberdare valleys, they would lengthen the *a* of *valleys* in mockery of the lengthened vowels of Welsh. And the fact that once the whole Welsh nation had their own language— were different—naturally set them apart. And in the crude social associations that exist, different meant 'funny'—peculiar and ha-ha.

In his classic guide *The Face of Wales*, published over fifty years ago, Tudor Edwards could condemn the valleys in a few dismissive images:

> The constant vilifying of the Rhondda has become a noxious habit. Certainly the squalor associated with technological achievement, with exploitation and unemployment is much in evidence. The towns are for the greater part mean, drab creations, each with its terraces of papier-mâché houses piled higgledy-piggledy on the gashed mountain-sides, each with its Victorian

neo-Gothic church ... each with its clan of Dissenting tabernacles ... Sometimes the surface of the river which fills the narrow tortuous valley is veiled with scum and the moulting trees are ringed with coal dust ... In the towns there are undertones of poverty relieved by great effort and courage. There is the black-faced minstrelsy of miners, like some sub-human—or super-human—race apart, on furlough from the grudging earth ...

It takes little for the reader of Edwards' purple prose to reach for his or her clichéd attitudes to the country, despite the caveat about the 'noxious habit' of taking a pop at valleys life with which he begins. For that cliché is founded upon centuries of mockery of the Welsh—and above all of the way they speak—by the English. Shakespeare was not above a little lampooning.

In Henry V, his character Fluellen is written specifically for actors to make merry with his words. When Gower bids him come 'to the mines' (in the late Middle English meaning of 'a subterranean passage dug under an enemy position—especially the wall of a besieged fortress—in order to gain entrance or, with explosives, to collapse a fortification') to speak with the Duke of Gloucester, Fluellen protests:

> To the mines! tell you the Duke it is not so good to come to the mines. For look you, the mines is not according to the disciplines of the war; the concavities of it is not sufficient; for, look you, th'athversary—you may discuss unto the duke, look you —is digt himself four yards under the countermines; by Cheshu, I think, a' will plow up all if there is not better directions ...

Shakespeare's lampoon is merciless: Fluellen is not only stupid (he mistakes the meaning of *mine* and interprets it as only a cartoon Welshman might) but swears *by Cheshu* (450 years later the accent remains unchanged) and the utterance is littered with clichéd Welshisms like *look you*.

Ten years after he quit the leadership of the Labour Party, Neil Kinnock is still probably Britain's best-known Welshman. Many claimed when he lost the 1992 general election that it had not a little to do with his Welshness, tapping into this deep-seated ritualized mockery of the nation by the English. Indeed, his particular way with words brought upon him the nickname 'Welsh Windbag'. 'The kind of lampooning that is pointed at the Welsh or used of the Welsh is to use phrases I've *never* heard used,' he protests. 'For instance, now, "indeed to goodness, look you!" I never, never, never have heard that used in my life.'

Kinnock objects, too, that what some call *Wenglish*—the English spoken in Wales—is rooted in the broader cliché of the 'valleys':

> All representational Welsh accents are South Walian accents. Nobody ever uses a North Walian accent. Secondly phrases are allocated to the Welsh which they never use and *Look you* is probably the chief of all of those. I've heard the word *boyo* but I could count it on the fingers certainly of two hands. People simply do not say *boyo*.

But *boyo* or no *boyo*, it was perhaps the resonant verse of Dylan Thomas's 1953 'play for voices' *Under Milk Wood* that finally fixed for ever our idea of what South Walian Anglo-Welsh sounds like. With its wild, rich wordplay, full of jokes—the scene is the village of Llareggub—and its characters like Nogood Boyo and Mrs Dai Bread One and Mrs Dai Bread Two, not to mention Organ Morgan, *Under Milk Wood* both celebrates and lampoons the culture and the language of the coastal towns and the valleys of South Wales.

And like it or not, it has become an (albeit small-scale) local industry, this Anglo-Welsh talk: a little glossary of such words, called *Talk Tidy*, has been assembled by John Edwards:

> I call it the 'Ida Syndrome'—the habit of saying *I do 'ave, I do like*, and the ultimate is *I do do*! I always quote the apocryphal story of two ladies shopping in Ponty market, saying one to another, 'Pink, I do like, but blue I do rather, but pewse [puce] ah, Deuce! I do go scatty for pewse!'

And Professor Nik Coupland of Cardiff University's Centre for Language and Communication adds a couple more standard examples. 'Popularly, Wenglish is taken to be those phrases that are stereotypically Welsh—the *isn't it?* tag or the *innit* tag, if you like. Or saying *by 'yer* or *by there* instead of simply *here* or *there*. Or saying *look you*' (as disputed by Neil Kinnock).

Much of the typical phraseology of *Wenglish* owes its distinctive shape to the indigenous language, as is the case of Hiberno-English in Ireland. Welsh grammar constructs sentences differently from English and there are many examples of direct literal renderings of phrases or sentence-order from Welsh into English. Nik Coupland observes:

> We have the *I do like it* and *I do do it* in some of the south-east Wales valleys. We have the double negation—the *I haven't done nothing* and so on. And these are clearly stigmatized as so-called 'incorrect' forms. There's this phenomenon that you could call 'fronting' which is to put words that you want to emphasize or if you like meanings that you want to emphasize up front in your sentences, saying something like *cold it was, mind you*. Now that kind of construction is available in Welsh. So it is an exact mirroring of the syntax of Welsh when people speak English. A transfer phenomenon if you like.

Most purely Welsh-speaking communities are concentrated today in the north of the country, but even in the basically monolingual English-speaking areas, the structures remain deep in the linguistic bedrock. Sometimes they even poke through the English tilth where no satisfactory equivalent exists: 'Welsh words are then borrowed into English discourse in one way or another —words like *hiraeth* (yearning) or *hwll* (spirit) or *tup* (silly)'.

And Neil Kinnock finds himself referring back to similar useful shades and qualities of meaning that the Welsh term supplies where the English equivalent is found wanting:

> If I was to speak of people who were 'arrogant' or people who thought they were superior, I would say that they were *crachach*, which literally translated is 'scabs'. Then again, if I was to cuddle a child I would use the word that my grandmother used to me which was *cwtsh*, and it is 'cuddling' but it's something even warmer than that; you know it really is getting together.

Cwtsh has a complex etymology which goes back to Latin *collocare*, meaning 'to lay in place', 'to lodge'. Through Old French (where it means 'hide') and Middle English it emerges as a dialectal form, *couch*, which then evolves into the Welsh *cwtsh*. 'And one place that it ends up', comments Dr Robert Penhallurick, Lecturer in English Language at the University of Wales in Swansea, 'is in this dialect phrase *to cutch down*. So it acquires a Welsh pronunciation—*couch* becomes *cutch*—and then that *cutch* comes back in to the local English.'

Over the course of four centuries, Welsh was literally beaten out of the people by many decades of oppression by the ruling English. Welsh-speaking schoolchildren were forced to wear a wooden collar round their necks if they were heard speaking any other language than English, and indeed the Act of Union of 1536 states quite specifically: that 'No person or persons that use the Welsh speech or language shall have any office within this realm.'

'The Act of Union basically made English the official language of Wales,' observes Robert Penhallurick.

> It meant that if you wanted to get on, you had to learn English, not Welsh. Welsh was not the language of administration or government or the legal areas; it just wasn't allowed. So Welsh speakers who were active in those areas would have to learn English. Amongst the mass of the population in most of Wales however, up until that time and for a long time afterwards, Welsh would be the first language.

These days, the core of users of Welsh is down to about half a million speakers, yet the spirit of that Welshness, says Professor Nik Coupland, lives on in the linguistic blend that is Wenglish.

> There's a particular point here that I think is important, too: as the Welsh language itself has declined over the years, I think the English language has taken on some of the functions of Welsh to capture that cultural identity for people who don't speak Welsh. And I think that's why people invest a lot—if I can put it that way—in their own Welsh-related forms of English speech. People are often very proud of the Welshness in their voices—they wouldn't like to give it up totally.'

Most distinctive, of course, is the accent. Some call it 'sing-song' (note again the derogatory connotations people immediately summon up) which is part of the inheritance from the Welsh language, and which extends across the border into Shropshire dialect too. Another feature of Wenglish pronunciation is the particular way in which the Welsh pronounce the *r*, which is neither heavily voiced—as in the rural dialects, for example, of the English south-west—nor unvoiced (as in standard Received Pronunciation). It is 'rolled'. Robert Penhallurick has a special interest in the way the English language has evolved in Wales, and has completed extensive fieldwork for the Survey of Anglo-Welsh Dialects, tracing the exact boundaries of different varieties of pronunciation:

> A rolled *r* in Wales would be diagnostic of strong Welsh influence or a lingering Welsh influence in that the rolled *r* is the main *r* sound in Welsh—trilled thus: *rrrr*. So where you hear it being used in English, it normally means there's still quite a strong Welsh influence there, and when we look at maps that describe the use of this *rrrr* sound in *English* words in Wales, there's quite a clear boundary that we see on these maps which correlates quite closely with Welsh-language areas.

From years in the knockabout, often cruel world of politics where personal idiosyncracies of every variety, but especially of speech, are pointed out, picked at and satirized without mercy, Neil Kinnock knows the score. But under protest:

> I hear people saying that the fact that I am Welsh and have a Welsh accent cost votes and many of them are serious people so I take note of what they say. I think it's very difficult to prove. There may be an innate antagonism towards Wales and things Welsh—'Taffy was a Welshman, Taffy was a thief—all I know is that even if it had been demonstrated to me that the price of an extra 100,000 votes was to scrap a South Walian accent, I wouldn't have done it. And I probably couldn't have done it either.

Whizz-Words of Oz

Heading out of Sydney towards the Blue Mountains, the Holden keeps firmly to the left lane of the Western Motorway. Pale green road signs indicate turnoffs to Parramatta and Liverpool in the loose, widely spaced lettering familiar from American highways; straight on lie Penrith and Katoomba. From a giant hoarding beside the road the smiling face of a middle-aged woman in uniform gazes at us as she cuddles a little child: the legend *The Salvos never give up caring.*

For someone with an eye—and an ear—for what's different and what's the same with the English language as you travel the world, it is hard not to be struck by the delicious little contradictions and echoes of other English-speaking communities round the globe. Here, as the proudly Australian car—a *Holden*, with styling and size that owe more to Detroit than Dagenham—heads out of town resolutely on the *left* side of the highway. And that road is not actually a *Highway* (although in this land of linguistic cross-fertilization, many are so named) but a *motorway*—the term known almost exclusively in the UK and one which baffles and amuses American visitors. Yet the average US driver would feel completely at home—if he or she bothered to notice such a detail—with the signage that keeps the driver informed: the lettering and the style, as well as much of the terminology, is taken directly from the American road network, even down to the pale green backgound and the shield design on which road index numbers are indicated.

Again, the British driver can feel both linguistically at home—and very much at the other end of the world—when confronted with the place names on the signs along this Western Motorway: *Penrith* sits comfortably alongside *Parramatta, Katoomba* next to *Blackheath*. In fact, when seeking directions to Sydney's famous Macquarie University, I was amused to be directed to the northern outskirts of the city and the suburb of Epping. Oh, and as for the hoarding advertising the *Salvos*, it refers, of course, not to rounds of gunfire but to the Salvation Army, universally known to Australians in the typical *-o* ending form of abbreviation that still strikes a British eye as slightly unusual.

And that is again typical of the linguistic experience of the British visitor to Australia. Close, resonant familiarity—just like home, down to *pasties* and *pies, fish and chips,* and *petrol* —and complete dislocation as a nexus of Aboriginal names or a piece of local usage hoves into view. It is very much a simultaneous experience of 'home' and 'away'. And while Australians are rightly proud of their own inheritance, individuality and indepedence—and there are many who will insist that the *Australian* language is what they speak, rather than English—the visiting Pom is struck by the repeated linguistic connections with back home.

Perhaps because our exposure in Britain to American culture is so pervasive, the notion of linguistic difference, the celebrated clichéd view of two countries 'divided by a common language', as Bernard Shaw is famously alleged to have put it, has become deeply entrenched. It no longer surprises us to find *drugstores* on the corner of the *block*, to use the *sidewalk* to avoid the *automobiles*; and even those annoyingly euphemistic labels *rest room* and *powder room* are beginning to make a slithering appearance in our lexicon. And if we don't yet take the *elevator*, we are certainly no longer surprised when Americans do.

Not so in Oz. The *lift* is what will get you there, the *toilets* are what you need to ask for (and public ones are as common a sight as they are back home—unlike the US), and if you need some medicine, you go to the *chemist's* just like in Britain. As in the UK, there is considerable cultural pressure from American global lifestyles—and thus linguistic fashion too. Yet Dr David Blair, Dean of Macquarie University in Sydney and an expert in the study of English as a global phenomenon, insists that Australians resist Americanisms with some force.

> The effect of American English is certainly significant, but Australians tend to reject it when they're aware of it. Now Australians are very proud to be Australian, they're very proud of their identity, their national identity—I can't foresee the day when Australians will say to themselves, well we're sick of being Australians, there's no future in being Australian, we'll all be Americans from now on. I think it would only be in that very unlikely scenario that American English would have captured Australian English.

So *gas* is still what powers your heating system, rather than your car, which still runs on *petrol*, and the famous Sydney bridge that links north and south of the city crosses Sydney *Harbour* (not *Harbor*).

'Spelling is a really interesting issue,' says David Blair, 'because this is what people tend to be most conscious of. They're not very conscious always of pronunciation or new words coming in, but they're very conscious of the way in which words are spelled. And people often have very firm views about what is American spelling and what is not.' Australians are therefore very aware that *harbor*, with an *-or* at the end, is American, and the *-our* ending is what they use:

And for instance, the word *colour*. If you ask an Australian 'How do you spell the word *colour*?' ninety-five per cent I would think would say, 'Oh, with *-our*.' But if you read Australian newspapers, about half of them use the *-or* habit. And what really interests me is that although we would say newspapers and printed sources generally are very influential on what people do in language, this now long-standing habit of Australian media has not carried across to individual usage at all, because people know that *-or* is an Americanism, and they resist it at an individual level.

And even when they are not necessarily aware of the American spelling fashion, there is a tendency to retain the orthography of the former homeland. Take the wheels on this Holden car of ours—what keeps them off the road? '*Tyre* retains here the old British habit of using the *y*,' observes Dr Blair, mindful that in America the word is always spelled with an *i*. 'Very rarely, I think, would we see *t-i-r-e*—possibly because there's a spelling clash between two different senses of the word *tyre/tire*.'

The similarities to British English, then, are as much what strikes the visiting Pom as the differences. Not surprising, really, given that the history of Australia is to a very large extent part of the history of Britain. In fact the ubiquitous Macquarie, a name which is today more Australian than it is British, was originally Scottish. These days, Macquarie's name crops up everywhere in New South Wales—he was one of its first governors—from the humblest of cafés to the grandest of boulevards in the centre of Sydney, not to mention the distinguished university over which David Blair presides, and the eponymous Dictionary which represents some of the finest Australian linguistic scholarship. But a language uprooted and replanted in foreign soil inevitably, as it evolves, slowly peels off from the main track of the mother tongue. No more so than in Australia.

For example, to begin with there were the indigenous peoples. Little wonder that the Aboriginal population had some influence on the language of the early settlers. *Kangaroo, koala, corroboree, boomerang, billabong,* and others were absorbed into Australian English, because they represented things or creatures that existed nowhere else. But the Aborigines contributed fewer terms than one might imagine—there were at least 200 Aboriginal languages in the continent and each had its own individual lexicon when the first settlers made landfall in 1770, so there was no standard local term across even fairly small tracts of the newly settled territory. Captain Cook, and the men and women who followed shortly after him in the so-called First Fleet, for the most part therefore stuck to what they knew.

Rather, the new Australian settlers did what settlers have done since voyages of discovery first were made, and named the new plants and wildlife they found after equivalents that were fondly remembered from back home. 'And so they would see something like a magpie, you know, a black and white bird, and think, "Oh that looks just like the magpie back at home", and so they would call the Australian bird a *magpie,* even though it had nothing to do with the English magpie.' Speaking is Dr Susan Butler, Executive Editor of the *Macquarie Dictionary,* whom we interviewed standing at the very heart of historic Sydney, known as 'The Rocks', in the shadow of the famous Harbour Bridge.

> They'd see a tree—very common around Sydney—called angophora, and say, 'Oh that looks like an apple tree, we'll call that a *native apple tree*'. And this pattern of naming things, *native plums, native cucumbers, native ducks,* and so on went on. A lot of these names have since been replaced: we now refer to an *angophora* rather than a *native apple.*

Some of the most toothsome contributions to the Australian lexicon, and the words which have made their way into national stereotypes, like *fair dinkum, cobber, tucker*, and so on, actually originated in British English, but only in a very limited dialect form, but which flourished and became generalized amongst Australian settlers. *Fair dinkum* is an expression that originally meant 'a reasonable amount of work'. Susan Butler explains:

> In *Robbery Under Arms* by the prolific nineteenth-century novelist Rolf Boldrewood, there's a quote where the bush-rangers are saying it took 'an hour's hard dinkum' to get to the top of a hill. So *fair dinkum* in effect means 'a fair day's work for a fair day's pay'. And so it's that call for justice and reasonableness and fairness in dealing with people which has been very strong in Australian English.

More exotic are some of the expressions with their roots deeply embedded in the reality of the Australian social and cultural experience. Like a *furphy*. 'There was a company called Furphy in Victoria that made pots and boilers and things like this, and they also then made water carts,' Dr Butler recounts. 'These water carts were used in the First World War, and the soldiers would gather around the water-carts and obviously gossiped as they gathered. So the information that was passed around in this kind of unofficial way was referred to as a *furphy*. A *furphy* is always proved wrong in the end, so it's always misleading rumour.' Other local flavours were contributed by convicts' slang and from the language of the gold rush of the late Victorian period.

But, regardless of all these obvious local lexical exoticisms, and the more familiar modern ones such as *barbies, tinnies*, and *eskies* (all essential contributions to the Australian leisure-filled summer: *barbecues, cans* (of beer), and insulated cool-boxes, from *Eskimo*), one of the elements that marks out Australian English most clearly and colourfully is its love affair with 'affectionate' endings.

There are two principal forms, and the three examples I have just quoted illustrate one of them to perfection: the *-ie* ending. The other, that we observed on the hoarding advertising the virtues of the Salvation Army at the beginning of this section, is the *-o* ending. 'The Salvos never give up caring' was the slogan, and the use of the abbreviation in *-o* is so common Down Under that it barely warrants attention. To British eyes, however, it seems as unusual and original— we have few, if any, formations in *-o* (unless they are commercial names like *Rolo*, *Polo*, and *Mintoes*). Australians have hundreds, and can, with a natural formation structure well and truly in place, coin an infinite number of new ones, as new terms come along that need a little linguistic caress. 'A lot of people think that the *-o* ending is negative,' observes Dr Kate Burridge of La Trobe University in Melbourne, 'and I know that's true in American English, and perhaps also in British English to a certain extent—*weirdo, wacko, wino, bozo, sicko*—but that's not the case in Australian English certainly.'

So *arvo* is standard Australian for afternoon, and as we see elsewhere in this volume ('Icky Bitty Babytalk'), any number of words can take the *-o* ending. 'I think if you asked me what was the most distinctive feature of Australian English, it would be the love of abbreviations,' concludes Dr Burridge.

> I think that at a time when our good old Australian lingo— words like *larrikin* or *okker*, you know, the *beaut blokes* and *bonzer sheilas*—they sound a bit passé now, certainly in the city, and when of course we're confronted by the American English influence as well, I think our love of abbreviations has not changed, and I think it's a way of showing Australianness in our English.

Fair dinkum, say I.

Word of Mouth transmission dates

CHAPTER 1: OFFICIAL CURRENCY
Spun Gold *August 2000*
Moolah Makes the World Go Round *October 2000*
Dear Sir, I Wish to Complain ... *July 1993*
Cut and Thrust *November 1992*
Lies, All Lies *July 1993*

CHAPTER 2: PERSUASION
The N-Word *February 1998*
Heart to Heart *January 1998*
From Soap to Serum *January 1996*
Cover Story *September 1999*
Working It Out *July 2001*

CHAPTER 3: HOMEWORK
Toujours la Politesse *August 2000*
Of Mogs and Dogs *February 1996, March 2000, December 2001*
Icky Bitty Babytalk *September 1995*
Never Say Die? *February 1996*

CHAPTER 4: MIND YOUR SPEAK
Nicely Spoken *January 2002*
To Er ... Er is Human *August 2000*
Rude! *August 1996, April 1997*
Crack the Whip and Put Your Foot Down *August 1999*
All-Purpose Filler *August 2000*
Kersplatt! *March 1994*

CHAPTER 5: MUSCULAR LANGUAGE
Football United *September 2000*
Surfin' NSW *September 2001*
A Little Birdie Told Us *July 2001*
Paying Court *July 2001*

CHAPTER 6: WORDING YOUR EATS
Words of Mouth *August 2000*
Organic Panic *August 1999*

Summer Sizzle *September 2000*
Cakes and Ale *September 2000, August 2001*
The Naming of Tarts *September 1999*

CHAPTER 7: BETWEEN OURSELVES
Ssshh! Don't Let On *October 1995, January 1998*
Put Words on Your Chest *August 1999*
Jazzin' it Up *January 1998*
The Ire of the Beholder *December 2001*
How Nice to Vada Your Eek *September 1995*

CHAPTER 8: THE NAME GAME
Naming Names *September 2000*
Coffee-Breaking the Mould *January 1999*
True Brit *August 2000*
How to Name a Plane *September 2000*
Appeal of Bells *August 1999*

CHAPTER 9: COUNTRY NATTERS
Writes of Spring *April 1997*
A Rose by Any Other Name *May 1998*
Woodcraft Folk *September 1998*
Flights of Fancy *April 1997*
Under the Weather *August 2000*
Fall Tales *September 1998*

CHAPTER 10: THE WORD HAS LANDED
Seated One Day at the Mouse-Mat *August 2000*
In-Flight Entertainment *August 2001*
Indeed to Goodness, Look You *October 1994*
Whizz-Words of Oz *September 2001*

Acknowledgements

We are grateful for permission to reprint copyright material in this book and especially for the following:

PAM AYRES: 'The Bunny Song' from *The Works: Selected Poems* (BBC Books, 1992), copyright © Pam Ayres 1992, reprinted by permission of the author.

JOHN BETJEMAN: lines from 'Church of England Thoughts Occasioned by Hearing the Bells of Magdalen Tower', *Collected Poems* (1978), reprinted by permission of John Murray (Publishers) Ltd.

RALPH BLANE AND HUGH MARTIN: lines from 'Trolley Song' from *Meet Me in St Louis*, words and music by Ralph Blane and Hugh Martin, © 1944 EMI Catalogue Partnership, EMI Feist Catalog Inc and EMI United Partnership Ltd, USA; worldwide print rights controlled by Warner Bros Publications Inc/IMP Ltd; reprinted by permission of International Music Publications Ltd. All rights reserved.

MARTY FELDMAN AND BARRY TOOK: extract from the script of *Round the Horne* first broadcast on BBC Radio, reprinted by permission of Lyn Cook, and Roger Hancock Ltd for the Estate of Marty Feldman.

NIGEL FORDE: 'The Naming of Tarts', copyright © Nigel Forde 2002, especially written for *Word of Mouth* and first published here by permission of the author.

JOHNNY MERCER: lines from 'Spring, Spring, Spring' from *Seven Brides for Seven Brothers*, words by Johnny Mercer, music by Gene de Paul, © 1944 EMI Catalogue Partnership, EMI Robbins Catalog Inc and EMI United Partnership Ltd, USA; worldwide print rights controlled by Warner Bros Publications Inc/IMP Ltd; reprinted by permission of International Music Publications Ltd. All rights reserved.

MICHAEL ROSEN: 'Not in Front of the Children', copyright © Michael Rosen 2002, especially written for *Word of Mouth* and first published here by permission of the author.

Index

This is a word by word listing of words and phrases treated as lexical items in the text. Foreign words are given in italics.

A
a bit of wellie 83
a bit strong 190
a cat may look at a king 77
a dog may look at a Bishop 77
à l'americaine 211
abs 65, 66
academicals 134, 135, 137
accordion scheduling 270
ackers 15
Acksly Angbay 179
Aggo-Paggo 181
Aggotalk 181
Aggy-Paggy 178, 181
ah, ahm 103
air rage 7, 104, 149
ajax 202
albatross 147
ale 154, 167–71
ale-conner 171
Alexandra 135, 137
all grist to the mill 168
ambo 86
angel 11–12
angel delight 173
anti-spin 9
appeal 229
arsenal 134, 135, 138
artbollocks 178, 192–3
arvo 85, 264, 288
as I was just saying 27

as soon as possible 19, 21
at a gallop 114
at the wheel 116
attract 44
aubretia 242–3
aubrieta 243
aunty 81
austringer 250, 251
autumn 236, 259–62
autumn of her years 259

B
baby talk, baby speak 80–2
babykins 86
backslang 178, 179–80, 181, 200
back-stall 143
bad 189
Bambi 66
banoffee 154
barbacoa 165
barbecorgy 166
barbecue 154, 164–6, 287
barbie 85, 154, 166, 264, 287
BAR-B-Q 165
barista 211
BBQ 165
be taken 89
been there, done that, got the T-Shirt 186
beer 154, 169
behind the wheel 116
being lost 87

bickie 81, 82
big wheels 66
Billy Bundles 14
bio-cosmetic 53
biodiversity 53
birdie 134, 144, 147
bit between one's teeth 114
bit of wellie 83
bitch tits 66
Black Wednesday 12
blinkered 114
bloom 55
blue 243
bluebottle(s) 134, 141
blurb 57–63, 121
blurbing 57
blurb-speak 40
blurb-writer 58, 60, 61, 63
blurb-writing 60, 62, 121
boardwalk 259
Bob Majors 206
bobby/ies 81, 82
bob(s) 230–1, 234
bod 201
body-boarder 140
bodytalk 66
bogey, bogie(s), bogy 144, 146–7
bogeyed, bogied 147
bogeyman 146
bolts 113
bona 196, 197, 202
boogie-board 140, 142

Bookie 181
bookie 83
boss key 269
boss of the moss 148
boy 45
boyo 277
brash, brashing 247
bread 189
bread and honey 189
breakdown 117
breaking bar 246
breathe one's last 89
brekkie 85, 86
brewer, brewster 169
brick flattened 156–7
brickfielder 257
bridal 170
bride-ale, bryd-eale 170
bridle 94, 114, 115
bring his back down 115
bring to the table 266
Bristol 206, 224
Brit 219–20
Britain 212, 214, 215, 216, 217
British 206, 212–20
British English 218
Britisher(s) 216, 221
Britishness 214
Briton(s) 213, 220
Brits 216, 219, 220

INDEX

brock 181
broody 238
bubbly 40, 44
buddleia 240, 242
bullseye 14
bumper to bumper 116
burgeoning 237, 238
butch 201, 202, 203
buy a pig in a poke 77
buy a ticket for the clue train 277
buzzard 147
byword in its own time 59
by 'yer, by there 278

C

camp, camp as Christmas 201
cams 139
cans 287
cant 198, 199, 200
cardie 82
careless talk costs lives 51
carsey 201
carts 201, 203
cask-conditioned ale 167, 168
castellanus 255–6, 258
castellatus 255
castles in the sky 255–6
Casuals 138
cat 74–8
catch a tube 134
catching waves 140
cat may look at a king 77
cat's miaow 78
cat's pyjamas 78
cat's whiskers 78
cavalcade 113
cavalry 150

cellophane bridge 148
cereal 169
Ceres 169
chafe/chafing at the bit 112, 113, 114
change(s) 229, 230, 231
change-ringing 206, 228–30, 234
changing up a gear 116, 117
cheval, chevalerie, chevalier 150, 151
chicken 201
chicken-legs 66
Chinese walls 267
chivalric 150, 152
chivalrous 134, 149
chivalry 149–52
chockies 82
chocky bickie 81, 82
Chrissie 85, 86
Christmas tree 66
chrysanthemum 244
clambunsculars 247
clang 126
click 130
click-clack 128
clip-clop 126
clue train 267
cobber 218, 264, 287
cock-eyed bob 257
cockle 14
codespeak 178, 179–82, 198
coffee 206, 210–12
cold cream 50
Colonel Bogey 146–7
complete failure 64, 65

completely knackered 114
compo 86
concept art 193
concept dining 158
condor 147
conned 171
cookie(s) 81, 83
cooler-box 66
Corinthian 138
cosmetic, cosmetics 46–56
cosmetic surgery 49
cossie 82
cottage 201
could you possibly just 71
County 135
courtesy 150
cracking a few waves 140
crack the whip 112
crash, bang, wallop 126
crash, crashes 117
crashing area 140
crocus 241
crosswalk 259
crown 231
cultivar 242
curtsey 150
curvy 44
customer care 98
customer charter 96
Cut 181
cutch, cutch down 279
cwtsh 279
cyber 268
cybercafé 268
cybernaut 268
cybernetics 268
cyberpiracy 268
cyberpunk 268
cyberslacker 268
cyberspace 268
cybersquat 268

D

death 68, 87–92
deconstruct 193
deeleebob, deeleebobber 123
definition 66
delts 65
dendranthemum 244
denotative 56
derro 85
de-ummer 102
de-umming 99
devaluation 12
dibs 2
diddleebob 123
diddleybo 123
diddleything, diddleythingy 123
die is cast 249
ding 126
dingdong 94, 123
dingus 123
dingy 123
dirty 178, 189
dish 201
dividers 265
do 'ave, do like, do do 279
doctor 4, 5
doctoring 5
dog 74–80, 81
dog and bone 79
dog Latin 181, 244
dog may look at a Bishop 77
Dogger, Fisher, German Bight 253
doggie(s) 81, 86, 87
doobree 118, 119, 123
doobry 94
dooda 118, 121, 123
doodad 123

INDEX

doofer 57, 94, 118, 123
doohickey 123
dosh 2, 15
double eagle 147
downpour 255
drainpipes 66
drizzle 254, 255
dry 212
dubes 200
dump-bin 58, 59, 64
duping delight 34

E
eagle 134, 144, 147
eco- 160, 161
eco-friendly 53
ecological 161, 162
economical with the *actualité* 32
economical with the truth 32
ecosphere 53
ecosystem 55
eeh 103
eek 195
Egg and Bacon 181
Eggo 181
eggy-peggy 180
eight-pack 66
elephant's ass 148
England 219
English 206, 213, 214, 215, 216, 217, 218, 219, 220
enjoy your meal 95, 96
enjoy! 97
er 94, 99, 101, 102, 103, 120
erm, er...m, errrm 94, 99, 101, 102, 103, 120
eskie 264, 287
Esperanto 179
euh 102, 103, 120
everything in our power 19
expire 89
extra 232

F
face-lift, -lifting 49
face-raising 49
failure 64
fair dinkum 287, 288
falconry 236, 248–53
fall 258–62
fall asleep 89
fall of the leaf 236, 260–1
farthing 11
fastening 57
fast lane 117
fecund 237
feely, feely-omi 202
fell 246
femme 202, 203
fertilize 237
fifth 233
film 83
fire-side chat 8
flat-bench flies 65
flavoured moo 206, 212
flitan 337
flotation aid 273
flyte, flyting 109–11
folding 15
foreign 214, 217
foreigner 212–13, 217
frankly 25, 29
freak 65
fried 65
front slide 142
fructify 237
fruitful 237, 238
fruity 233
fry your thighs 66
f'ship, f/ship 44
fuchsia 240
fundamental 233
furphy 287
FX 8, 126–8

G
gadget 122, 124
gasser 178, 190
-gate 32
gateau 159–60, 173
gay 195–203
gee 82
gee-gees 82
generosity 151
generous 151
gentilesse 151
genus 151
get on the clue train 267
getting shredded 66
gewgaw 123
gig 189–90
girl 202
gizmo 122, 124
glad eye 238
glass ceiling 267
glutes 65
go into overdrive 117
gob 246
Goddis good 170
godiva 14
going to meet their maker 87
golf 144–8
gorilla 14
grande 211
Grandsire Bob 234, Majors 233, Triples 230
gratin 159–60
grazing 7
greasy spoon 210
Great Britain 216, 218
green 147
green shoots of recovery 32
green wellie brigade 81
gridlock, gridlocked 116
grinding 168
grip it and rip it 147
grist, grist to the mill 168

grunkle 126
GSOH 40, 44
guns 65, 66
gutters 143

H
haar 256
hack squats 65
hag 247
half-angel 11
half-crown 11
hams 65
handkerchief 81
hanky, handky 81
hanky-panky 81
harmless 212
haute cuisine 157
have a nice day 95
have the bit between one's teeth 114
have the whip hand 114
have, having issues with 266, 267
headstrong 114–15
heckythumpers 124
high and stinky 148
hold your horses 112
holding folding 15
holding the reins 116
hole in one 147
holistic 161
hootenanny 121, 123
hot cat 78
Hotspur 135, 136
how may I help you 97
hum note 233
hypocoristics 80–1

I
I do 'ave, I do like,

INDEX

I do do 279
I think the question you're asking is 26–7
I want to make it perfectly clear 25–6, 29
I wish to complain 15–21
I'll have to hurry you 27
I'll spot you 66
I'm glad you asked me that 27
I'm sorry but 74
Ida Syndrome 278
-ie 82–86, 288
if I may finish 27
improved 42–3
in the pocket 190
in yerk 251
indeed to goodness 277
innit 278
inorganic 164
inscription band 232
intellig 44
ironing out the wrinkles 55
is there any chance 69
issues 266
it's in the pocket 190
it's written all over your face 36
itsy bitsy 83

J
javahead 211
jazz 187–90
jazz talk, jazz-talking 188–90
jess, jesses 236, 248–9
Johnny Longpockets 15
jump jet 222
just-in-time 270

K
kangaroos in the top paddock 167
kersplatt! 94, 125, 126
keyhole 2
kick 140, 141
kick over the traces 114
kiddies 81
-kin(s) 86
knackered 114
knackers, knackers yard 114, 118
knick-knack(s) 121, 123
kohl 48

L
lallies 196, 197, 199
Lancaster 222
largesse 151
lats 65
latte 206, 212
latty 196
lazy wind 257
leather-queens 203
left-arm spin 5
lefts 140
let me be perfectly clear 26
let me be perfectly frank 26
let me give you a straight answer 28
let me just say this 29
let me just say 33
let the cat out of the bag 77
level of comfort 274
lid(s) 134, 140, 142
life in the fast lane 117
like a butterfly with sore feet 148

like a dropped cat 148
lip 233
lip-gloss 50
lipstick 50
little white lies 31
living life in the fast lane 117
locking the stable door 117
lonely hearts 44–6
look you 276, 277, 278
lop and top 247
l/term r/ship 44, 45

M
mackeral sky 258
Macquerie 285, 286
Madison Avenue 31
maggie 75, 86
make a U-turn 116
make do and mend 51
make it my mission 98
make it perfectly clear 25–6, 29
Management By Walking About 265–6
Management By Walking About Without Purpose 265–6, 269–70
mares' tails 258
market 172
marketed at, marketed to 172
marketing 47, 55, 171–5
mash-tun 168
Mathma 181
may I just say 27, 28
MBWA 265–6
MBWAWP 265–6, 269–70

menuspeak 154, 155–60
menu-spin 159
metho 85, 86
method, methods 230, 234
mews 249
Mexican overdrive 117
might I be so bold 74
miss, missed the clue train 267
mission statement 96
mistral 257
mizzle 254, 255
moggie 75, 77
molly 201
money 2, 10–15, 189
monitor 11
monkey 14
moo 206, 212
moolah 2, 10
morphing 7–8
motorcade 113
Mountie 81
movie 83
Mowse 249
mozzie 86
Mr Mustard 14
muggin' lightly 188
mulley groove 232
multishirk, multishirkers 269
multishirking 268, 269, 270
multiskilled, multiskilling 269
muscle-bound freak 65
muscle-marys 66
muso 85, 166

N
naff 201, 202

INDEX

native 286
natural 162
nellie, nellie queen 201
nevis 14
new 41–3, 174
new and improved 42–3
New Labour spin 5
Nicespeak 96–98
Nimrod 226
nine ounces 14
no pecs – no sex 66
noblesse 152
no-fun 212
non-smoker 44
Notions 178, 181
nouvelle cuisine 155
n/s 44
n-word 41

O
-o 86, 283, 288
ogle, ogle riahs 200
old 41, 42
omee 200
omi, omie(s) 178, 196, 197, 199, 200, 202
omi-polone 199
omy 200
oncer 14
onomatopoeia, onomatopoeic 94, 125–32, 169
oojamaflip 120, 123
oojamaflop 120, 121, 123
-or, -our 284–85
organic 154, 160–4
organic chemistry 164
organic farmer 161
organic farming 163
organic gardening 163
Orient 136–7
ounce 14

out the back 134, 139, 140, 141
overdrive 117
overtakes, overtaking 117

P
pack it in 112
paddle 140, 141
paint 48
pallone 200
palone, paloni 200
paloney 200
panny 233
par 145–8
par for the course 146
park, parked 116
parking a problem 116
parky 256
parliare 199
parlyaree 198
pas devant les enfants 178, 180
pass away, passing away 87, 91
pass over 89
passed on 92
pavement 259
peal 229
pec-deck 66
pecs 40, 65, 66
pelf 15
perfectly clear 25–6, 29
perm 190
phonoaesthetics 111
phwee 131
pig in a poke 77
Pig Latin 180, 181
pin-drop syndrome 270
plain bob 230, 231, 234
Plain Bob Doubles 231
Plain Bob Minimus 231

Plain Bob Triples 230, 231, 234
planespotter(s) 221, 226
plant names 239–45
plastic surgery 49
please fly with us again 274
Polari 196–203
pollie 85, 166
polone, polones 178, 199, 200
polony, polonies 196, 199
pow! 126
prairie-dogging 271
precisely where I stand on this matter 26, 29
prezzie(s) 81, 82, 85
pumped 65
pumping iron 66
pup 78
pure food 162
pursue/pursuing/ pursuit of excellence 86, 96, 98
push that iron 66
put a horse's back up 115
put someone's back up 115
put your best face forward 50
putt(s), putter(s) 147–8
putting the cart before the horse 114, 117

Q
quads 65
quaffed 169
quality, service, and value 96
queer 200, 201
quern, quern-stone 168
quint 233

R
radiant 238
rage 7, 104, 149
rain 254–5
random bullshit generator 266
rangers 135, 136
real ale 167–8, 170
recovery 13
rein in one's feelings 114
rejuvenation 55
repetitions 64
reps 64
reserves 13
respun 19
revving up 117
rhino 15
riah 200
rich 233
ride a tube, ride on a tube 142
ride the clue train 267
rights 140
ring 229
ringing the changes 228–9
Ring o' Bells 229, 231
ring of truth 37
rip(s) 140, 141, 143
ripped, ripped abs 66
road rage 7, 104, 105, 112, 115–16, 149
rocket-fuel 212
roke 256
rolfing 144
rookie 81
rouge 48
Rover 75
rovers 135, 136
r'ship, r/ship 44
rub of the green 148
rudery 106–9
Rug 181

295

INDEX

S
saddled with 114
Sally Army 85
Salvos 85, 166, 282, 283, 288
sarnie 82
Sassenach 219
scotale 170
Scotch mist 254
scot-free 170
scots 170
Scottish 206, 214, 216, 220
sea-fret 256
sea-roke 256
Seattle 211
seeks, seeking 44
self-starter 117
selling someone a pup 78
selva oscura 245
separate flotation aid 273
service sector 95
sexy 44
SFX 8, 126
shilling 11
ship-shape and Bristol fashion 216
short 211
shower 254, 255
shredded 66
sidewalk 218, 259, 283
sim 44–5
sirocco 257
sisyrinchium 242
six-pack 65, 66
sizzling 127
skinny 206, 212
slap 40
sledgehammer 111–12
smellies 82
sn- 86
snap, snapping 108–9
snedding 247
snowman 147
soft day 254

Sopwith 224
sound-bite 5, 7
sound-bite culture 7
source 266
southerly buster 257
sovereign 11
sparge 168
sparing no effort 19
speak/speaking/ speaks to the hand 141, 142
speed humps 142
spin 3–9, 28
spin doctor, spin-doctor 4, 6, 9
spin doctorate 5
spin doctoring 7
spin machine 2, 9
spin war 5
spinnan 4
spinner, spinster 170
spinners 5
spinners 58, 60
spinning 3, 5, 7
spinning a yarn 5
spinster 170
Spitfire 222, 227
sponduliks 2
sprag 247
spun 19
Spurs 136
squidge, squidging, squidgy 129
squiggle 129
squirk 129
squirm 129
stag-headed 246
star on top 66
steady seller 59
stealth bomber 222
Stedman Triples 206, 230
stepping on the gas 117
stinger 141
stoop 251–2
striated 66

strong 190
stubbies 166
subvert 193
succour 238
supermarket rage 149
surf rage 7, 104, 140, 142
surf-cams 139
sustainable 161
swoop 251–2
synaesthesia 86

T
take a ride on the clue train 267
take life at a canter 114
talkies 80
talking the talk 64
talk to the hand, because the face isn't lisening 141
tall 211
tavern 169
TBH (to be had) 199
teacheress 46
tear-tape 57
teddy 81
tee 148
teeny 86
teeny-weeny 83, 86
tee-shirt, tee-shirt-speak 178, 182–6
telly 82
testoon 11, 12
that's a very good question 27, 28
that's the cat's miaow 78
that's the cat's pyjamas 78
the box 142
the Brits 219
the cat's miaow 78
the cat's pyjamas 78
the cat's whiskers 78

the die is cast 249
the Fall of Man 260
the green 147
the jazz 187
the new 41, 43
the n-word 41
the question I think you're asking is 26–7
The Rains 255
the reserves 13
the rub of the green 148
the truth is 30
the truth will out 30
the tube 142
thieves' cant 198, 199
thin 233
thing 119, 120–1
thingummy 94, 119, 120, 123
thingummybob 118, 119, 120, 123, 124
thingummyjig 57, 118, 119, 120, 122
thingy, thingies 118, 120
third 233
three ounces 14
three sausages short of a barbie 166
thwack! 125, 126
Tiddles 75
tierce 233
tight 233
tinkers' cant 199
tinnie(s) 85, 154, 166, 287
to be had (TBH) 199
to be perfectly frank 25
to make it perfectly clear 25–6, 29
to put someone's back up 115

INDEX

toile 50
toilet preparations 50
toiletries 49–50
toilette 50
tone 233
tow-lines 140
trade 199
trains 140
trams 140
trannies 203
triple eagle 147
triples 230
truc 119, 120
tube 134, 142–3
tune 233
turgid 239

U
'umming' and 'erring' 99–103
um(s) 94, 99, 100, 101, 102, 120
under par 147
unguents 47
unique selling proposition 44
united 135, 137, 138
United Kingdom 215, 216
unspun 9, 27
uplighters 265
USP 44

V
vada 195, 202, 203
vanishing cream 49–50
varvel 248
vascularity 66
vasistas 121, 122
Venerie 251
VGSOH 44, 45
vintners 169
viper 188
vision statement 96
vroom-vroom 94

W
wads 15
walkies 74, 79, 80, 87
walkie-talkies 80
walking the walk 64
wanderers 135, 136
want to make it perfectly clear 25–6, 29
washboard abs 66
Watergate 32
weasel words 19, 23, 62
weather 236, 253–8
web-cams 139
wedge 15
wellie 83
wellie(s) 81, 82, 83
Welsh 206, 216, 217, 275–81
Welsher, Welshy 217
Wenglish 264, 277–8, 280
wet 212

whadjamacallit 119
wham-bam 94
wharfie 85
whatchacallem 120
whatchacallit 120
whatever 120
whathaveyou 120
whatjamacallit 120
whatnot 120, 121, 122
whatsit 120
whatsitsname 57, 94, 120, 123
whatyoumacallit 120
whip hand 114
wholefood 161
wholegrain 161
wholemeal 161
wholesome 158, 163
whumph, whumpf 126, 131
widget 122, 123
widowmaker 246, 247
willy-willy 236, 257
Winchester Notions 181
with due respect 74
with great respect 23–4
with respect 23–4
with the greatest respect 29

with wings 212
WLTM 44
wolf trees 246, 247
women's toiletries 49
wonga 15
word-spinning 47
working-wounded 270
workout(s) 64–66
worm-burner 144
wort 168
Wotsits 122
would it be possible 73
would you mind terribly 71
written all over your face 36

Y
-y 82, 84, 85
yeast 170
yerk 251
yob 180
you're welcome 95
yuck 127

Z
zap! 94, 126, 127
zapped 126
zapping 7
zhooses, zhoosing 200
zing 126